# My Life,
# My Letters
# & My Loves!

## Exploring An Ordinary Life!

By

Alida Henriette Struze

*My Life, My Letters & My Loves:*

*Exploring An Ordinary Life*

Alida Henriette Struze, author

Michael T. Petro, Jr., editor

PetroPublications.com

Printed in the United States of America

ISBN-10: 1517440254

ISBN-13: 978-1517440251

# Dedication

I dedicate this book to those who kept urging me to write it!

To the memory of my family who loved me!

To all "my kids" who brighten my life!

To friends who have been a real gift!

To God who blessed me always!

# Acknowledgement

I would be remiss if I didn't thank Michael T. Petro, Jr., my editor and publisher. Without his help, this book would not have been published. We started working together in the summer of 2014 to take out all the copyrighted material from my private Christmas letters, and we continued to meet every week. I never knew all the things that had to be done to get a book published and Michael made it seem routine. The fact that we were both organized and had an editing goal each week made the book get done faster than expected. Not only did he do a good job of editing, but when I would get concerned and wondered if anyone would want to read this simple book, he would encourage me to continue because he felt it was worth publishing. THANK YOU MICHAEL!

# Table of Contents

# Foreword

My family and I met Alida a month after Christmas letter number 28 was mailed or hand-delivered. I was the new pastor at the Lakewood Baptist Church, and she was, and still is, an active member and leader. Her first words of greeting included a much-appreciated offer: "I am a social worker, and I work at Legal Aid. If I can help you, call me."

Over the 38 years I have known Alida, I have marveled at her compassion for others in their needs, her friendship and service to her 1939 Lakewood High School class, her strong support and deep concern for issues concerning ecology and wildlife, her ability to encircle friends as family and share her care and love with them, and her faithful commitment to her church.

I have witnessed Alida's quiet outreach to others grow into widely recognized appreciation. There are many who could speak of her friendship as an RTA bus rider traveling to and from work in downtown Cleveland. The "Bus Group," sparked by Alida, looked forward to workday contacts, dining out bi-monthly, and annual Christmas parties at her home. Without fanfare, and before beautification plans were being spread around the city, she purchased and planted flowers on West 6th Street near Legal Aid. And, the list goes on…

In writing this book, Alida has responded to the request of her friends to share more of her life with them. She has written an "open book" that allows us to appreciate what she calls an "ordinary life." In doing so, she has, by example, made it easier for each reflective reader to be more thoughtful, be more forgiving, and be more loving, caring and appreciative while living his or her own autobiography. Certainly, my family and I, and Alida's many friends and colleagues, have been blessed to be a part of the continuing extraordinary life of a dear friend.

The Reverend Doctor William G. Noyes, Retired

November, 2015

# Introduction

Little did I know when I started writing my Christmas letters in 1950 that they would be the reason this book is written. At first I would send about 100 letters, but as they became more popular, I would have 700 copies printed. Three or four hundred would get mailed and I would fold and hand out one to everyone at work and church. I never left anyone out. Many receiving the letters would send a note or speak to me suggesting I write a book. They wanted to know what life was like when I was a child and more about mine and my family's life until 1950 when the letters began. Several times I started writing but got so far and stopped because I thought the book would be too simple. I kept being asked, "When are you going to write the book?" One friend threatened to lock me in a room with no phone to force me to begin writing. I decided my friends really wanted this book, but I knew I was going to need help. Ask and you shall receive!

The Christmas of 2013 I was invited to a gathering at the Sai Gon Plaza in Cleveland, Ohio where Gia Hoa had invited five authors who briefly described their books. Before I left, I spoke to one author who gave me his business card and I gave him one of my Christmas letters. When I got home I read the card and discovered he was also an editor and publisher. Just what I needed! I was busy planning for our 75th class reunion from Lakewood High in June, 2014 so waited until that was over before calling Michael T. Petro, Jr. Ambivalent as I was, the book was started.

You should know this book will not read like a novel because it was put together in sections. It will never win a Nobel Prize, because it is a simple, personal history of my life over a period of many years. In it you will find articles I have written about some things as they happened and others nice to remember. I have used very few names in some chapters and changed some names for privacy sake.

No matter where I meet people they say "Don't stop your Christmas letters. We look forward to them." That always amazes me. I wish I knew how long I can continue writing them. At my age, only God knows!

# Part One:

# Early Memories

# Chapter One

# **Innocence Abounding**

Be forewarned, as you read this first chapter you may perceive a sense of sadness in my writing. It is genuine and unintentional. As I put the following words on paper I felt a sense of sorrow in the realization that the country I grew up in and loved so deeply has changed so dramatically over the years — and not always for the betterment of my fellow Americans. We have lost what we cherished most: simplicity, civility, and a sense of community! However, in other chapters you will find the expression of a wide range of emotions, and I wish to share them all with each and every one of you!

"Those were the days," as Archie and Edith Bunker sang at the beginning of each episode of the popular 1970's sitcom titled, *All in the Family*. I look back on those days when I was a child and wish that every child today could have the same experiences. We lived in a totally different society than we have today. Our neighbors had the same morals and values and were like an extended family. If a child did something wrong and the neighbor told the mother, the neighbor got thanked and the child got spanked. One soft spank usually ended the problem and all the mother had to do from then on was give the child a stern look. When I was in college a child psychologist said mothers and fathers who disciplined their children may have made them neurotic, but without parental guidance children are more likely to develop character disorders.

When I sit on my front porch, either day or night, I see very few neighbors relaxing on their porches. This was not so during my childhood. After supper people sat on their porches chatting with neighbors, maybe getting news of someone's problems or achievements. This frequent, informal chatting strengthened our relationships. This socializing might go on until it was time to prepare for bed. There were no decks in the back yard to keep families isolated. Being neighborly meant welcoming new people by taking them something to eat, like a fresh, home-baked pie or cake. How nice! How neighborly!

Like today, there were people who needed help. But when I was in elementary school only the poorest kids wore jeans and the children were embarrassed if they had holes in them. This makes you wonder why young people today pay good money to buy jeans made with holes. If there was a needy family all the neighbors would help. One food item needy neighbors would receive looked like white margarine, which came with a packet containing some yellow ingredient. The two would be mixed together so it looked like butter. This began at the beginning of the Great Depression.

We grew up without fear. We could keep our side door unlocked all day and not fear someone entering without permission. Some people didn't even lock their doors at night. Children could ride their bikes everywhere without fear of being kidnapped. Sometimes a group of us, still of elementary age, would gather just to talk in the early evening, but we knew we had to be home by dusk. I remember mothers packing a brown bag lunch and letting a group of us children walk to what was then called the Brookside Zoo. Now it is called the Cleveland Metroparks Zoo. We would look at the animals in the only building on the zoo property, then check out Monkey Island, eat our lunch under the trees, and walk the two or three miles back home. We wouldn't think of vandalizing anything, we weren't afraid of anything or anyone, and we just enjoyed the walk — as only children can!

The community in which we lived still had lots of fields full of beautiful wild flowers. Across from our house was a little pond and we loved to look at tadpoles and hear the sound of frogs. There were at least three baseball diamonds, but with so few cars we could play baseball on the street. The curbs served as first and third base. It was amazing that windows didn't get broken very often. Now cars line the streets and every field where children could once play are filled with houses. Butter cups, Queen Anne's lace, daisies, and other wild flowers, which taught us to value nature, are all gone!

Those were days when honesty, trust, and being as good as your word were honored. We could go away for a day or a week, leave furniture on the porch and it was still there when we returned. Hobos were men who liked to ride trains to see parts of the country. They had a reputation for being of good character. Sometimes one would come to the door asking for food. If dad was home the hobo would eat indoors with us. But if dad wasn't home mom would feed him on the back porch steps. Sadly, today we must be very cautious, and the practice of welcoming a complete stranger into our homes is no longer recommended.

Before the Great Depression we had neighborhood clam bakes. My dad, a sheet metal worker, made a huge steamer. My mom, two aunts, and a neighbor, cleaned the chickens — which didn't come in pieces back then. It must have taken hours to cut the chicken, take off all the feathers and singe the pin feathers over the stove. They would put the chicken, clams, sweet potato, and sweet corn all together in gauze bags. They were topped with celery and butter. Today, I have not had a clam bake that tasted that delicious!

We didn't have to worry about children being obese. We ate healthy food. As hard as my dad worked, he would plant a garden every year. We ate nutritious veggies, and mom would can some for winter. Many homes were built with fruit cellars in which to store the canned goods. She would also make jelly and catsup that were delicious. We did eat some things that are now considered unhealthy. As an example, if we had a pork roast on Sunday, Monday morning mom would send one of us to the store to get round rye. On it we would spread the grease from the roast with a little salt and pepper. It was so good! We didn't know about cholesterol back then. Women made pie crust with lard, but it had a wonderful flavor.

There were some children who were overweight but usually they had serious health problems. Most children were the proper weight. We were outside practically all day in the summer getting exercise and making friends. We played hopscotch, jump rope, hide and seek, and other games that kept us moving. The girls played jacks and the boys played marbles, catch, and baseball. There were roller rinks and ice rinks. We all had roller skates and in the winter sleds were used on a hill on our street. We didn't get rides to school; our feet were our transportation. Few women drove and older children didn't have cars. We didn't have sidewalks when we first moved into our house and we kept losing our rubbers that protected our shoes from the mud.

Children didn't sit in front of the radio for hours but did their homework and went out to play when it was done. Parents and children alike valued education. We wanted to do our best, wanted to be there every day and didn't want to be late for school. Our mothers knew when we went to school we were safe; that we had excellent teachers, and when we graduated we were ready for college and wouldn't need remedial classes. My mother made it clear that we were to do our best because even if we were gray-haired and in a wheelchair we were still going to graduate! After World War II ended my brother Walter became the first in the family to go to college, and I finally became a freshman at age 32.

Children were allowed to be children and were not treated like adults. We talked to one another, but now they won't know how to communicate later in life because of texting. We knew how to add and subtract in our heads, but because of calculators today they need computerized cash registers. Children won't know how to write because today educators want to eliminate cursive writing on top of not teaching penmanship and how to hold a pen or pencil.

Children, being children, take for granted how hard their parents work for them. When I think about how women labored in those days, doing housework with equipment that didn't make tasks easy, I feel sad. They used washing machines in cold basements, and hung the wet clothes to dry in basements in the winter. In the summer women took heavy baskets of wet clothing outside and hung them on clothes lines. They hoped it didn't rain and then had to take them down when dry. Just about everything was ironed. Men's shirts had to be starched and sprinkled with water to dampen them before being ironed. It was almost an art form getting the shirts ironed without a wrinkle or scorch in them. Washing machines had wringers that got most of the soap out of the clothing, and when they were again rung out of two tubs of water the clothing was clean and soap free. Scrub boards were used to get really dirty spots out. I wonder how mothers managed laundry for sheets and clothes for five people, plus cooking meals, ironing, and cleaning — and all with what now looks like ancient equipment! Cakes didn't come in boxes. Everything was done by hand. If you wanted chicken you bought a live one which got wrapped in newspaper to take home. It pecked at people on the streetcar and had to be killed at home. That job went to the man of the house.

As soon as a woman married she was expected to quit work, be a homemaker, and before too long have a child. Very few mothers worked until World War II when they were needed in factories to replace the men who had gone off to war. My mother and other women in the neighborhood went to help the war effort, but I'm glad she was there when I was little. It was so good to have her open the door and I would be surrounded with the smell of what she was cooking for supper, with maybe cake for dessert. We all ate every meal together. We would wait a while for dad, who might be late because he was so tired he slept past the streetcar stop. There were no fast food places or hundreds of restaurants; mothers were our chefs.

When I started writing this chapter I realized how simple those early years of my life were and how much they shaped my perspective as an adult. I named this chapter Innocence Abounding because when I was a child it was a simple, innocent time. In the 1920's and 1930's children were respected and allowed to be children. Adults now wish we had civility, common sense, and an attitude of caring — like we had before the cultural revolution of the mid 1960's. Let's look at how life was like day by day in the early part of my life:

When we think of food, we think of stores. There were no huge stores like we have now; which have put many small, family-owned stores out of business. No matter if it was a grocery, hardware store, or barber shop, the owner knew your name and you knew his; it was so personal and friendly. There were no bar codes on food. You took your grocery list to the store, which often had sawdust on the floor, and maybe a barrel with pickles in it. Item by item you would tell the grocer what you needed and he would go to a shelf to get the item and write the amount on a slip of paper. He would add all the items and give you the bill. (No computerized cash registers then). The same thing happened if we went to the West Side Market, which we did many Saturdays. When Walt and I were little some merchants gave us raw hot dogs we could eat right there; the meat was so delicious!

We had Blue Laws that required all stores to be closed on Sundays, which made it a quiet day of rest. Dad would take us to a movie or museum, or maybe a nice ride with the family. Drugstores might have been open. Every drugstore had a soda fountain. Ice cream cones were two scoops for a nickel. The East Side Market has been replaced with a sports arena, but the West Side Market has survived and has about one million visitors each year. Both markets remain an integral part of Cleveland's history. No store would be open on a holiday. Holidays were respected for their meaning and shopping frenzies were unthinkable! Thanksgiving and Christmas were for family time and not shopping time. Stores didn't play Christmas music and have decorations up until AFTER Thanksgiving. We couldn't wait to visit downtown Cleveland during the holiday season. No one went downtown in their work clothes or everyday clothing; we didn't go without getting dressed up and looking our very best! When we arrived downtown we loved to feast our eyes on the mechanically operated Christmas decorations in the display windows of the May Company and Taylors. The huge tree in Sterling Lindner's was a beauty! Today there are no more big stores downtown. How sad!

There were also home deliveries. Farmers would bring their veggies and fruit in season to the neighborhoods. People would buy baskets of tomatoes, peaches, strawberries, and other fresh fruits and vegetables, and much of it got canned. If we wanted bakery or ice we had cards to put in our home window, and merchants would come to the door with some bakery or ice. The cards for the iceman had 25 or 50 on them so he would know how many pounds to bring. He would have a heavy leather mat on his shoulder on which to put the ice. How he managed to go up stairs with that heavy weight is still a mystery to me. He would put the ice in what we called our ice box, under which was kept a container to catch the water as the ice melted. While the iceman was delivering, children would get on the back running board and grab little pieces of ice. Milk came in bottles and most homes had a milk box on the side of the house. In the winter the cream would rise to the top and sometimes run outside the bottle.

Every house had a coal bin in the basement. When there was a delivery of coal a basement window would be opened and the coal shoveled into the coal bin. Dad spent many hours shoveling coal into the furnace to keep us warm on cold days. When we started using gas heat in later years the bin was removed.

There were other merchants and salesmen who came to the house. Insurance men came to collect money, as did a merchant who sold all kinds of household goods that were quality material. Most of the blankets and sheets we had we got from him, and he would deliver his merchandise to his customers, who would pay by installments. There was one man who came to sharpen knives. One of the most fascinating was the paper rags man who would yell "paper, rags" so fast it sounded like he was saying "paperex." He was known for his horse and wagon, and for picking up and collecting all kinds of what we might call junk, or recyclable material today. I was told his shouting was so loud that children could hear him from inside their schoolrooms.

Doctors made home visits, called house calls, even at night. They wouldn't dare do that now. Drug dependent people would prey upon them, knowing they were carrying medications they could use. My family personally experienced many house calls. If we were so sick we couldn't get to the doctor's office he would come to our home. We knew him for such a long time he really understood our family and extended family, which enhanced his practice with us. Doctor Joe, as we called him, let his wife go to Europe ahead of him so he could operate on my "second mother," the aunt who lived with us. Dr. Joe was like part of the family. I don't know what we would have done without him!

It was a custom in those days to just "drop in" to visit family and friends. A lot of us had no phone. They would be happy to see us and we would be glad when they surprised us with an unexpected visit. We would often play croquet with our visitors. Players used mallets to drive a wooden ball through a series of hoops placed on the ground. They would try to hit away the opponent's ball. Visitors never went home without having something to eat, along with a cup of homebrewed coffee. If we didn't have anything to eat one of us kids would go to the store and get some cake for our visitors. One time we visited a distant relative who didn't offer us anything. We were both quite little. As we were getting our coats on my brother suddenly said loudly, "We can't go yet, we haven't had anything to eat." I'm sure we made a hasty retreat.

Remember when you bought a phone, plugged it in and that was it? Now you buy a phone and it takes hours to program it. Nothing is simple anymore. Things you bought years ago lasted forever because they were made right here IN AMERICA. Now phones and other things are obsolete when you buy them, or will need to be upgraded shortly after they are purchased.

When I think of entertainment, a happy memory of our entire family sitting in front of the radio would come to mind. We listened to Jack Benny, Burns and Allen — who were so funny we laughed until we had tears in our eyes, and they never said a dirty word. On a Sunday dad might decide to take us to a ball game. You didn't need a reservation. We just went down to the stadium, could afford the low price and even a hot dog which tasted so good then. One of the cheapest things we could do was go to movies. Then we had five theaters in our city. Now there are none. Often there would be double features and one would be a Western. Some theatres would give away dishes, or on Saturday afternoon some might have contests for kids doing the hoola-hoop. The movies were suitable for the entire family. They were not filled with all the sex and violence from which we have to protect children now. At the end of a romantic film the couple shared a simple kiss, or the groom would pick up his bride and take her into a room, and that was it! Shirley Temple, Fred Astaire, and Ginger Rogers helped get us through the Great Depression and World War II with movies that left us smiling. It was at the movies where we could watch newsreels of the current events we had heard about on the radio. Usually there was a short feature with Betty Boop, Laurel and Hardy, or maybe Donald Duck or Popeye. The *Palace* would also have big bands and comedians that were hilarious and clean, or a couple little people that danced beautifully, along with other performers.

In those early days there were no charge accounts. If a woman needed a new washing machine (as they were called then — and there were no dryers), she would save nickels and dimes until she had enough money to pay cash. That was a good way to stay out of debt. The first time I saw credit cards advertised I knew it meant trouble for some people.

We had three newspapers: *The News*, *The Press*, and *The Plain Dealer*. The only one left today is *The Plain Dealer*. Paperboys stood on corners and other high traffic areas selling their papers. There were no home deliveries. If something traumatic happened the boys would run down the street yelling, "Extra, extra, read all about it!" We might hear about the Dionne quintuplets being born. Maybe there was one murder a year, and not the many tragic deaths we hear of nearly every day today. What has happened to us? I often say, "This isn't the country I grew up in," and many older people agree.

It seems no matter where we were, we would see the organ grinder with his monkey. The man would play a very small organ which had a truly unique sound, and the monkey would collect money from the crowd of listeners. It was always fun to watch the two of them work.

The price of postage was affordable and the postal service wasn't in debt. A letter cost 3¢ and if it wasn't sealed (which never made sense to me) it was only 2¢. A post card was just 1¢. Sometimes we had two deliveries per day, and the same mailman delivered to our home for many years.

In the 1920's there were many homes without plumbing. We had a relative who had to pump water into her sink, and when she washed clothes she had to heat the water and put it into big tubs. She had to heat her heavy iron on the stove. Her outhouse was attached to the house somehow, but in various parts of the city others were outside and unattached. That is one thing that is no longer a problem.

Streetcars were the only form of transportation. They had a motorman and a conductor. The conductor kept a record of where the streetcar was in case of an accident. They ran often and were clean. Sometimes you had to start where you lived and transfer downtown to an Eastside or Westside one. On the Westside people could transfer at Brookpark Road to what was called a Dinky, which would transport people to Snow Road. Dinky's had wicker seats, a small coal stove for warmth, and could be run at either end. Buses and the Rapid Transit appeared much later.

Even seasons have changed. We knew winter would turn to spring and we would need a spring coat. Now winter often blends right into summer. June used to be the month for weddings because you KNEW the weather would be good. Summer used to turn into fall and children going back to school began to wear warmer clothes. Now summer and winter bump into each other so our bodies don't have time to adjust to the climate change. I decided we have only three seasons: summer, winter and orange barrels — now used to warn people of construction!

Emails are full of stories recounting some of the things we used to do, like drinking out of the garden hose when thirsty. That would appall some people today. Does this help you understand that life wasn't easy years ago, but it was much simpler, friendlier, safer, and more relaxing than the age we're living in today? Technology may be good in some ways, but it is making life more difficult in other ways. I'm sure there are things I have missed that you remember. If so, enjoy the memory and smile!

# Chapter Two

# The First Twenty-Nine Years!

Previously I wrote of how things were for everyone many years ago. On October 4th, 1921, I was born into a mysterious world of unknowns. I have come to the year 2015, and as I look back to write this chapter, I am absolutely amazed at all I have experienced in the first 29 years. After that period, my life exploded like a colorful firecracker.

Throughout my life, the family closest to me included my parents, Elizabeth and Walter, my brother, Walter Jr., born December 8th 1922, and my mother's sister, Minnie, who always lived with us and was like a second mother. As children, Walt and I called her "Pinkie" and that became her nickname. Our extended family was mom's sister, Mildred, called Mil or "Body" by Walt and me (Who knows why?); Uncle Henry, their daughter, Genevra, whom they adopted when I was seven, and Uncle Heinie (Heine in German, Henry in English), mom's bachelor brother who always lived with them. We were always together but visited other relatives. For some reason we had hardly any relationship with dad's side of the family. In later years I briefly met two cousins on dad's side of the family and we regretted that we had not known each other as we grew up.

My parents had been married about seven years and unable to have a child. Pinkie, who never married, worked with a woman whose name was Alida. Alida had a friend who was expecting an illegitimate child, which in 1921 was not socially acceptable, so she placed the child for adoption. It was arranged for my parents to legally adopt me. (See Chapter Thirteen, Discovery And Decisions) I have no idea where I lived before they brought me to my new home. When I was five months old my mother got pregnant and Walt was born on December 8th, 1922.

Of course my name became Alida. I loved the name because when I grew up every girl, it seemed, was named Mary or Anna and I was glad mine was different. Years later I discovered my natural mother had named me Mary Ann. A name book said the name Alida came from the Middle East, a place known for its fine cloth, and especially its purple cloth — and I love purple! I always had compliments on my name but the biggest compliment came when four of my friends each named one of their children Alida: my secretary at Legal Aid, a friend from Thailand who was in my class at CWRU, a tap dancing teacher who named her child Emily Alida, and my Karen friends in church made me happy when they named their second child Alida Moo Thaw, who is now almost two years old. The other Alidas are close to 40 years old now, and one Alida surprisingly became a social worker. I'm glad to know that as long as the Karens are with us, there will always be an Alida in my church.

Life, compared to today, was so different, so safe, most people had the same values and morals, and your neighbors were like your extended family. Whatever you bought lasted forever and wasn't obsolete the minute you walked out the door. Most things were made in America and were not made with toxic materials such as lead. Unfortunately, we were not aware of how manufacturers were polluting the land and water until the Cuyahoga River caught on fire. Hopefully new laws will change destructive practices.

Where we lived, Walt and I just had to walk down the street and into the playground and we were at school. When Walt started to go to school with me, neighbors would call us Mutt and Jeff (based on the comic strip) because he was tall and I was so little. Mom would tell us she would call us twice, and if we didn't get up we would be late for school. We were sure to be up because school meant a lot to us. We ate our breakfast listening to Gene and Glenn on the radio. Their theme song was "Hello, hello, hello," and I can still remember every word of their opening song. Gene would take the role of a woman and the banter with Glenn was hilarious. I still use one of the words spoken by Gene just for fun. Cinnamon was pronounced "cinnamonamon!" The part of breakfast I didn't enjoy but kept us healthy, was the cod liver oil, followed quickly by half an orange to cover the unpleasant taste.

We had wonderful teachers at Thoreau Park. A 4th grade teacher kids warned me was tough. True, she wouldn't put up with nonsense but was kind and taught us life lessons I never forgot. At the end of the year she would pretend we were at a picnic and made up a story with our last names. I was dessert, Struzelcake! I kept in touch with her until she died. We had penmanship and learned how to write and how to hold a pen or pencil. We didn't have calculators so we knew how to add, subtract, multiply, and divide in our heads. I wasn't great at math. Thanks to my mother who helped me night after night, I learned the multiplication tables. At least we knew how to make change! We learned good English, how to write a paper, and didn't need remedial help in college.

We had recess at school so we got plenty of exercise, but when we got home we also played hop scotch, hide and seek, and jump rope. Boys played marbles and girl played jacks. One never sees a chalk mark for hop scotch on sidewalks anymore. We used our imaginations and made up games and we read a lot of books.

I joined the Brownies and learned to make sheets with hospital corners, which I still do today. The best thing I learned was their motto, "Always Be Prepared," which has guided me throughout my life. Later, when I worked as an adult, I was teased because I kept so much rain gear in my desk, but when it rained I had a line of people standing near my desk asking to use it. I was prepared!

It was in elementary school that I learned I had some acting and singing ability. I had the lead in every operetta from the 1st to the 5th grade and was scheduled for the 6th grade operetta, but some mother wanted her daughter to have it. I was still in the cast.

Days off from elementary school were a special treat when we would go to Pinkie's office for the day. She worked for the old Cleveland Railway taking care of records in the red brick building on Bradley Avenue. She would give Walt and me the job of taking clips off old papers and we would run around on big carts or climb ladders carefully. We would look forward to Pinkie's lunch hour when we would visit a nearby dime store, and of course come back with some treasure. Mom and Aunt Mil would cook pork chops and potatoes on a hotplate Pinkie had. We would have a good meal and go home happy, having had a special day at "Pinkie's office."

I learned to love nature because we had fields filled with wild flowers, such as buttercups, daisies, Queen Anne's lace, and many others. A neighbor had a lilac hedge that must have been eight feet tall and was the length of their large house. It was so beautiful at lilac time. I was sad when I learned the new owners cut it down, but glad that I have that breathtaking picture in my memory. The wild flowers and a pond across the street from our house are all gone, filled with buildings. The fields were also filled with a couple ball diamonds where boys loved to play and baseball was their favorite sport. We had a modest home with no garage, but plenty of land on which Pinkie could plant flowers and dad would plant a vegetable garden. Isn't it strange that I was born on Saint Francis of Assisi Day, went to a school named for Henry David Thoreau — both nature lovers, and in later life I have become an environ-mentalist?

I'm so glad mom was a full-time homemaker and didn't work outside the home. It was so good to come home from school and have her open the door. She was such a great cook; and to come home hungry and smell the roast, meat loaf, or cake we would have for supper was real perfume! It was comforting to know that she was always there for her children.

I just happened to be there when a new kid on the street joined my brother and some other boys. I might have been in the 4th or 5th grade. He was about three years older. His brown eyes smiled before he did, and from that moment Ned was part of my life and my life's pattern was set. One night when a bunch of us were playing ping pong, he sneaked a dime store picture of himself to me so I assumed he felt the same about me. I put the picture in my *Bible* and it is still in the same place today. The rest of the story you will find in Chapter Eleven, My Love Story.

Holidays were always wonderful. How my mother and aunts did all the cooking, baking, and decorating, plus wrapping gifts, I'll never know. Aunt Mil baked bushels of all kinds of Christmas cookies and gave them all away. I waited all year for her butter cookies and am so glad I got the recipe, which everyone wants! One bite and you become an addict! When Uncle Heinie, mom's brother, joined us, there was beautiful music. He had taken piano lessons from an excellent teacher and was so good he played for silent movies. I loved him playing Strauss music or the *Poet and Peasant Overture* — and all by memory! Walt and I had our own Santa Claus at a very early age. A while after we ate, Uncle Henry (mom's brother-in-law) would say he had to put coal in the furnace. It wasn't long before we heard footsteps on the porch and there was Santa with a pack on his back filled with gifts. We had nuts, cookies for the reindeer, and sang a song to Santa. With a "Ho Ho" he left and soon Uncle Henry, who had a perfect body for Santa, returned.

That lasted until I was in the 3rd grade and came home with a note for mom. As I recall, the teacher said there was no Santa and I called her a liar because, "My mother says there is a Santa and she doesn't lie to me." We were at Aunt Mil's a block away at the time. Mom sat Walt and me on a small couch and proceeded to tell us the awful truth. I don't recall our reaction but years later when I was about 48, I answered the door and there was Santa once again. After a minute with an apology he said, "Oh, I have the wrong house!" He was looking for the child next door. This may sound crazy, but for a few moments I was a disappointed child, and the feeling was real. I giggle when I think of it now. I'm glad I had those few years of fantasy and the years when Christmas was about Jesus and not so commercial. The Christmas gift we made for mom at school and wrapped in tissue paper she loved more than some expensive item we could buy.

People we knew didn't travel to Europe in the 1920's. As stated earlier, because of Blue Laws everything was closed on Sundays, so it was very peaceful. Sometimes we went to a show with dad or he would take us to the Art Museum. On the spur of the moment we would go to the ballpark to see the

Indians and eat a hotdog. A reservation wasn't needed and it cost very little. The farthest we traveled was to Lisbon, Ohio and less frequently to Cherry Tree, Pennsylvania which was between Oil City and Titusville. We had step-relatives in both places. Sometimes Uncle Henry's mother and mom's aunt, both of whom we called "grandma," would come along to Lisbon wearing blue serge dresses and shoes that laced up to the knees. Mom's aunt, Grandma Grebbein, would visit us often when Walt and I were little. She always made sure I had a chocolate cake for my birthday. Little Walt would want to sleep with her, so to get some rest she told him she had fleas.

Uncle Henry had a beautiful voice and yodeled. As we traveled he would teach us songs from World War I and others of that time period like *Beautiful Ohio* and *I Want A Girl Just Like The Girl That Married Dear Old Dad*. It was the beginning of my love of singing. Mom would always take a leg of lamb and her delicious mint sauce to Lisbon. Amelia had an oak table that had room for all of us and her five children. They never knew we were coming but they were always home and glad to see us. The older kids would take Walt and me for a walk and we would cross a river on a swinging bridge, which was a bit scary! Milkweed was abundant so bees were not in danger as they are now. We always went home with a basket of vegetables. That generation is no more, but the third generation is happy I keep up the tradition of visiting them once or twice a year, and I continue the tradition of bringing food.

In dad's Chevy, that had big jugs on the fender for water and milk, we would go to Cherry Tree. What takes about three hours today took all day when I was a young girl. We would leave early in the morning and it might be dark when we got there. One time it was dark and raining and we had to ask another farmer to guide us to the farm. This was a real farm that had an outhouse with a *Sears Roebuck* catalog for tissue. My mother and aunts would sew sheets together which would be filled with hay for children and women to sleep on, and the men would sleep in the barn. The first thing Walt and I wanted to do was to have one of the older children take us into the woods. That childhood experience in the woods enhanced my love of nature. I can still feel the coolness of the forest in the summer and the smell of fern and rich loam. It also increased my love of trees. Those visits helped me respect farm animals which again gave me an appreciation for God's creation. We grew up knowing chicken didn't come in pieces. In the city people went to the market, chose a chicken which was wrapped in paper, and if taken home on the streetcar might peck at people. The man of the house had the nasty job of putting it to sleep. Sounds crazy but I didn't mind the smell of manure which then was natural and not toxic like it is today. The air was cleaner too. Next to the house was a field which men used for ball games which were a must before we went home. Things were so simple and so good. Because of the distance in those days we only went to Cherry Tree maybe once a year, but I'm so glad I have those memories.

Although my parents and Pinkie grew up with some religion and believed in God, they didn't join any church in later life. We didn't say grace at meals nor were there Bibles in our home. I was in elementary school when my classmate asked me to go to her church and my parents didn't object. There was no Protestant church nearby but a minister started one in his basement. When a new building was built on State Road the church took one of the spaces. The church was close to my home so I went to morning and evening services. For special days I would be asked to memorize something to recite. My parents would come to support me and in season would bring lilacs and tulips or peonies for the altar. After a while some very conservative people took over the church and spoke against shows, playing cards, cosmetics, etc. I must have always been a liberal because young as I was I did not like that. Every evening the pastor would invite anyone who wanted to follow Christ to come forward. One Sunday I did. I don't know what they thought about a child coming forward. I don't recall them ever talking to my parents and they never talked to me. It didn't matter because our time in our home was coming to an end, but that wish to follow Christ was the beginning of, I like to say, God shoving me where He wanted me to be — step by step. My favorite hymn was *Love Lifted Me!*

One sweet memory I have of my childhood was my dad taking me to the drugstore for a 5¢ double dip ice cream cone; every drugstore had a soda fountain. It was a warm day and he had my little hand in his big rough hand. I remember trying so hard to whistle with no success as we walked. Years later I whistled beautifully. I can picture that little tyke blowing air, not music.

Sickness in the family started early. My mother and Aunt Mil had gallbladder operations and then were kept in the hospital for weeks. The two families always helped one another during illness and Pinkie took over when mom was ill. My dad worked so hard as a sheet metal worker at *Quality Body and Top* on Carnegie, and a lot of his earnings went to doctors and medicine. When I got older one day I asked, "Dad, how do you stand it?" His answer I never forgot was, "Well kid, that's life, you have to learn to have patience." What a role model he was!

Walt and I each had a Jew's harp (It's in the dictionary) and we would play *Twinkle, Twinkle Little Star* together. Uncle Heinie played the piano like a professional and mom decided to provide us with piano lessons. It didn't take with Walt but I loved the lessons. I had only taken lessons a short time when the teacher had a recital. A very short beginner's piece was mine to play. I thought it was so nice that as the older girls finished, an usher would bring them a lovely bouquet, probably from their family. I was shocked and delighted when an usher did the same for me. I never see a snapdragon without remembering that loving bouquet from my family. Lessons continued for just a short time because the Great Depression had touched our home and mom could no longer afford the cost of 50¢ for my lessons. I had enough lessons that I was able to keep playing on my own, but took more lessons later in life.

For Walt and me life was comfortable, but suddenly in 1932 everything changed. The Great Depression had reached our home like a terrible monster. Our landlord wouldn't let us stay and just pay the interest like his brother allowed my uncle to do. We had to move. The uprooting was traumatic and depressing. We moved to the upstairs of a double on Easton, off 93rd and Kinsman, which at that time was a German neighborhood. No animals were allowed so we lost our dog, Chester, and cats, Jake and Lena, that we loved. Visitors were shocked when they saw Jake and Lena drinking out of the fishbowl, but never touched the fish. Walt went to the 6th grade at a school on Kinsman and I went to the 7th grade at Audubon which was known as a rough school. I missed my old friends and was suddenly with children of many cultures, which was a learning experience. One teacher sat with his feet on the desk peeling an apple, unlike my former teachers' behavior. I would run home because I heard girls were assaulted in Woodland Hills Park. It was the only time I ever wanted to run away from home, but I knew better. Being in the operetta *H.M.S. Pinafore* helped and for some reason I never forgot the words: "Things are seldom what they seem, skim milk masquerades as cream." I loved acting. Mom enrolled me in tap dancing which was cheap and discovered a new talent. We were all lonesome so dad would drive us once or twice a week to see my aunt and uncle who lived in our old neighborhood. I missed going to church but I never forgot God. As for clothes, we didn't have many new ones. I would look back and say I had one dress on me and one in the wash. How my parents managed I'll never know. Many days for lunch mom would send us to the store for rye bread and big baloney on which we would put the catsup she made before we moved. It was delicious. We never were hungry.

It didn't help that mom had three operations in the year we were on Easton, needing a special nurse each time because of complications. Pinkie would lend dad money for the nurses. One cold morning as dad was having breakfast he asked me if I could rub his neck which ached from the work he did. When I finished he said, "How could anyone with such little hands have so much strength in them?" Years later I would have appointments at work for lunchtime back rubs. I apparently have a gift of comforting, or just therapeutic hands. Many nights I dreamed we were going back to our beloved home where I wanted to see my friend I met in the 1$^{st}$ grade, and kept in touch with her until she died when we were both 90!

We entertained ourselves doing jig saw puzzles. Sometimes we would manage to go to the *Palace Theater* where we saw live news; we only had the radio at home. There was always a short feature like Betty Boop, Laurel and Hardy, or Popeye. Vaudeville was wonderful. Every big-band came to the *Palace* and we loved the beautiful music. There were hilarious and clean comedians, tap dancers, a brother and sister who were midgets who danced ballroom-style, and magicians. Whoever was there when we could afford to go eased our unhappiness. Actually movies with Shirley Temple helped us get through many troubling times. Movies were almost always the kind the entire family could see. There was no nudity! A kiss was the most sex allowed. In Western movies we expected guns, but movies of the 1920's didn't have the violence that we have today, so I now stay away from violent movies! When the circus came to town it was an annual treat for us to enjoy clowns, the marvelous performers, and especially the animals. We would go home happy, looking forward to the next year.

There were two bright spots in what I call the worst years of my life: 1932 and 1933. We looked forward to going to Euclid Beach Park for the Cleveland Railway and Al Sirat Grotto picnics. (See Chapter Fourteen, Euclid Beach Park) The second was one day Pinkie told Walt and me if we saved money so we would have something to spend, she would take us to the *Chicago World's Fair*. We had been saving money, but we lost it when our bank failed. When we got some back we bought our first bikes. Pinkie made each of us a little blue string bag so we could save $25 which she would match. She was a brave woman taking two kids ages 10 and 11, but I have a feeling between the Great Depression and mom's illnesses she thought we needed something cheery. When we got off the bus in Chicago, we walked the streets carrying our bags looking for a rooming house — which were common in those days. I don't remember how long we were at the fair. *Maxwell House* was just introducing their coffee and samples sold for 15¢. Walt wouldn't pay that much but I did. We each brought home a chameleon and enjoyed watching them change color. On the way home it poured. An author on the bus started singing Lena Horne's *Stormy Weather*. I wrote to her and asked about her books, which she graciously informed me were a bit too adult for a little girl. At least she answered!

Then came the exodus. Pinkie made arrangements with a woman she had worked for to buy her home. The friend, whose husband had died, wanted to spend winters in Florida and she would stay with us in the summer. In June, 1934 we moved to Lakewood. We were so happy to be in a house again — and such a lovely one! Mom had someone help her clean the woodwork three times until it was "spic and span" before we moved in because the previous owner was no housekeeper.

Walt and I had a long walk to our new school but it was good exercise and an excellent school. I was in the 8$^{th}$ grade when I met Ruth Burger, who became a lifelong friend. Years later she had three boys who are now in their 60's and some of those I call "my kids," and to whom I'm "Aunt Alida." We found friends we played with and I still keep in touch with some. To help with finances mom would bake her delicious kuchen and sell it.

Our new neighborhood was a melting pot of cultures and economies. There were Italians, Slovaks, Polish people, and Irish, and though we were still feeling the teeth of the Great Depression, some had very good jobs. I will always be grateful that I got to know all these people and their ways. At Christmas I got to taste the Italian and Polish bakery. I loved seeing my Slovak and Polish friends taking a basket of food to church at Easter to be blessed by the priest. The baskets were always covered with a beautiful cloth. My Slovak friend would invite me to eat some of the blessed food with her. While they spoke their native language at home, they made every effort to learn English because they were proud to be American. One summer I learned a lot of Polish as I helped an immigrant to learn English. One Polish friend said, "Lidka, you learn too well. Soon we can't talk in front of you." I reminded her that that wasn't polite anyway. I was "Lidka" to them. Some Saturdays my Polish friends would take me to their Polish church hall a block away to dance. I really liked ballroom dancing but Polkas were a lot of fun! One elderly man said, "How come you dance Polkas so well and you weren't born in Poland?"

One of the loveliest things we did, and almost everyone knew how to do, was ballroom dancing. When couples did the bridal dance they did a beautiful waltz and didn't move from one foot to the other like they do now. Children were always included in weddings and other social functions so they learned how to celebrate them. Parents would take their children on the dance floor and teach them how to do ballroom dancing. What is called dancing now is more like exercise and a partner isn't necessary. Music was soft, so it was possible to talk with people sitting at your table.

Mom found a hairdresser on our street who worked out of a room in the back of her house. After a while I became friends with her and her sister. They went to the Slovak church, Saint Cyril and Methodius, only two blocks away. After a while, because I had no church, I went to church with them just to be in a place of worship and feel closer to God. Their cousin was a priest, who even in those days, when there was division between Catholic and Protestant, would say masses for my mother and even came to our house and ate with us. Some Sundays we would visit Father Paul and he would treat the three of us to a show and dinner. We were like family to him. He knew I would always be a Protestant and he respected that.

Soon I was in high school where, unfortunately then, they had sororities and fraternities — which kids did not know how to handle and made the Great Depression raise its ugly head. There were the "Have's" and the "Have not's." We who were the "Have not's" couldn't sit at the sorority table for lunch and write on the Year Book page at graduation that the sorority sisters wrote on. It is good that the school no longer has those two groups. I wasn't with the kids that went to football games and didn't even want to date because of my early love. My 8$^{th}$ grade friend lived close to me and we were in about the same position. I always have said she was brighter than me but I excelled in shorthand which she had to quit. We both loved a cappella choir and it was there I discovered I had a God-given high soprano voice. At gatherings when people would get around a piano and sing, people would ask who had the high voice. A substitute teacher heard my voice and liked it. My voice became my identity.

In my senior year I shocked myself by entering the Interscholastic Solo Contest. I never had any lessons as others did. Thank God that substitute teacher was teaching that day. I told her what I had done and she immediately said she would coach me. We chose *Villanelle*, a coloratura song in French which ended with a high B-flat. On May 13th, 1939, I sang for the judges and was the only soprano from Lakewood High to get a first rating. I cried all the way home I was so happy. It is the happiest memory I have of the Great Depression years. Every year after that on May 13th I would send a note of gratitude or phone my voice coach. At 25 and 50 years she got a dozen red roses. We were friends until she died.

Graduation in 1939 meant meeting a goal, but also meant finding a job. Many in my high school class went to college, but I didn't have the finances. In my class book I said my goal was to be Alida in Aida. The Great Depression was still in force and I filled out many applications. Pinkie knew the manager of the dime store we loved as children and got me an application for a Christmas job. I was hired to work at the jewelry counter at $10 a week. A job was a job and I enjoyed talking with people. What a thrill it was when I got a letter offering me a job at the Federal Reserve Bank at $15 a week. I started there January 1st, 1940. The jobs we did then, sorting checks and running 2,500 checks on an adding machine and balancing them, are now all done by computers. The best part of working there was that in 1941 another lifelong friend, Beulah Neal, came to the bank to work. I sang at many weddings but was happy to sing at hers when she became Beulah Carey and eventually had "my first kid" Neal, and then Roger and Drew, to whom I'm still "Aunt Alida." Neal died of a sudden heart attack and I miss him. There was also Rita Boroviak, who asked me to write letters to her brother Dutch during the war. Both women were my friends until they died — after lifelong friendships!

The only fan letter I ever wrote to a movie star was to Ronald Reagan. I wrote the letter after watching him and Jane Wyman in the movie *Brother Rat*. After we came out of the show I told those I was with that he would become a star. He did send me a post card saying "Thanks Alida." I saved it because it was part of my teen years. When he became president I put it in my safe deposit box.

In 1946 a cousin decided to leave her job at the Illuminating Building, but told her boss about me before she left. I was offered a job and took it so I could begin to have normal hours and maybe begin to live a little. Now I see it as one way God was guiding me gradually to where He wanted me to be. The Illuminating Company was next door to the Old Stone Church and had noonday services every day. The first day I went I felt at home again in a Protestant church. There weren't many attending but some would hear me sing and invite me to their church. I kept feeling I was supposed to be doing something other than being a clerk, but I didn't know what and had no money for college. I became friends with the associate pastor and his wife and would go to the evening services with them. For seven years I went every day on my lunch hour, praying I would find what God wanted me to do. Our time is not God's time. Some days I would be depressed and would call Reverend Garner and tell him I was in a gloomy mood. He would have me come over and talk to me while he had lunch. When he knew he was going to move to a church in Michigan he suggested I find a church where I lived where I could be of service. He knew I wouldn't be inclined to take a streetcar downtown on Sunday. Though there weren't a lot at the noonday services, Reverend Garner said if he just reached one person he would be happy. He reached me! One Christmas when mom just came home from the hospital and it was a bit gloomy, the door bell rang. There was Mrs. Garner who took time from her Christmas to bring me a Goodspeed translation of the *New Testament*, and in it Reverend Garner had written a personal message to me. The gloom was lifted. Every Christmas Eve I phoned my "other family" after they left Lakewood. I'm still in touch with their daughter.

I was 25 when I found the Old Stone Church, and it was at that time doctors had diagnosed my mother with severe depression and in need of shock treatment. Pinkie and I would take turns going with dad to take mom for her treatments. The doctor would talk with mom to find out what she did during the week. He discovered mom, Pinkie, and a neighbor overdid going to Bingo — which I learned to dislike! The doctor felt it was too much for mom. He had mom go to a room, and with nothing to put her to sleep as they do today, he gave her the shock treatment. Then, one of us would sit with her until she awakened. We were given no instructions. She would be half asleep when dad would come and help us get her to the car. When she woke up at home she was fine until the next weekend when we went through the routine again. I don't remember how long that went on but she was in a number of mental hospitals. I felt bad for mom being sick and bad for dad who worked hard to pay hospitals and doctors. I would go out with friends occasionally for enjoyment, but there wasn't much laughter in our house. The last four months of her life mom was in a nursing home. It was sheer hell for me to place her there for safety's sake, but written in Chapter Fifteen, The Other Side Of Hell, was what the patients did for me.

When I learned the wonderful choir director at Lakewood High was the choir director at Lakewood Baptist I was thrilled. I called him to see if I could join the choir to use my voice in honor of a singing teacher who had died, however, I did not want to become a member. I knew I would have to be baptized by immersion, which I grew up thinking was strange. T. R. Evans welcomed me. After a few years of warmth and friendship from the members, the feeling of comfort in that church, and remembering that little girl going forward to say she wanted to follow Christ, I decided to join — BUT immersion was still a problem! I told Reverend Garner about my concern, and he said he would go ahead of me in the water to prove I would be giving up something special. I talked to Reverend Lomas on Saturday and he said, "My sermon tomorrow is, 'You are not far from the kingdom but not near enough.'" We were singing the last hymn on April 22nd when I decided to go forward to join the church. I swear I saw the words "God Is Smiling" in the hymn book before I went forward but never found them. I was the only one baptized on May 21st, 1950. Mom had some of my Baptist friends over for lunch, and that afternoon I never sang better than I did at a recital another singing teacher had arranged.

I joined the church in 1950 and in the same year made a shocking discovery you can read about in Chapter Thirteen, Discovery and Decision. It was good I had faith and now had a church home which I believed helped me at that time. As you will find in my Christmas letters, we lived through a lot of history along with others called "The Greatest Generation!"

You will find in the Christmas letters that follow these first 29 years of my life that God had a lot of surprises in store for me. The letters start out rather blandly, but get more active as years go by. I did things I never thought I would do nor thought I had the courage to do. I realize, looking back, many decisions I made were really God guiding me to become what He wanted me to be — a social worker!

# Part Two:

# Christmas Letters

When I joined my church I got so active I didn't have time to write a lot of notes to relatives and friends. I felt my writing would look like hieroglyphics if I sent a separate Christmas note to each person. So, to stay in contact with the people who were important to me, I decided to write just one master letter for everyone, and thus the annual Christmas letter was born. As one reader said, my Christmas letters chronicle the history of my later life and all the amazing changes that came with it. People often tell me to never stop sending my annual Christmas letters because they find them both inspiring and comforting. This, of course, continues to surprise me because I see them as just ordinary letters. It warms my heart each time I am told my letters brightened someone's Christmas holiday. At my age I don't know how long I will be able to continue to compose and mail my letters. I will continue as long as I am able!

Chapter Three

**Ten Christmas Letters
From 1950 to 1959**

# 1st Christmas Letter, December 14, 1950 (At Home)

Dear friends,

I know this is a breach of etiquette, but I'm afraid it's the only way you would all get a full-length letter from me this year. It's hard for me to believe that a few years ago I was wondering what I could do with my time, because now I am wondering if I will ever have a little time to waste.

The main reason for my being so busy is the fact that I joined The Lakewood Baptist Church in May. I sang in the choir for a year and finally decided that I would like to be a member. Believe me, I'll never forget that day. I was no sooner a member than I became involved in activities for the Baptist World Alliance, which was in July. There were many rehearsals for a 5,000 voice choir, as well as a pageant. It was an experience I wouldn't have missed for the world.

All summer I was an usher at the church. When September rolled around choir started again, and I also took over the duties of a third-year Primary teacher. I guess it's true that the teacher gets more out of the teaching than the children get out of the teacher. But really, friends, even though there are times when I wonder if my nerves can take it, I wouldn't miss one of those Sunday school sessions. Just being with those kids makes one feel like a new person. We have a Junior Choir at church now, and I get the biggest kick out of seeing some of "my kids" in their robes walking proudly up the aisle. They'll never know what they have done for me!

We have potluck suppers at church on Wednesday nights and they are great fun. So, you can see that a great deal of my time is spent in my "second home," my church! That's one nice thing about Protestant churches; there are so many jobs that a person can do, and that really makes you feel like a part of the church. For Christmas we're going to present a Living Nativity Scene on Detroit Avenue. I'm supposed to be Mary for a half-hour, get warm for a half-hour, and rotate in this manner for three hours. I will be doing this on the 22$^{nd}$, 23$^{rd}$, and 24$^{th}$ of December.

Just so you won't think I spent every minute in church, I can assure you that I have continued my singing lessons, although I have also mastered that great passion I had for music. I still love it but it doesn't bother me anymore. I take several lessons a month just to keep in touch with it. But as far as worrying about a career, I've grown up and discovered that someone can love their hobby without making it a full-time career! I'm also taking a course in typing and shorthand at Wilcox College two nights a week. I took an aptitude test during my vacation and was advised to review those subjects. I'm getting along surprisingly well considering my age. Ah, yes, I was 29 this year!

Just to keep your records straight, I'm not married yet and I'm not going steady. Lately I've wondered where on Earth I'd find time for a man if I had one. Once in a great while I have a date, but I've been so busy it hasn't made much of a difference to me. We thought for a while that my brother might be weakening, but that romance faded into nothingness also.

Mom is still suffering from a nervous breakdown. It's been two years since she got so very sick. We finally changed doctors and are hoping this one will do her some good. She is staying at my aunt's house because we can't leave her alone all day. My Aunt Min, whose nickname is "Pinkie," has taken over most of the housework, but I manage somehow to get the cleaning and some of the ironing done. What would I ever do without my wonderful aunts? When I count my blessings they certainly head the list.

Dad hasn't been too well, but he goes to work every day and never complains. Believe me, I can learn some lessons on how to have patience from just watching him. Walt is quitting his job at Crile Hospital to take a job as a salesman for Armour & Company, selling the drug products they make. His pre-med training may come in handy yet! He was just 28 and might be Army bait! The time he spent in the Merchant Marine isn't counted as service.

I'm still working at the CEI and have asked for a transfer, but they don't seem to have much of anything at this time. The personnel manager was wonderful to me, and so was my boss. I've seriously been thinking of going into full-time church work, but as yet I don't know just what to do. I'd probably need more education, but couldn't afford that. The only reason I'd hate to leave my present job is because I wouldn't be able to go to the Old Stone Church every day on my lunch hour. What a relief it is to find refuge and peace for a half-hour each workday. We've been working overtime for the past month or longer, so what little time I had to myself was consumed by extra work.

It's about 1:00 a.m. and if I'm going to get up for work tomorrow, I'd better start signing off right now. I still have to take my bath and get ready for bed. I certainly hope this stencil turns out alright. I never typed one before so you will have to forgive any errors you find. I'll try to type a personal note on each copy for you, but this was the only way I could write a half-way decent letter to each of you. There must be at least a million things I forgot to tell you. Oh yes, I forgot to tell you how much I enjoyed our blizzard. I never had such a wonderful rest, and I felt just like a kid again shoveling snow. Needless to say, I felt like an old lady the next day! I only missed one day of work, and that was because I really didn't try too hard to get there!

Please don't think that I've forgotten any of you because you haven't heard from me. My conscience has been killing me! I certainly hope this letter finds you all well and happy. I mean it when I say I've never been happier in all my life than I've been this year. I guess it is good for one to be busy.

Goodbye for now, and may God bless you and yours during this holiday season and all through the coming year!

All my love, Alida

# 2<sup>nd</sup> Christmas Letter, December, 1951 (At Home)

Dear friends,

So help me, I don't know where the past year went. Last year at this time I thought I would write to each of you at least once or twice during the year but, alas, here I am stenciling one again.

If you were to ask me what I've done this past year, I would find it difficult to know where to begin. In July, four of us went to the beautiful Baptist Conference Center in Green Lake, Wisconsin. We stayed there several days and went on to the Dells. They were lovely! Next we visited the Schlitz Brewery in Milwaukee, and we ended the week by spending a day in Chicago. It was a long trip, and I was glad to get home.

For my 30<sup>th</sup> birthday in October my dad took a few days off and drove me to Battle Creek, Michigan, where we spent a couple of days with my dear friend Reverend Garner and his family. That was a glorious trip for me because there is nothing I love better than to drive along the highways in October and enjoy nature's paintings. The trees were one heavenly mass of color and I came home feeling refreshed and ready to face anything.

Need I say that church work has kept me more than a little busy, but I have enjoyed every minute of it. I'm looking forward to being Mary in our Living Nativity Scene again this year. That is our church's contribution to the community at Christmas time. Of course, there is also choir work, and again this year I am a Sunday school teacher. Yes, it keeps be busy, but I wish I could convince everyone I know that there is nothing so satisfying as giving your time and service to God's work. You may all think I'm getting terribly "churchy" but, believe me, everything I've needed in the way of Hope, Faith, Friendship, and Courage, I've found in my church!

My cousin got married in September and I was the "Old Maid of Honor." We had a shower for her, which was a humdinger! All in all we had a lot of fun. My folks are threatening to raffle off Walt and me next year if we don't get married. I haven't had much time to look around for a husband. For a while I was going with my old friend, George. But I guess he has gone the way of all men and once more I am on the loose! During the year I helped one of my "friends" get his Master's degree in Engineering at Case by typing the rough draft for his thesis. Night after night after night I worked on that darned thing until I finally had to take a day off from work to sleep, but it was a good experience.

I took a course in typing and shorthand, or a "review" I should say; only to find I hate it just as much as ever. After a year I'm still thinking of changing jobs, but I still don't know what I want to do. Off and on I've continued singing lessons, but I don't know why! I don't have the time to practice so I might as well give it up. Half the time I don't even come home for supper. You know, friends, something has happened to old Struzie. After sitting around doing nothing for years she suddenly got on the ball. Truthfully, though, I think I'm getting too old for this pace. I've been taking the vitamin pills my brother sells for Armour's. If you guys need a tonic, let me put in a plug for Armour's Liver, Yeast and Iron. They sure do pep me up when I need something!

A friend of mine that loves to sing just moved across the street from me. The neighbors will probably have to install shatter-proof glass in their windows. Betty and I are looking forward to many happy hours of singing together. I imagine the neighbors will be requesting *"Far Far Away."*

As we approach Christmas I thank God that my family is well. Mom has been ill off and on during the year, and my brother was quite ill for several weeks, but he's alright again. He got a questionnaire from the Draft Board the other day. He was 29 Saturday, so I hope he's safe. That may sound selfish but he had enough during the last war, although his time in the Merchant Marine isn't counted as service.

My Uncle Pat wants me to go to New York with him and my aunt in January. I'm looking forward to it; the change will do me a lot of good because I've been quite tired. If and when I get there I'll try to contact those of you who live in the East.

Well, friends, this may or may not be a very informative letter. I won't know until I read it over, but at any rate, I've had a chance to say "Hello!" I'm not lying when I say I do think of you often, and remember each and every one of you in my prayers during the year. It's been nice writing to you again, and I hope and pray that the year ahead will bring each of you all the things you cherish the most.

May God bless you and yours,

All my love, Alida

P.S.

I'm very sorry I didn't get this letter in your Christmas mail, but circumstances beyond my control prevented it. I must tell you about our "unusual" Cleveland weather. We had a terrific snow that lasted almost a week. Last night it poured and tonight it is freezing, so you can imagine what it's like walking and driving. If it stays this cold, I'll be a very cold Mary in our Living Nativity Scene on Christmas Eve. We had our pictures taken Wednesday, and they will be in the Press Saturday. Someone said on the streetcar tonight that the weather will break soon. Believe me, if it doesn't break, we will!

We aren't exchanging gifts this Christmas. It's just too much expense for my folks. But it really doesn't matter; friendship and love all year round mean more to me than a gift tied with ribbon at Christmas. I've loved getting all your cards. It's so much fun to come home from a long hard day at work and find cards from so many friends. It always makes me feel very rich!

Once more I'll say Au Revoir (The girls at work laugh at me because I like languages, so I sent them a German card anyway!)

# 3<sup>rd</sup> Christmas Letter, December 12, 1952 (At Home)

Dear friends,

It seems like only yesterday that I sat in this same spot to write my 1951 letter. It seems as if the older I get, the shorter the years are. Maybe we just appreciate time more. The best way to tell you about this year is to start at the very beginning — and a wonderful beginning it was! I started the year by going to New York City with an uncle and aunt of mine. For several years they had invited me, but I had always declined the offer. We were there for one week, and it took me 10 weeks to get back down to Earth. We had a suite of rooms at the Park Sheraton and I loved it. Several times we had breakfast sent up to our room, and for me that was a lot of fun.

We ate at Lindy's almost every day. My uncle said he never saw anyone eat so many pickles, but I'm the old "pickle kid," and would rather eat pickles than Lindy's famous cheesecake. They had the most wonderful sturgeon sandwiches at $1.75 each, but they were worth every cent of my uncle's money! We went to Radio City Theatre and saw *Call Me Madam*. Several mornings my uncle and I got up around 6:30 a.m. and we did the things my aunt wasn't interested in doing, such as taking a ride on the Staten Island Ferry and walking through Central Park.

My aunt and I had one glorious day of shopping. I got several dresses at Saks 5<sup>th</sup> Avenue, plus two hats and gloves. One day my uncle decided I needed a new coat, so he took me to one of his friends. When I walked into our hotel I was the owner of a lovely gray Persian lamb coat. It was truly a delightful week, and of course I was able to appreciate it twice as much because my uncle wouldn't let me pay for a thing, except the clothes and coat. I had fun, but was strangely glad to get back to Cleveland. One loses one's perspective in a place like NYC. You're surrounded by mink, lights, and high living in general. That's why it's easy to forget that you are still the same little cog in the wheel that you were back home — and not the whole wheel! Well, it was loads of fun and I wouldn't have missed that week for anything.

In February my brother took off once more for the Merchant Marine, and since he left he has been to Denmark, Greenland, and Japan. He seems to like the adventure, not to mention the good wages, and he does have many advantages inasmuch as he is a radio operator. In his last trip he saw Honolulu, Manila, Yokohama, and many other ports in the territory. He was home for several days last month, and we were all so glad to see him. But he has gone again and once more is headed for Japan.

March and April were uneventful, except for the usual income tax headaches. Then came May! It was then that my church asked me if I would like to go to Green Lake to represent the church at the Laboratory Training School for Sunday school teachers. I decided that if I could talk my boss into giving me an extra week without pay I would go. Fortunately, I'm in the good graces of my boss, and so I began to look forward to another vacation at the end of June. I doubt if I can make those of you who have never been there understand what a wonderful time I had. I stayed at the hotel and had a room overlooking the lake. The woman I shared the room with loved beauty as much as I did, and we both hated to go to bed at night. The moonlight on the water was so beautiful. During the day we studied, worked with children, observed others teaching, and learned new skills. Does that sound like work to you?

Honestly, I came home more refreshed and relaxed and HAPPY than I have been in years. The first week we were there the missionaries and workers for the Indians were also there. I met many wonderful Indian friends, and even learned the song *"My God and I"* in sign language. I don't know what contributed the most to my two weeks of complete happiness. Perhaps it was the beauty of Green Lake, or perhaps all the wonderful people I associated with. Maybe it was the fact that the two weeks I walked hand-in-hand with God and found in the richness of that experience the happiness we are all looking for. If all is well at home I'm going back to Green Lake — for the next three years at least!

I could go on and on, but I do in a few sentences want to tell those of you who were there with me, that when I came home I kept my promise to quit choir and devote my time to the second hour of church school with children. I have a different teacher working with me every week. This makes it difficult, but we are seeing the results of having a unit carried through. We had a wonderful unit on Burma. With the help of my flash camera we made a chart of our church friends. We had a happy experience planting bulbs and sharing them with other departments, as well as with sick friends. Believe me, I came home exhausted and wonder how on Earth Florence Stansbury managed to get through two weeks of teaching both children and adults. However, it is worth every bit of the effort just to hear parents say their children want to stay the second hour.

I have been doing more visiting in the homes and wonder why I never did it before. The parents just love to have you come, and the children are overjoyed to have a visit from their teacher. All in all I can only say "Thank God for Green Lake." I'm still receiving dividends from that simple investment of two weeks of my time. Thanks to all of you who have written to me. I think of ALL of you so often. Recently I heard a Negro baritone sing *"Lord, I want to be a Christian,"* and I was suddenly sitting in our Primary room with all of you. It's funny how those two weeks together formed a bond of friendship that I'm sure will last forever. To my other friends, I want all of you to know that even though I have been busy, I have forgotten none of you. You have been in my thoughts and prayers more than you can know. Kay, it was so good to get your notes and the pictures of your children. Also, it was wonderful seeing you when I was in New York!

I have tried changing jobs, but so far nothing has come along that I want. I missed an excellent chance as Receptionist-Secretary at the Illuminating Company because I had no typing and shorthand experience. I'm still singing, and have a lot of fun singing duets with a baritone friend of mine. I couldn't possibly mention in this letter all the things I've done this past year. There has been time for everything but sleep!

I'm sorry to report that my mother has been ill for a month. She had two bowel operations, and we haven't known from one day to the next how she'll be. I don't know what people without faith do at times like these, but I have certainly been grateful for mine! It is only in the words "Thy will be done" that I have found any comfort. I wish I had another stencil so I could write more, but I believe I have covered the highlights in my year. I hope and pray that all is well with all of you. I hope you will have the happiest kind of Christmas, and that the blessings of the day will remain with you in the coming year!

GOD BLESS YOU AND YOURS, Alida

# 4<sup>th</sup> Christmas Letter, December 21, 1953 (At Home)

Dear friends and relatives everywhere,

By now you must be thinking that I must have crossed some of you off my Christmas card list. For a gal who always had cards out two weeks in advance, this greeting is really late. But as you read this letter I'm sure you will understand the delay.

The year 1953 started off as usual for me, but it certainly took some very surprising turns. Nothing unusual happened until spring, when I became creative. One morning on my way to the corner I composed a poem as I cautiously stepped over the worms, which the spring rain brought to the surface. The poem was published in *The Plain Dealer* and accepted by the *Baptist Leader*. Believe me, it pays to be crazy!

> Gentle, gentle spring rain
> To nature you give birth.
> I wish you'd just bring out the flowers,
> And leave worms in the earth.

In May I finally served on a jury, and never was paid so well just to have fun. I got $5 a day, and in two weeks was on one case. The rest of the time I worked jig-saw puzzles. Well, it was a good racket and a good experience. I thoroughly enjoyed every minute of it.

June came and during that month I came down with a slight case of pneumonia. I was home from work for three weeks, and then went on my vacation to recuperate. For my vacation I went back to Green Lake, Wisconsin where I enjoyed myself so much last year. Once again I attended the Lab Training School for Sunday school teachers and came home with many new ideas and a lot of inspiration. I didn't have time to eat between trains, and it still amuses me when I remember talking to the woman next to me on the train. She not only was friendly, but gave me practically her entire lunch to eat.

Now hold on to your hats friends! Old stick-in-the-mud Struze came home from Green Lake, and after a month of going crazy trying to decide what to do, I decided to go to college — AND DID! The 19<sup>th</sup> of September found me at the Baptist Missionary Training School in the great big city of Chicago. You know, sometimes I still have to pinch myself to make sure it isn't all a dream. All my life I wanted a college education, but never knew exactly what I wanted to study. There was always a desire to learn more about the *Bible*, and even though I thought I would be a happier person if I'd only go away and learn something, I just hated to give up the "security" I had. Knowing I wouldn't have a pay check coming in every week scared me to death. But somehow, with God's help, I found the courage to take the step.

So far I have enjoyed every minute of school and have made a very satisfactory adjustment. I have a wonderful roommate, and that is half the battle. One day I told her that in preparing decorations I was going to use the turkey motif. Ruby said, "Roommate, you use such big words like turkey." That struck me so funny that I almost woke up the dorm laughing. We always seem to get the giggles at midnight. I also have a "Big Sis" named Carol Welch, who is the most adorable girl in the school. She's only 20, so I should be her Big Sis, but at BMTS age doesn't matter too much. Saint Francis said that it only takes one sunbeam to drive away many shadows, and that is what Carol meant to me a few times when I wondered if I had made the right decision. She had truly been a "sunbeam" to me. Never a night goes by without her coming in to say goodnight to me and I in turn wake her every morning. I don't know if that is a fair exchange or not!

I have loved learning again, and amazingly enough have had excellent grades. This term we studied Astronomy, General Psychology, Devotional Life, Field Work Guidance, Freshman Orientation, and English Composition. Golly, it thrills me to know the Earth is 8,000 miles in diameter, that all stars are gaseous, and that I have a central and peripheral nervous system. I don't think I'm getting egotistical. I have never felt so humble in my life as I have in the face of the vastness of the universe and the miraculous workings of our bodies.

If you ever want a well-rounded education, live in a dorm for a while. One night I discovered I had blankets but no mattress. Another time I went to the USO to help serve lunch to the boys, and when I returned my roommate had turned the room around. Also, the legs of my pajamas had been sewn, and my bed was short-sheeted! For those of you who don't know how to short-sheet a bed, you take the bottom part of the top sheet and bring it up to the head of the bed so that when the unsuspecting person goes to bed, he can only get his feet down half way.

For my birthday, the girls had a little get-together in my room — and I was really surprised! I think more popcorn is popped at BMTS than anywhere in the world, and at Christmas one walks down the halls enjoying the beautifully decorated doors. We have a kitchenette on each floor where we can cook, and there is a utility room on each floor where we do our personal laundry. Our sheets and towels are cleaned in the school laundry. We do have to keep our rooms clean, and also help with the housework in the rest of the building. This cooperative living cuts the tuition fee a lot. The meals have been wonderful, although I still enjoy getting a box of homemade cookies from my mom!

During the term we had two holidays. One day all classes were cancelled and the school hired two buses to take us to the dunes in Indiana. At the dunes we spent a day just relaxing on the beach and roaming through the woods. It ended with a wiener roast. Then there was Thanksgiving, and we were off for both Thursday and Friday. I spent the day with some friends in Chicago and appreciated their kindness. Truthfully, I haven't seen too much of Chicago. I did visit the Adler Planetarium and the Field Museum for Science class. But other than going to church on Sunday and two visits to a theatre to see *The Robe* and *Martin Luther*, I didn't go out too much. We have a grand candy shop nearby which serves the biggest sodas and sundaes, and we bike up there once in awhile. I'm glad to say that I've been very happy, and only wish I had taken this step a long time ago.

As I close this letter I want each of you to know that you are in my thoughts and prayers often. I never appreciated my friends as much as I have since I'm away. There is always a letter from someone in my box. If I were as rich in money as I am in friendship right now, I would have nothing to worry about. But I'm sure the Lord will find a way for me to get through. My one prayer is that God will bless each of you at this holiday season and through the coming year. I intend to stay in this country to do Christian work, so you will be hearing from me.

I love you all, Alida

# 5<sup>th</sup> Christmas Letter, December 20, 1954 (At Home)

My dear relatives and friends everywhere,

Christmas is such a happy time of year! It is a time when we like to think of giving and sharing. I especially like this time of year because for me it is not only a time of giving and sharing, but also a time for remembering. As I address envelopes to each of you, I like to take a little time to remember the part you played in my life. I may never be a millionaire, but as far as friendship is concerned, I often feel like the richest woman in the world. There are times when I'm at school that I feel very lonely. I feel very far away from you and wish I could pick up the phone and call you, or have the time to write notes like I used to write. When I got home for Christmas vacation and saw the huge stack of cards, I realized once more that no matter where we go in life, real bonds of friendship are never broken. My heart was lifted by your many expressions of love and friendship and they are the most treasured gifts of this season.

Some of you are no doubt wondering how I'm getting along in my new adventure as a "school girl." May I say that I have never been happier in my life, and I find that each day is a new adventure in the realm of knowledge! My only regret is that I must eat and sleep. I would much rather be able to spend every hour in study. College is not the easiest thing in the world, and especially at BMTS. We not only have all our class work to do, but we share in the housework. We also seem to have endless committee meetings to attend. Believe me, I'm grateful for the 14 years of work — which disciplined me to use my time to good advantage. All in all I didn't have as rough a time last year as I thought I would have, and, believe it or not, ended the year by getting scholastic honors. When I looked back on my first year, I realized that I had not been alone in this venture. Without God's help, and without all the thoughts and prayers of so many of you, I could never have accomplished so much.

My Aunt Min, who retired this year, and my cousin, Genevra, came to Chicago to take me home in June. Before we went to Cleveland, we stopped over in Battle Creek so I could see my dear friends, the Garner family. I spent a few weeks at home just relaxing, and then went to Green Lake for my third year in Lab School. This year I specialized in Kindergarten work and always enjoyed my two weeks. If it is at all possible, I am going to go to Green Lake again this summer for my fourth year, which means I will graduate from Lab School. If I don't get a diploma from some place it won't be my fault!

When I got home from Green Lake I went back to the Illuminating Company to work for several months, and then was off to school again. It was so good to be home, and I must apologize to many of you whom I just didn't get a chance to visit. I had such good intentions, but the two months flew by so fast I don't know where they went. Our house was very lonesome in a way this summer because, not only was my brother gone, but our dear dog died. Many of you know that she was the "baby in the family." Even now when I think of home I have a difficult time realizing Tippy just isn't there anymore! Walt is still in the Merchant Marine and seems to be enjoying it. He has made about seven trips to Japan, Korea, and Indo-China. I wish you could see my collection of dolls and other souvenirs Walt has so thoughtfully bought for me.

And so, after spending a wonderful vacation at home, I went back to Chicago and began my sophomore (suffer-more) year at BMTS. I have a new roommate who collects donkeys of all things! Say, do you think that's why she got me for a roommate? Ha! Our room is small but it has two closets, which is fortunate. We have four filing cabinets and three bookcases in the room — which makes it look like an office! We don't dare leave any food around or we have a whole army of ants descend upon us. The only reason we have this trouble is because the room is right off a brick terrace. One night we had ants all over the filing cabinets. Maybe they wanted an education, too!

Our courses are so interesting this year and the teachers just couldn't be any better. Having been at Green Lake, I found Christian Education was simple, and the teacher we have for Old Testament History has made the *Bible* come alive for us. I never realized the Old Testament could be so interesting! Sociology is fascinating, although a little difficult, and History of Civilization has really made me open my eyes. Our History of Civilization teacher is a "Master of all trades." Not only is he a minister, but he writes music and articles. He knows unusual facts about everybody who has ever lived, and can tell you the anatomy of every living thing. He has written speeches for Jose Ferrer and Ralph Bellamy, to mention just a few, and he has a heart that is just as big as he is. Ben is a Negro and one of the most wonderful Christians I've ever known. He teaches not only what he has learned from books, but also from what he has learned from life. He has a sense of humor, which is a great asset in making a course interesting. I will have these four subjects all this year, although Sociology will be replaced by Social Psychology and Political Science in the next two terms.

Things at home have been about as usual. My Aunt Min was in the hospital at Easter, and this Christmas season finds my dad and Uncle Henry both on the same floor at St. John's Hospital. Both have had operations. At least they are keeping each other company. I can count our blessings and say that I'm glad that things are no worse than they are now! Some of you have written to me and told me of the sorrow you have had in your family this year. May I say that I am very sorry and pray that God will give you the courage and strength you need as you face your challenges.

I haven't had letters from some of you for a long time and would love to know what you are doing. To Grace and Peggy in California, and Kay back east: how are you anyway? It was so good to see so many of my Green Lake friends again this year, and it was like old times being back at the Illuminating Company with the girls I worked with. You can well imagine that the thing I look forward to most when I come home is seeing all "my kids." "My family" is growing up! It has been so wonderful of all my friends to share their children with me, and I certainly enjoy them!

This letter isn't as newsy as I wanted it to be, but I am writing it in a big hurry, so you will have to forgive me. I have reached line 53 on the stencil, which means I must begin to say goodbye for another year. I always hate this part in my Christmas letter because I wish I could just go on and on. I hate to say goodbye even in letters. Again may I say "thank you" to all my relatives, friends, and my church family, for all you have done for me throughout the year. I only hope that someday I can repay all your kindness. I pray that this will be a truly wonderful Christmas for each of you, and that the blessings of this season will remain with you and yours throughout the coming year.

GOD BLESS YOU ONE AND ALL!  Love to you, Alida

# 6<sup>th</sup> Christmas Letter, December 17, 1955 (At Home)

My dear family and friends,

How wonderful it is to be home again, and if the calendar didn't say so, I would never believe that a whole year has gone by since I last wrote to you. It has been a year packed with so many things, it is no wonder I have lost track of time.

My sophomore year at BMTS was a most enjoyable one, but at the end of the year it was a good feeling to know that I had reached the half-way mark. Because I worked very hard and the teachers were very generous, I once again received scholastic honors at the end of the year. I tell you this in all humility for I know that without God's help I could have accomplished nothing!

Summer jobs were hard to get and I was extremely tired, so I decided for the first time in 15 years that I would just relax and do whatever work came my way. First of all I went to the Lab School at Green Lake where I completed the course I was taking and came home with a much-cherished diploma. No sooner did I get home than I was offered a job as Kindergarten Supervisor at the Young Adult Family Conference which is held in the Abbey area in Green Lake in August. This proved to be a very rich experience, and I will never forget the sight of 38 families sitting in family groups having their evening devotions together.

In between my two trips to Green Lake I spent a week at the Sunday School Convention in Cleveland. There I had a lot of fun working in the exhibit booth of the *American Baptist Publication Society*. There were some weeks when I had nothing to do, and I filled that time by doing some volunteer work at my church in the morning. I spent the afternoons enjoying the sunshine in my backyard. While enjoying the sun I pulled weeds, and by the time I pulled out all the grab grass, we had no lawn! I also wrote some letters and several articles, and I sold one of my articles to the *Baptist Leader*. You will be interested to know that while I was at the Family Conference, a photographer and reporter from *Life* covered our activities. It was a new experience to watch them work. If these pictures get into their issue covering Christianity, I will get a thrill out of knowing I was there when they were taken.

One of the nicest things about the summer was that my brother managed to be home for a week. I had not seen him for over a year and a half. Dad was on vacation at that time, so we really had a family reunion. To add to the joy of the summer we got a new puppy, and what a darling ball of fur she is. Somehow she got the name of "Susie," but a better name would probably be "Foxy" because she doesn't miss a thing. She's really a panic and keeps my family busy and happy.

And so the summer came and went and the next thing I knew it was time to pack my things and return to the big city of Chicago to begin my junior year. Cleveland may have its faults, but I would never trade it for Chicago. I never go to the Loop without being overwhelmed by the number of stores, and I always wonder how they all manage to make money. The size of the Loop makes Cleveland's shopping center look like small town stuff, but I'd still rather shop at Higbee's than at Marshall Fields. Be it ever so humble, I guess there is no place like home!

The junior year has not been an easy one, and I have felt pressure this year more than in other years. The courses this term were Missions, New Testament History, Social Group Work, Recreational Leadership, and History of Social Thought — with my favorite teacher, Mr. Ben. Throughout the year we will have New Testament History, but the other subjects will be replaced with Mental Hygiene, Social Problems, Social Case History, Storytelling, Drama, Choric Speech, and Introduction to Literature. I am doing my field work in a German Baptist church where I'm teaching a Leadership Training class.

Last term I taught Introduction to the *Bible*, and this term the course offered will be Survey of the Old Testament, although I don't know how I can cover the material in the Old Testament in nine weeks! I am grateful, however, for the opportunity to try my hand at teaching, and have thus far enjoyed it very much. Other than my regular housework, which is cleaning the Public Relations offices, I do three hours of secretarial work for our Academic Dean each week.

Each year the junior class gives a formal banquet and some kind of entertainment for the seniors. My class elected me as the chairman of this affair. It has been a valuable experience to guide the planning of our junior-senior event, and if I get nothing else out of this experience, I am learning how to keep 21 girls happy all at the same time! Most of the big decisions were made before we came home for Christmas, and thus far we have hopes of really surprising the seniors with a gala affair.

The second week of my Christmas vacation will be spent at the Student Volunteer Movement Conference at Ohio University in Athens, Ohio. We will discuss the place of missions in the world today and the theme is "Revolution and Reconciliation." Half of the delegates will be American and half will be foreign students, so it should be a most worthwhile and challenging week.

There is one thing I want to get off my conscience. It pains me to think of all the birthdays I have missed these last few years. I used to love to send cards, and still do, but there are days at a time when I don't find time to even look at my birthday book, and before I know it your birthdays have slipped by. This is really a scotch way of doing it, but may I wish all of you the best kind of birthday now in case I forget to send you a card during the year.

As I opened the many, many cards that were waiting for me when I got home, I was once more thrilled by the strong bonds of friendship which neither time nor distance can erase. There is a verse in Scripture which is so appropriate for this Christmas season: Love never ends. (1 Corinthians 13:8) When all the ornaments are put away, and the beautifully wrapped packages and gaily-decorated trees are no longer in evidence, one thing will remain, and it will be just as fresh and lasting as it was that first Christmas day — Love!

I wish each of you would read the 13th Chapter of 1 Corinthians this Christmas season. Perhaps we don't find the usual Christmas story, but I'm sure we find there the real Christmas message. You have all given me so much: your time and money; your hope when I was in doubt; your faith when I thought I had no faith; and your love, which means more to me than all the rest. THANKS!

May God Bless You and Yours at this season and throughout the coming year!

With all my love, Alida

# 7<sup>th</sup> Christmas Letter, December, 1956 (At BMTS)

My dear family and friends,

Once more the Christmas season is here, and I am always glad for this time of year when my thoughts turn to my family and friends. I remember you all year, but I just don't seem to correspond because of the busy round of daily activities. This year I am writing from BMTS because a change in our school schedule prevents my getting home before the 21$^{st}$, and in that case you might not get the letter until Easter! In any event, it is good to come into your home to bring my warmest Christmas greetings!

The spirit of Christmas is everywhere at BMTS. Last night we decorated three trees and made wreaths for the doors. We sang many Christmas carols, and even Santa Claus came to visit us. Tonight we will have about 200 guests coming to the school, and we will present our Christmas play. I'm sure that next year I will miss the kind of Christmas celebration we have here at BMTS. I wish you could see the doors in the dorm; just about every door has some kind of Christmas decoration on it, and some girls are very artistic.

It is hard to believe that four years have slipped by, and on June 3$^{rd}$ I will be a graduate of BMTS. These have been such happy years, and sometimes I wonder why I didn't take this step sooner. However, I'm glad for the 14 years I worked. The experience I gained in the working world gave me many insights that I have been able to apply to the factual knowledge gained here, and thus my studies have been far richer.

Last year I had a rich experience in being Junior-Senior Chairman. This year I was elected president of the senior class, and thus far I'm enjoying my studies.

Because I got a scholarship to the Writers and Editors Conference, I was able to go to Green Lake, Wisconsin again this summer. As always, I felt spiritually refreshed when I got home. It is good to get away from the noise of radios and the glare of city lights for a week or two, and find amid the wonder and beauty of nature the kind of peace and quiet which makes one feel very close to God!

Some of you know and some of you don't know that on August 20$^{th}$ my father passed away after having several strokes. My brother was in Okinawa and couldn't get home, and mom wasn't well, but my very wonderful aunts were here to help as usual. There have been times when I wondered if my faith would be strong enough to sustain me through a death in the family. Through dad's death I learned how much our faith can mean to us; how much the love of God can strengthen and comfort us. I discovered the real truth in God's words: "I will never leave thee, nor forsake thee." (Hebrews 13:5)

On September 3$^{rd}$ I returned to school to begin my senior year. You may wonder what I intend to do after I graduate. God willing, I will begin working on my Master's degree in Social Case Work at Western Reserve University. I would like to do Industrial Counseling or Church Social Work, and in either case would need another degree. As long as I am in the swing of studying, I might as well go on. But of course, a lot depends on whether or not I can get into the school, and whether or not I can get a scholarship. I'm sure if this is God's will, He will help me find a way — as He has done in the past!

Doesn't life take amazing turns? If anyone had told me four years ago that I would be thinking of two more years of study at this point, I would never have believed it; but then five years ago I never would have guessed that in June of 1957 I'd be a college graduate! God has been so good to me, and He has worked through so many, many wonderful people in order to bring me this far.

Perhaps you would like to know that I have a very large and beautiful room this year, and at the present time have it all to myself. It is nice to have a roommate, but it is also nice to be able to study from morning to night if I wish without anyone interrupting. I often pop a batch of popcorn and invite the entire third floor to share it with me, and I don't get any refusals. We have a fine group of girls on this floor and I've really enjoyed being with them.

We have some very interesting foreign students again this year. The countries represented are Denmark, Switzerland, Puerto Rico, and the Bahamas Islands. Among our faculty there are two Negro teachers and Mr. Chou from China. Our education is made richer by the fact that we come in contact with so many fine teachers and students of other races and cultures. I find it is true that God created us all equal. I have a difficult time trying to understand why we can't learn to live together in the spirit of brotherly love. This might help to bring about peace on Earth and good will toward men!

The time has come for me to say Au Revoir for another year. But before I do, I want you to know that my heart is full of gratitude to all of you for being such a good family and such loyal and faithful friends. Whatever I have accomplished, I have not done alone. You have all helped me in a multitude of ways, and I daily thank God for bringing each of you into my life!

At this Christmas season I pray that each of you will come to know God as I have learned to know Him. I pray His blessings will be showered upon you and yours this Christmas season and continue through the New Year!

With all my love, Alida

# 8<sup>th</sup> Christmas Letter, Christmas 1957 (At Home)

My dear family and friends,

Once more our thoughts are turned to the holiday season and those we like to remember at this special time of the year. My memories have been going back to my childhood when I would hopefully, and yet a little fearfully, wait for Santa Claus to come. We would have candy and nuts ready for his reindeer, and it was always a thrilling moment when we heard the tinkle of bells and then his footsteps on the porch. When I discovered a few years later that Santa was really my jolly, lovable Uncle Henry, Christmas lost some of its childhood magic, but I will always cherish the memories of those days.

Many things have happened since I wrote to you last Christmas, and of course the outstanding event for me was my graduation from the Baptist Missionary Training School. I received a Bachelor of Religious Education degree and at last have the education I always wanted. More importantly, in preparing for Christmas service, I found the kind of happiness that comes from feeling that one is doing the kind of thing which gives meaning to life. It was hard to say goodbye to all my Chicago friends, but I have discovered that real friendship lasts regardless of time or distance. Do you realize I haven't seen some of you for almost fifteen years, and yet I still feel there is a tie that binds our hearts in real affection?

Speaking of friendship, I think you should know that the woman who mimeographs this letter always takes time from her busy holiday schedule to get the letter ready for me. She has two fine children, and her home is always aglow with warmth and cheerfulness as well as gay decorations.

It would have been good to go back to work after four years in college, but it seems that God had other plans for me. I had a deep conviction that the next step for me to take was to go on for my Master's degree in Social Work. I was accepted by the School of Applied Social Science at Western Reserve University in Cleveland, which enables me to stay at home while working on my degree. This isn't an easy course, and commuting from one end of town to another every day doesn't help. But, I'm getting used to it now and am thoroughly enjoying this new field of study.

We have classes several days a week, and the other days I have field work at the County Welfare Department, Public Assistance Division. In the various agencies in which students work, we put into practice the theories we learn in the classroom. Most caseworkers at Public Welfare have a caseload of about 80-90 clients, but thus far I have only four. I visit my clients in their homes and am learning the disciplines involved in helping people to help themselves.

There are times when this work is heartbreaking, but there is much satisfaction in knowing one is helping others in a constructive way. Even though I am not in a church setting, I feel I am doing missionary work in a very real and meaningful way. I'm not sure where I will be or what I will do when I finish these two years of study, but I am preparing myself for whatever task God has for me in the future.

It's beginning to seem as if I'll never be anything but a student, and I'm afraid that when I start working I will be so spoiled I'll think I should have three months off every summer, two weeks at Christmas, and a week for spring vacation.

My family is doing fairly well. Mom and my Aunt Min, who we affectionately call "Pinkie," are keeping busy. I don't know what I would do without them, because they have made it possible for me to devote all my time to study. Walt was home all summer, except for three weeks he spent in Scandinavian countries. We hated to have him return to the ship again, but he loves his work as a radio officer on the merchant ship. Susie, our two-year-old dog, is a real comedienne and keeps us laughing all the time. She is full of tricks and her eyes have a devilish twinkle in them. She loves all kinds of raw vegetables, fruit, tea, coffee, and fresh pastry. What a dog's life she has!

I would love to hear from some of you so I would know what is happening to you and your families. Peg and Grace in California; the Cooks in Florida; my old Federal Reserve pals; and all the rest of you, my thoughts and prayers are often with you and yours. And here is a special message for the BMTS class of '57: I hope you are all enjoying your various tasks in Christ's service. I understand Betty Musselman got married. Congratulations to the happy pair! May I urge each of you to send me any change of address so I can keep the records straight for our round-robin letter! By the way, how is the first letter progressing? I hope it will be back to me the early part of the year so I can get another one started.

May God bless each of you at this Christmas season and may you feel His presence and guidance throughout the coming year.

With all my love, Alida

# 9<sup>th</sup> Christmas Letter, Christmas 1958 (At Home)

My dear family and friends,

Once more the holiday season is here with all its glitter and sparkle, with gaily colored decorations and beautifully wrapped gifts; with an air of expectation and mystery. Ears are tuned not only for the sound of Santa's sleigh bells, but for the voices of angels singing "Peace on Earth, good will toward men."

As I sit here by the window looking at the snow falling gently, I am glad we have had an old-fashioned holiday season so that children can use their sleds and make snowmen. Somehow I have always been awed by the quiet beauty of winter; so white and peaceful, and I really enjoy shoveling snow — as strange as that may seem!

It is a good feeling to be able to look forward to June, for that will be the end of six years of college. Even though at times I was a typical student and fretted over exams and papers, I am sure that I am going to miss school because never again will I have the privilege of spending eight hours a day just for study. I've learned a little bit and, what is more important, have discovered how much more there is to learn.

What will I do when I'm finished with school? That is a good question and I don't know the answer as yet myself. It is quite likely that I will work in a social agency for a year or two to get the benefit of supervision. This may not be missionary work in the narrow sense of the term, but in its broadest and deepest meaning it certainly is. This summer when I worked for County Welfare and had 58 cases, I worked harder than I ever have on any job. However, at the end of the day I would feel that, despite my fatigue, I had been doing the work that God had intended for me. This year my field work is with Travelers Aid, and I come in contact with many young people in the Detention Home and with unmarried mothers who are seeking help away from home. In both these agencies I have found that, not only do people need material things, but they need most of all to know that someone cares about them.

This Fall I had a rich experience in another area when I taught a six-week leadership training course for Primary teachers. I love teaching others, so this was a thrilling experience, and I was delighted to have 22 students in my class.

As for my family, I am glad to report that we are all feeling pretty well at the moment. My brother has been home for two months and will return to the ship the first of January. This is his first holiday season at home in many years, and it has done us all a lot of good to have him here with us. He has made two guitars while home; one is electrical. It must be nice to have so much creative talent. He has been taking excellent movies of his trips, so we feel we can share in his adventurous life. Our pup, Susie, is a little comedienne, and we never have a dull moment when that bright-eyed rascal is around. She does everything but talk, and in her own way does that too. We have always had intelligent dogs, but this one is the smartest of them all.

A word to the BMTS class of '57: I never did find out where the last round-robin got stopped, and if any of you have it, mail it to me and I will see to it that it is sent on. I will be glad to start another one if you will please send me your correct addresses; otherwise there isn't much point in doing so.

This may be my last Christmas letter to my friends in town, so I would like to share with all of you — both near and far — some thoughts I have about the gifts you have given me these last six years. You have given me money and other tangible things, but the gifts I have appreciated the most have been friendship, loyalty, faith, hope, and love.

I never took friendship for granted, but in these years that word has taken on new meaning. Even though I haven't been able to keep in touch with some of you as often as I used to, there has been a constant stream of letters, phone calls, dinner invitations, and warm welcomes. Because you have been so loyal, I have never felt completely alone. In those times when things seemed the most difficult, one of you would remember me in some special way that would warm my heart, lift my spirits, and give me hope and courage to go on for the next "round."

I can't over-estimate the gifts of faith, for it was that faith which I have found through so many of you which has led me into a host of new experiences. Without faith I would never have ventured to college, and I'm certain that it was God's constant presence with me that enabled me to do as well as I did. I never went back to college after any vacation without going in to see my pastor for a chat and a word of prayer. When I entered my freshman year, Reverend Lomas, my former pastor, said, "If you take the first step in faith, God will do the rest." I found that there is real truth in that statement.

To sum this up I can say that you have given me the gift of all gifts — love! Whatever else has been behind all the wonderful things you have done for me, the root of it, I'm sure, is love! At this Christmas season we think of how much God loved us. He loved us so much that He sent His Son into the world to proclaim that love. Surely He is still proclaiming it through people like you!

Whatever life may bring, I will be eternally grateful to all of you for helping me to have six of the happiest years of my life. When I accept that Master's degree in June, God willing, I will do so with humility, for I will know that it not only represents six years of hard work on my part, but it also represents an investment on the part of each of you.

At this joyous season I can wish nothing finer for you than the kind of gifts you have given me. I pray that the spirit of this season, so full of love and wonder, will be with you and yours throughout the coming year to make every day of 1959 a rich and wonderful experience. God bless you, everyone!

With all my love to all of you, Alida

# 10<sup>th</sup> Christmas Letter, November 27, 1959 (At Home)

My dear relatives and friends,

It seems a little early to write this Christmas letter, but the first snow of the season inspired me to get busy, and, frankly, this has been such a wonderful year for me I can't wait to share it with you.

In June I ended six happy years of study when I got my Master's degree. It was a real thrill to march with hundreds of other students across the campus, and I had to keep pinching myself to prove I wasn't dreaming. When I graduated from BMTS only my faithful Aunt Min, or "Pinkie" was able to be there. So I was happy when I got my Master's because my mother, aunt, my friend Dorothy, and a neighbor were able to share my happiness. I can only say that I feel a real miracle took place in my life and it has proven to me again that, "with God all things are possible!"

With my education completed — though I know I still have much to learn — and my bank account depleted, I had to think about a job. The only place I really wanted to work was at the Family Service Association, and that was the first place I applied. I had dreaded the chore of job hunting, but my problem was solved easily because Family Service hired me. I took the entire summer off and began to work on August 24<sup>th</sup>. I have loved every minute of my work and am now officially a social caseworker. I have my own office and make appointments with my clients who come in to see me. Our agency deals with personal and marital problems and parent-child relationships. There is never a dull moment and I find the work challenging and satisfying, although as in everything, there are discouraging moments. After 14 years of doing clerical work (which I hated), again I find myself at times wondering if I'm dreaming! Not only do I like my work, but for the first time in my life I feel I am where God wants me to be!

My summer vacation was an active one. Pinkie broke her wrist in January and was not able to do the yard work. I thoroughly enjoyed spending two and three days a week in the yard cutting grass and trimming hedges. I also had the thrill of planting tomato and pepper plants — which actually grew and produced! By the end of the summer I had a beautiful tan from being out-of-doors so much. The days I wasn't in the yard I was busy in the house cleaning cupboards, closets, cabinets, and last of all, the fruit cellar. This may sound like a strange vacation, but after six years of mental work I found myself enjoying physical labor. Of course I took time to visit my friends, and as soon as school was over I took a weekend trip to Chicago.

My brother's car is now in my name, and having the Mercomatic drive makes it quite easy to operate that vehicle. I'm still extremely nervous in traffic, but little by little I'm gaining confidence. Actually, I wish I had learned when I was sixteen and had more courage!

My family continues to have its battles with illness, although on the whole, this has been a better year than some. Pinkie really had a rough time with her broken wrist because arthritis set in. It is almost a year since she fell and there are still some things she cannot do with her hand. But for a woman 74 years of age, I think she has done remarkably well. Mom has periodic spells of depression, but other than that she has been doing well. Walt was home for a few weeks and we're hoping he may get home for Christmas. But in any event he will have several months of vacation this spring or summer. He looks wonderful, but then I've always been prejudiced where he is concerned.

Susie keeps getting funnier all the time. I wish you could see her licking on a sucker. We hold it for her and she licks and licks and sometimes puts her paws on the stick so it looks as if she's holding it. She learned to crawl over the gates we had up to keep her in the kitchen. So now she has the run of the house and sleeps on my aunt's bed. She likes to be covered up and stays that way all night. If only I could get pictures of her in some of the positions she gets into I could make a fortune. She has us all convinced that she is the smartest, cutest, and most human-like dog that ever existed.

This letter tells you of two "miracles" in my life: The thrill of getting a degree and the joy of a new vocation. But the real miracle took place 10 years ago when I found Christ and joined my church. My wish for each of you is that you might find Christ in Christmas. I pray that Christmas will be not just a time for giving and receiving gifts, but a time of remembering the real meaning of Christmas! May you experience not only a sentimental feeling about a Babe in a manger, but may you experience the living presence of Christ, the Prince of Peace, who said, "...Lo, I am with you always..." (Matthew 28:20) He can and will work miracles in your lives as He has in mine!

Whether you are near or in the distant land, my thoughts and prayers are with you and yours, not only at Christmas time but throughout the year. Your friendship is still my most cherished possession!

God Bless You Everyone, Alida

Chapter Four

**Ten Christmas Letters
From 1960 to 1969**

# 11<sup>th</sup> Christmas Letter, December 4, 1960 (At Home)

My dear relatives and friends,

Here it is again, that wonderful time when we remember all those who have had some share in our lives. How rich life is because of friendship; how empty it would be without all of you! Other years have gone by swiftly but this one, in keeping with the jet age, zoomed out of sight before I knew it, leaving only the vapor trail of memories to prove it was here at all.

Last Christmas was one of the nicest we had in a long time because Walt was able to be home for a few days, and he flew back to celebrate New Year's, too! I had so much fun shopping, trimming the tree and getting the house decorated for Walt's arrival.

Nothing exciting happened until the end of May when Walt came home for three months. During his vacation he spent three weeks in Central America, and I'm now the owner of a beautiful skirt from Guatemala. Later he spent one week in Sandusky fishing and filled our freezer with his catch. Next he built a peg-leg cabinet for part of the stereo set he brought home from Japan. I have been getting my fill of beautiful stereo music and especially enjoy it on Sunday afternoon when I'm relaxing.

Toward the end of June Pinkie suffered from a slipped disc and arthritis in her back. She was in the hospital for three weeks. It took her a long time to get over it, but she eventually bounced back as usual and helped me clean up the yard this fall.

While Aunt Min, whose nickname is "Pinkie," was in the hospital we worked like beavers around here taking the wallpaper off the dining and living rooms and hallway. Thank God the wallpaper was off the bedroom walls, but we took the furniture out of all four, painted the walls and put down new carpets in each room. A friend helped Walt and they worked until the wee hours of the morning. During my vacation, which began the first of July, I finished painting odds and ends like closets and the attic way. For the first time in my life I got some practical experience with a putty knife and paint brush. After two hectic weeks of painting Walt was glad to be called back to the ship to rest. What a mess we had, but the house looks so much nicer. It was worth it!

Again this summer I did all the yard work and enjoyed it. I found courage to use the electric hedge trimmers, and to my mother's surprise I still have my ten fingers. Our yard was just beautiful this summer and we now call the backyard "Susie's Park."

Susie is five-years-old now and continues to be a source of fun and companionship for us. The minute we sit down she cuddles up to one of us. Her love of shrimp tells us she has expensive tastes. She still loves her vegetables, fruit, and fresh coffee cake dunked in coffee. I'm sure she doesn't know she is a dog!

I still get lonesome for Chicago, so a friend and I took a weekend trip to see some of my friends there, and I showed her through BMTS. We stayed with Laura and James Hill, and one evening the four of us enjoyed a smorgasbord at the Kuhnsholme. I'm satisfied now that I've finally eaten there and have seen one of their puppet operas.

Between work, church, and home I manage to keep busy. I still like my job although I'm convinced I'll never know enough to be able to figure out the complicated emotional and physical makeup of people. Although this work can be frustrating at times, I'm still glad I'm in this field and feel fortunate that I'm with an agency that has such high standards. At church I'm on the Social Progress Commission which meets once a month, have attended circle meetings, and have just finished a six-week leadership training course for Primary Department teachers. In January I am to begin teaching an adult class and wonder where I'll find time for preparation. I'm on the Speakers Bureau at work and am slated for three of four speeches during the year. At least I can't complain about life being dull!

On December 10th I'm having the agency Christmas party at my home and that should be fun. We have already purchased Walt's plane ticket for arrival December 24th and departure December 26th. He won't be home long but we're glad he can be here even for a few days to share Christmas with us. So Christmas is for us as well as for you, a time of anticipation and sharing of fun, friends, goodies, and good will. To the smell of cookies baking, the sound of jingle bells and children's happy laughter, friends join me in adding a sincere wish that your Christmas will be bright and gay, and filled with the joy and good will the angels proclaimed the night the Prince of Peace was born. May the New Year bring you and yours Prosperity, Good Health, and Happy Hearts!

With all my love to all of you, Alida

# 12<sup>th</sup> Christmas Letter, December 4, 1961 (At Home)

My dear relatives and friends,

This is my 12<sup>th</sup> annual Christmas letter, and as I scanned the others today there were many things I had forgotten. The common threads that ran through them all were my deep appreciation for your love and friendship through the years and my gratitude for all God's blessings, and these two will never change.

Last year's letter ended with my happily anticipating the agency party at my home and the arrival of my brother for Christmas. The party was a big success with a fun-filled pot luck feast, and Walt did get home for several days to make our Christmas a very happy one. We regret that this year, unless some miracle occurs, he'll be on his way to Honolulu for the holidays. His ship should arrive in New York tomorrow, the 4<sup>th</sup>, and he might come home for a day or two now, but Christmas seems out of the question.

The early part of this year was uneventful except that I became Chairman of Children's Work for the Cleveland Baptist Association, and was asked to go to the National Conference for Children's Workers at Green Lake, Wisconsin in June. I began my month's vacation in the middle of June and journeyed to Chicago where I stayed with friends overnight, and the following day we drove to Green Lake. It was a lovely trip, and I was happy to see Green Lake and many dear friends once again. My plan was to spend a few days in Chicago on the return trip, but a year of hard work and a week at the conference left me totally exhausted. So, I spent one afternoon with Laura and Jim Hill and left Chicago that night.

The maritime strike delayed Walt's plans, so he began his vacation the day I returned from Green Lake. This meant I was able to be home with him for three weeks. Two of those weeks were spent running to Lakewood and St. John's Hospitals. My mother was in one hospital with a slight depression, and my Aunt Mil was under observation in the other hospital. Walt and I did a lot of odds and ends around the house, bought a barbeque grill on which we cooked many luscious steaks, and in general had a busy time. Just to get away from all the turmoil for a day or two, we took a fast trip to Ithaca, New York. We were enthralled by the beautiful Appalachian scenery and visited Cornell University campus. We stopped at Corning, New York for a visit to the famous glass center where we saw the expensive Steuben glass being made. How I would love to have bought some, but the price prohibited my even thinking about that.

Walt talked me into going fishing with him on a party boat. For the first time in my life I bought a license and learned how to use a rod and reel. Soon I found that just sitting and waiting for fish to bite could be rather relaxing. The first day we came home with three fish. The second day we had nine, and I caught my first two. On the third day Walt and I went out alone at night and the fish caught me! After catching 18 fish quicker than Walt could take them off the hook, the lake suddenly got rough. There I was, the only one from among the 25 to 30 people who got seasick. For two agonizing hours I was either leaning over the side of the boat or just lying on my back — too sick to even be embarrassed.

Walt was sympathetic but couldn't help laughing, and I laughed when I could because that is about the only defense one has against seasickness. I couldn't go to work the next morning and felt the effects of that excursion for several days. That was the end of my fishing for the season, but Walt went to Canada where he got pike that made ours look like minnows! He brought home a small five pound pike, which he baked. It was delicious! All I can say is that life is full of new experiences! The house was suddenly very empty when Walt returned to the ship in the middle of September, and we are looking forward to his next vacation. While he was home he set up a tank of tropical fish and we are now "baby-sitting" with them.

Everyone got in on the health problems this year. My aunt, Pinkie, and I both had the flu at the same time and were laid up for a week. Several weeks ago Pinkie had a cataract removed from her right eye and will have the other eye operated on in six months to a year. This has been most painful for her and she doesn't look too good, but she has always had a lot of bounce so I think she will be alright. While Pinkie was in the hospital, our dear little Susie got deathly ill and had me up all night on Saturday. Luckily the Vet was open Sunday morning and we took her for a checkup. She had something like the flu, and after being in the animal hospital for several days she was put on a special diet of canned dog food — which she refused to eat! We catered to her as usual and prepared soft foods she liked, such as peas and beans, and she was soon back to normal.

I still like the work I'm doing for the Family Service Association. I meet many different kinds of people and hear about many problems. Sometimes it is emotionally tiring, but it is also very rewarding to be able to prevent divorce and keep a family together, or to help parents better understand their children. For the first time social workers can be certified and because I met the necessary qualifications, I now have a lovely certificate hanging in my office. The worst part of the job is the dictation, which is never finished, but on every job there is something that isn't easy.

As always I find real joy in my church and in being of service when I can. I was scheduled to teach a leadership training course in Story Telling this year, but that was about the time I had the flu. I was almost grateful that not enough people signed up for the course so it was cancelled. I just wasn't up to teaching at that point. But I did enjoy visiting members of the church during our every member canvass and found a warm welcome wherever I went.

And so I come to the end of another Christmas letter with the age-old prayer that you will find the true meaning of Christmas amid all the hustle and bustle. As you give and receive gifts may you remember the gift of love God gave us: His Son, Jesus Christ! "And His name shall be called Wonderful, Counselor, The mighty God, The everlasting Father, The Prince of Peace." (Isaiah 9:6)

With all my love to all of you, Alida

# 13<sup>th</sup> Christmas Letter, November 18, 1962 (At Home)

My dear family and friends,

If the stores weren't decorated and our Public Square all trimmed for Christmas, I would have a hard time believing the holidays are just around the corner. My main impression of the past year is summed up in saying — 1962 flew! This has been a full year with much accomplished and even more left undone because of lack of time. I'm so glad Christmas gives me a chance to reaffirm my affection for so many of you whom I just don't get a chance to contact during the year.

The early winter months of the year passed uneventfully and the spring thaw meant house cleaning time. Last spring we had a man do the worst of the cleaning and that was a big relief because mom and Pinkie can't do it anymore, and I just don't have the time. The Saturday before Easter I decided I needed something to go with my purple suit, and on the spur of the moment went to a furrier and within 15 minutes had selected a lovely cerulean mink stole. I've wanted one for a long time and have enjoyed it.

My vacation was scheduled for July and for several months before that I was busy getting dictation caught up while doing extra work on a recent project for the agency. By the time my vacation arrived I was so exhausted all I wanted to do was rest and that is what I did. I took the entire month all at once and spent the first few weeks just loafing. The third week found me taking my annual pilgrimage to Chicago where I stayed for two days with Laura Pahl Hill. I saw my friend Chris Chou, and those of you who know Chris will be happy to learn that he is engaged to a Miss Wang, and the wedding will be around Christmas time.

Unfortunately, Walt was unable to be home during my vacation this year. A friend and I went to Hiram, Ohio to watch the Cleveland Browns practice, and from the way they played this year they never stopped practicing. Maybe next year will be better. The first day of my vacation I blossomed out in hives, and I still have them though my dermatologist has them under control now. She doesn't know what is causing them nor how long they will last.

Walt got home in August for several months and as usual took a fishing trip to Canada. He bought a Ford station wagon to haul all his equipment. Fishing wasn't too good, but he brought home a pike and two bass. We baked the pike, and one Saturday while mom and Pinkie were gone, Walt and I had fun experimenting and came up with the most delicious steamed bass and Chinese fried rice I've ever eaten. After my experience with getting seasick last year, I left the fishing to Walt this year. He will be in or near Japan for Christmas and we'll miss him.

As always, fall brought with it a full schedule. For six weeks I was teaching a leadership training course on Monday. I was also taking class lessons in driving on Wednesday and my road lessons were on Saturday morning. Walt gave me his '51 Mercury so I have something to drive — if I ever learn. I was doing real well until the teacher took me out on November 17<sup>th</sup>, which was a rainy day with slippery leaves on the streets. He told me to stay to the right on a curve which was a mistake for the next thing I knew we were confronted by a telephone pole. Fortunately, I was going slowly enough that the car and the pole were spared, but my pride was badly damaged. Better to do that now than later I guess, but I can assure you I have new respect for slippery roads, curves — and telephone poles.

The days ahead promise to be full with a six-week leadership training course I'll be teaching for new teachers in my church on Sunday nights. I'm also trying to find time to practice driving with the hope of having my license by the time the temporary permit expires. It will take all your prayers to get me through the driving test I'm sure, so please start saying some extra ones right now.

No year would be complete in our house without some illness. Mom has had arthritis in her back and Pinkie will come home November 21$^{st}$ after two weeks in the hospital. This time she had two tumors in the roof of her mouth removed along with her upper teeth. She's getting tired of a liquid diet but will be on it for a while yet. Even Susie got in the act and had to go to the Vet a few times this year. The minute we put the collar on her she begins shaking and doesn't stop until we walk out of the hospital. She is still so lively it's hard to believe she is seven years old.

My job as caseworker with Family Service continues to be interesting and challenging. I've been with them three years now and feel as if I've just cracked the surface in terms of all I have to learn. The new director of our branch is now my supervisor, and he is a very bright and learned person from whom I'm sure I will learn much. This is the first time I've had a male supervisor and so far all is well. There are times when I get so tired I wonder why I ever got into this field, but the satisfaction that comes with helping others is so rewarding that it helps me forget my tiredness. If only you knew how many people are reaching out for someone to talk with and to help them with their problems! So many people are reaching out for kindness, understanding, love, and affection. Many are reaching out for just one word of encouragement or hope. On the days that I am most tired I try to remember these words of Jesus: "Verily I say unto you, Inasmuch as ye have done it unto one of the least of these my brethren, ye have done it unto me." (Matthew 25:40)

I am so grateful to God for the many friends He has sent into my life, and I truly consider my family and friends my greatest treasure. I just wish I would wake up Christmas morning and find you all under my Christmas tree. It would be so nice to have you all under one roof. What a wonderful reunion that would be! I know that is impossible, so the next best thing is to hope and pray that God's richest gifts will be bestowed on each of you and yours this Christmas season and be multiplied in the New Year!

May I leave you with a thought a friend shared with me a few years ago, and I've always thought it so lovely: "Forgiveness is the perfume the flower casts back upon the foot that trampled it."

With all my love, Alida

# 14<sup>th</sup> Christmas Letter, December 1, 1963 (At Home)

My dear family and friends,

This morning I awakened to find the Earth blanketed with our first snowfall, and at noon I heard the Cleveland Messiah chorus, but I'm still finding it difficult to compose this letter. I'm not sure if the spirit of Christmas just hasn't hit me yet, or if the tragic events of the last few weeks made the things I've done this year seem trivial. At any rate, I find myself struggling with deeper thoughts than the ones I usually put in a Christmas letter.

Just to keep the record straight, I can say this has been a quiet year and most of my energy has gone into trying to keep agency work caught up. I did less church work but will make up for that when I begin a three-year term on the Board of Christian Education this January. As of this letter, my mother, aunt, and Susie are well and I am glad for that.

Walt came home in May for three months. He took two fishing trips to Canada, and on the second I went along. While Walt flew to an outpost camp to catch the big fish, which he did, I stayed in the main camp for three days. I found it very therapeutic to be away from all the familiar faces and surroundings for a few days. I thoroughly enjoyed making new friends, and was completely refreshed by the scenery. All during the trip the words of *"America the Beautiful"* kept running through my mind. We should thank God each day for one of the most beautiful countries in the world; for the mountains and valleys, the cold of the North and the warmth of the South, the green of the Eastern states and the desert brown of the West; for the variety of races, creeds, languages and cultures — and all this freedom, too! I have always appreciated my American heritage, but my appreciation was enhanced when I visited Greenfield Village and the Ford Museum in Dearborn, Michigan. I ended my vacation feeling more patriotic than ever!

Walt was determined that I would get my driver's license, and he patiently but firmly forced me to drive while he was home. On August 17<sup>th</sup> I took the test and much to my surprise, I passed! Now I have to find the courage to drive alone. Actually I need a smaller car that is easier to handle than the old Mercury!

And so another year has come and gone, and once more we are getting caught up in the purchase of gifts and wrappings to show our love to others. I hope we will each pause for a moment to thank God for the gifts He has given to us. May the holidays, this year, be for each of us a time of happiness, but also a time of deep thinking and rededication to those principles and values upon which our nation was founded. May our words and deeds prove that "In God We Trust!"

Thank God for His indescribable generosity to you. — 2 Corinthians 9:15, Phillips translation

With all my love to all of you, Alida

PS

    To BMTSers: I would like the class of '57 to know that the $7 that was left in our treasury, and which you turned over to me as President of the class, has been put to good use. I spent a few cents on the two round-robin letters which apparently didn't get around, and last month I sent a check for $7 to Colgate Rochester in the name of the class of '57. That's better than keeping it any longer!

# 15<sup>th</sup> Christmas Letter, November 22, 1964 (At Home)

My dear family and friends,

Last Sunday I wrote letters sitting out-of-doors enjoying spring-like weather. Today I'm glad to be inside and out of the almost zero temperature with Susie cuddled up close to me as I think about my annual letter. This has been a year full of surprises from beginning to end, and it has been a busy and happy year as well.

I began the year by keeping my New Year's resolution to entertain all my friends to whom I owed invitations. The first four or five weeks of the year were spent having one set of friends after another over for dinner, and I thoroughly enjoyed it. February is usually a slow month for everyone. I'm always glad for the brightness of Valentine's Day with its eternal message of love to warm our hearts and add flavor to an otherwise dull month. And if, for you, there is one who stands out above the rest to whom you can say, "I love you; I always have and I always will," be glad, for there is nothing finer in the world than to love and be loved.

In April the Lakewood High class of 1939 celebrated its 25<sup>th</sup> anniversary. We had a Dinner-Dance at the Pick Carter Hotel. Reunions are always fun, but it was hard to believe that so many years had gone by. It is even harder to believe that 20 years later, in 1959, I got my Master's degree from Case Western Reserve University.

Little did I think at this time last year that in May I would be working at the downtown office of Family Service. When I was transferred my clients thought I was getting a promotion, which was sweet of them. In a way it is nice to be downtown again, but it is also costly being close to the stores.

At the end of April Walt came home and, as usual, the house seemed more alive with him around. He was home until the middle of July, and in those months we gave the barbeque grill a good workout! He decided to build an airplane — an amphibian. Before we knew it, production began in the basement and Walt worked so many hours I kidded him about getting time-and-a-half for overtime. The bulkheads he made are stored in the attic, and if we can get a garage or barn he can begin to assemble it next year. It will probably take three to four years, but in one of these letters I'll be telling you that we are flying or have flown to Canada to fish. He is working on some parts aboard ship, which is making this trip more enjoyable.

While Walt was home we visited friends in Tillsonburg, Ontario, so he could get at least one weekend of fishing. He and Spike got two good catches, which we fried immediately, and those were the two best meals I ate all year. A man near Tillsonburg is building a plane. Walt and Spike decided to visit him and came back with the hilarious tale of how he is building it in the middle of his living room — with his wife's blessing! Luckily it is an old frame farmhouse because he has to tear out one wall to get the plane outside. While he was home Walt also built me a large bookcase and painted an abstract picture to go above it. For my birthday he sent me an oil painting of a lovely woodland spot with a cool-looking river flowing along. He is sure it's full of fish!

As usual I took the entire month of July for my vacation, and I had another surprise in store. I didn't think I would go anywhere, but my last week found me traveling through the New England states – and what an enchanting trip that was! The Adirondack Mountains in New York were so fresh and green, and speckled with the blue of so many lakes, such as Saranac Lake and Lake Placid. Ausable Chasm, also in New York, is a must for every sightseer who wants to feel close to nature. We went on to Vermont via a ferry across Lake Champlain, and then on to the top of Mt. Washington in New Hampshire to see the U.S. Weather Station. The eight mile ride to the top is beautiful beyond description, and the descent is terrifying until you get halfway down.

The scent of pine permeated the air in Maine as far East as Skowhegan, but in the picturesque resort town of Camden the smell of pine gave way to the smell of the ocean, and there I had my first lobster salad. Boothbay Harbor was nothing to write home about, but Gloucester, Massachusetts, with its many seagulls and artist colony at Rock Neck, was everything I had pictured. There was a beautiful painting of the sea on display, and I hope I can afford to buy it on my next visit. Next we went to Boston, Lexington, and Concord, where history came alive! Especially impressive were Paul Revere's home, Old Ironsides, and the experience of sitting in a pew in the Old North Church. While in Boston, I saw my dear friend, Doris Emery, and it was a treat to be with her again. Probably the most beautiful part of the trip was the return home over the Mohawk Trail (Route #2 in Massachusetts), which is correctly called the Switzerland of America. I treasure the many pictures I took and came home feeling more refreshed than I have in a long time.

As usual I've kept busy in church and am now Chairman of Children's Work on our Board of Christian Education. It is fun to be working in the children's division again even though I'm not teaching. I was asked to be on the committee to select a new Director of Christian Education, and BMTSers will be surprised to learn that after much searching we called Pat Newland. Pat was one of my classmates and little did I think when we graduated that one day she would be leading the program of Christian Education in my church. I'm sure she, with her past experience, will give us the kind of leadership we need.

As for my family, mom, now 70, has been in pretty good health this year except for an occasional bad spell. Pinkie, at 79, is still cutting grass and raking leaves. I have to get up early in the morning to shovel snow, or she would do that, too. She sprained her ankle last week, and we were all glad it was no worse. I celebrated my 43$^{rd}$ birthday this year and am fit as a fiddle, though the battle of weight is beginning, and it is a losing battle as long as mom continues baking. The closest thing to driving I'm doing is pedaling the exerciser I bought. And our Susie, now nine, is still alert and full of fun, and we all hope she will live to be a million!

As I write this letter, Thanksgiving is just a few days away and I'm sincerely thankful for the happy year that is ending, for all of you who have meant so much to me through the years, and for the coming Christmas season with its message of Love and Hope! May the blessings and the loving spirit of the season remain with you, and may 1965 be as happy and full of pleasant surprises for you as 1964 was for me!

With all my love to all of you, Alida

# 16<sup>th</sup> Christmas Letter, November 30, 1965 (At Home)

My dear family and friends,

Because I cannot think of any original way to begin my 16<sup>th</sup> annual Christmas letter, I guess I can do no better than to borrow from the Apostle Paul's letter to the Philippians: "I thank my God in all my remembrance of you." Joan Walsh Anglund voices my feelings in her lovely book, *Christmas is a Time of Giving*, when she wrote, "Christmas is a time of family and good friends meeting once again…for everyone it is a time of magic when troubles melt and once again the world is young."

This has been an ordinary year in many ways, but a good one! I had a lot of fun getting reacquainted with Pat Newland, my BMTS classmate, who came to my church as Director of Christian Education. We thoroughly enjoyed working together and after having two BMTSers running loose at once, Lakewood Baptist will probably never be the same. We also found time for fun. We saw *The Roar of the Greasepaint*, a Victor Borge concert, and we ate at some of the newest and finest dining places. Pat found out there is still some life in "Grandma Struze." (I still love that BMTS nickname). Pat did an excellent job of revitalizing our Youth Division, but, alas, November 28<sup>th</sup> was her last day with us. We hated to lose her but are happy that we were able to launch her on the road to happiness. She will marry Norman Hayes on December 23<sup>rd</sup>, in Middletown, Ohio.

Walt got home in January for a month because of a dock strike. His vacation began the end of May, and was extended to the end of August because of a second maritime strike. Production began on the plane and the skeleton of the fuselage went together piece by piece, and what a thrill it has been to see it take form. I was Walt's general flunky, expert only in giving encouragement. The hottest day of the summer found Walt building an extension on the garage so the plane could be stored for the winter.

My vacation, the month of July, was relaxing and refreshing as always. I got some exercise helping cut down a big tree in our yard, and I proved I could handle a saw. When Walt determined he needed a vacation from plane building, we decided to visit Canada for a week. With no definite destination in mind, we headed for Temiscaming in Quebec. An information center suggested we go six miles farther to Kipawa. My heart sank when, in the middle of a rain storm, we came to what looked like a wet version of the "Wild West." On one side of the road, which ended in Kipawa, was a small, uninviting building known there as a hotel, a general store, and a parking lot. On the other side was a small railroad station, docks, and water. As Walt made inquiries about fishing camps, he was "lucky" enough to meet the owner of one of the camps who assured him that meals would be furnished, and a boat would pick us up at noon the next day and take us to the camp 25 miles away. About 15 minutes before we were to leave, a phone call came for us which sent us scurrying into the store to buy steaks, chops, hotdogs — and I was on K.P. The scenery was breathtaking back in the wilderness, and the log cabin was clean, comfortable, and had indoor plumbing. But facing me in the kitchen was the big, jolting surprise: an old-fashioned stove! Gas? No! Next to it was an equally jolting pile of wood. I swallowed hard and decided this was the time to be flexible, to adjust, and to keep my mouth shut. The wood proved to be green, and I wish I had a movie of the two of us cooking chops one night. Walt was blowing on the fire, trying to keep it going while I watched the chops and wondered for an hour if they would ever get brown.

Our first full day there was Friday, and the weather didn't cooperate. While Walt looked out the window all day to see if it would stop raining, I played solitaire until I couldn't see! The temperature was in the 40's every night, and I slept with three wool blankets and socks on. Walt would get up at 6:00 a.m. to make a fire. All I can say is, I'm glad I wasn't a pilgrim!

On Saturday the sun peeked out, and I decided to brave a day of fishing. I put on Walt's life preserver which made me look like Mae West. I couldn't wait for the huge shore lunch our guide promised us. We went to a distant shore and portaged through the woods for 10 to 15 minutes fighting off mosquitoes all the way while carrying all our gear. We finally came to a beautiful lake where we fished all day. This camp was run by an Irishman, and he and his brother, who acted as our guide, lived up to Irish tradition, and we caught more fish stories than fish. By lunch time Walt had caught one large fish (which I wanted to take home) and one small fish, while my score was zero! The guide probably could have killed us, but Walt wanted me to know what a shore lunch was like, so the one little fish got filleted and fried by the guide — and eaten by me! Our guide, I think he preferred Canadian Club to Canadian fishing, but he was one of the rogues you couldn't help liking, and his Irish humor was better than the silence of some of the Indian guides. We had better luck fishing in the afternoon and even I caught a walleye that weighed about four to five pounds.

This may not sound like much fun, but I wouldn't trade that week for all the sumptuous vacation spots. It was good to be away from TV, horrid headlines, and complex city life. Sitting there in the boat, surrounded by the wonders of nature so unspoiled by man, and only the songs of birds to break the silence, made me wish I could stay forever. I thank God that my little Brownie reflex camera caught the magic of that spot. I have the picture of trees, sky, and water, enlarged and framed, hanging in my office to remind me in the midst of a hectic day that there is still some peace and quiet in the world. I was also impressed with how clean and lovely the forests are where man has not been, and wished we could do more to make litterbugs and billboard advertisers realize they are destroying the beauty of America.

My family had its share of illness this year with my cousin, Genevra, and Aunt Mill having serious operations. In November Uncle Henry had a stroke and a few weeks later my mother had a slight heart attack. She and my uncle were in the same hospital. At the moment everyone is home and doing fairly well. My Aunt Min, better known as "Pinkie," is still very active for a lady almost 81. Susie is still boss of the house. She sleeps more and won't go to bed at night without her toy, but is still lively for a poodle who will be 11 in July. I've had a little bursitis, but if that is all I ever have I won't complain. I enjoy my work at FSA, though I would gladly forget the constant dictation, and I continue to do what I can in church. Walt may be in the Canal Zone at Christmas time, and we will miss him during the holidays.

And so, like the year, this letter is coming to an end. It has been fun sharing some of my year with you, and as I mail this letter to each of you I will wonder what you did this year and pray that only good fortune found its way to your threshold. Christmas is a time of family and friends; a time of peace and joy; a time of giving and sharing; and most importantly, it is a time of hope and love. May the truth of these words find its way into your hearts and into your homes! And I pray that at the end of 1966 you may be able to say of each friend, each day, and each new experience, what I can say so sincerely about each of you: I thank my God in all my remembrance of you!

With all my love to all of you, Alida

# 17<sup>th</sup> Christmas Letter, November 26, 1966 (At Home)

My dear family and friends,

As I begin this 17<sup>th</sup> annual greeting to you I can think of no better way to describe the past year than to borrow from our Chinese friends and say this was the "Year of the House." Actually it was a rather uneventful year compared to some, but in terms of energy expended it probably topped most.

From January through April, days went by without anything to report except for a few social events and an unusual round of activities at church. Then came May and "Project House." For two months I came home from work every night and WORKED. I hired a young fellow to paint and after two months we felt as if we had adopted Bob. Mom enjoyed cooking for a young man with a healthy appetite, and Bob never refused an invitation to eat with us. He finished our house just before Uncle Sam got him. I went through all eight rooms plus the attic, basement, and fruit cellar, and didn't leave a stone unturned. Light fixtures were replaced as well as switches and wall plates. I got well acquainted with paint remover and varnish, and I'm sure the rubbish men were most unhappy with the load of stuff I had waiting for them every week. I was looking forward to resting the three weeks I took off in July, but I worked harder than ever, getting up a 6:00 a.m. and working until nine or ten at night. I spent two hot July days in the attic sorting through my college and church files, and now I have two files instead of four.

Through all the days of hard labor I kept thinking of my dad and appreciated more than ever how hard he worked around here. If it were possible to look down from heaven I'm sure he was laughing, shaking his head and saying, "I never thought my girl could do that." Neither did I. The big reward for all this was that I lost 10 pounds — which was a relief!

One reason for all the hard work was so that Walt wouldn't have to think about the house when he got home, and you can bet he was surprised and pleased when he walked in because I had not told him what I was doing. He was home from August 3<sup>rd</sup> to November 7<sup>th</sup>, and concentrated on his plane as well as doing odds and ends around here. Almost every day he worked from 6:00 a.m. to 6:00 p.m. and was glad to just sit and relax in the evening. About 9:00 p.m. he was ready for a pint of ice cream. This year he got the controls in and the first thing next year the FAA will inspect it, and then he can begin to cover the plane. It's bedded down for the winter in the garage, and I will check it periodically just to be sure it is alright. My job is still that of general flunky, though this year I was promoted to hostess when Walt had groups of fellows from the FAA here to see the plane and kibitz. Like Walt, I'm tired of the question, "How will you get it out of the garage?" The answer is simple: the wings are put on at the airport. Question two is always, "Will you really fly in it?" I'm sure Walt will, and as far as I know now, I will also. The plane has to be flown 50 to 60 hours before passengers are allowed onboard. Home built planes are well-built, because no man will do a sloppy job on something he is going to fly himself, and they are well inspected. The little red plane in *The Blue Max* was a home built plane.

Walt and I had planned to go to Canada the first week in October, but I chickened out when the weather got bad and spent my last week of vacation at home — working! Pinkie was having the trim on the house painted and storm windows installed. Walt and the man next door installed an incinerator, and I cleaned up the mess. We spent an entire day just taking old varnish off our front door. Before he left, Walt bought some material and made iron railings for the front porch steps. On the inside his creative ability is evidenced in three lovely oil paintings he did while aboard ship, which I had framed.

The year brought with it some sadness. In September my old and dear friend, Beulah, lost her husband, Lewis, after a year's battle with a tumor of the brain. Many of you remember how I adored her first child, Neal, who is now almost 21. She had two other boys, Roger, 15, and Drew, who is nine. I sang at their wedding and have so many happy memories of Lew and his kindness to me.

As for my annual report on the family, I'd say we did pretty well this year with mom hospitalized for a heart spell only once for about a week while I was in the midst of all the work. Her eyes are very bad and she can't read the paper. It's a good thing she has all her recipes memorized. We are combining our Christmas card list this year because she can't see well enough to write. Pinkie still works in the yard, but rests more in between. I hope I'm going that strong at almost 82. She took a bus trip to Lincoln, Nebraska all by herself to attend a Townsend Club Convention, and that was almost too much for her.

Thank God Susie is still with us, and every year we wonder more and more what we will ever do without her. She was 11 on July 25th. I bought us all chocolate cup cakes for supper, and we helped her celebrate. She loved the fudge frosting. She was quite ill for a few weeks with a kidney infection, and was getting up two to three times a night. If whining didn't arouse me she would awaken me by hitting my head with her paw, or by walking all over me. For the second time in two years she had a swollen face and had to have some teeth removed. It's a good thing she's learning to like jello! She sleeps a lot more. As soon as mom goes up to rest in the afternoon, she is right there with her, but at night she insists on sleeping with me. Every night about 8:30 she cries until I give her about 20 licks on a Tootsie Pop. We've had cute dogs before, but we all agree Susie beats them all in being bright, fun to be with, and almost human.

It is so spring-like outside it hardly seems like the end of the year and time to send Christmas greetings. But the spirit of Christmas should be in our hearts all year, and the love we feel for one another should be expressed joyously in every season. If ever the world needed love it needs it now, and it seems to me the greatest comfort and reassurance we have is our knowledge that God still loves us. Let's hope men everywhere will learn to love one another and live in peace. So at the end of another year I thank God for all of you, and pray your Christmas will be a blessed one and your New Year flavored generously with hope, faith, and love.

With all my love to all of you, Alida

# 18<sup>th</sup> Christmas Letter, December 4, 1967 (At Home)

My dear family and friends,

Today I received my first Christmas card and decided I had better get busy and write this letter. If last year was the "Year of the House" then this year was the "Year of Many Changes." Changes really began at the end of 1966 when our Parma relatives decided they were going to move to Florida. For a family as close as we were this was a shocking change and we hated to see them go. February saw Aunt Mil, Cousin Genevra, and my Uncle Henry, who was my childhood Santa Claus, leave for St. Petersburg. They have what sounds like a lovely trailer.

Spring found me busy in the house and yard. This was the first year Pinkie, now 82, could not work in her beloved yard. I bought shrubs for the front and worked hard on the grass, spending a fortune on fertilizer. My reward was a fungus that made the backyard look sick. The tomatoes I raised made up for the grass; some of them weighed at least a pound! For the house I decided to get custom made drapes and have the furniture reupholstered. Every bit of it had to go back because of poor workmanship. I guess no one cares how they do things anymore!

One of the biggest changes came in my job. Early in the year The Legal Aid Society decided they would like a social worker on their staff. This is to be a Demonstration Project from one to three years. I volunteered for the job and learned my boss had me in mind, which was very nice. On September 18<sup>th</sup> I walked into two rooms that were storerooms, and it was a thrill to begin from scratch to turn them into attractive offices, one for me and one for my secretary. I'm proud of the results. It has been so nice to work with young lawyers dedicated to helping the poor. I have gone to court with them, attended their staff meetings, and have decided the only way to get through life safely is to be married to a lawyer. I have a new respect for law and lawyers. I'm afraid I'm getting spoiled being on my own. It is a rich opportunity and I am grateful that I was chosen to do this bit of pioneering. I am still part of the Family Service staff and can return to FSA when the project is over.

Sad changes came when we lost four of our immediate neighbors, all of whom we had known for about 34 years. With their deaths came other changes as their families moved. Changes like these I can do without.

A happy week of the year found Walt and me in Camp Chimo. The camp is on an island in Lake Temagami, which is about 80 miles north of North Bay, Ontario. That first week of September was just beautiful, and I spent three days in the boat with Walt and Charlie, our guide. I have pictures to prove I caught three lake trout; two of them weighed five pounds. I had to work hard to bring them up from 300 feet. Walt had pulled the trout rod for hours and caught nothing. I took his fishing rod to give him a rest, and within 20 to 30 minutes I caught the three trout. The other day Walt did all the catching and I never got a nibble.

Charlie cooked us delicious shore lunches, and I thoroughly relaxed amid all the beauty of nature. On the way back to camp one day the guide spotted a forest fire which was the result of a careless camper. Walt and Charlie didn't hesitate to dock the boat and go through the brush with what little equipment we had to try to contain the fire until the boat came from camp with a pressure pump and hose. It was exciting and I was proud of them. The last few days we were there the weather got cold. It was 33 degrees in North Bay and I swear it was 23 degrees in our cabin. I got up in the middle of the night to start a log fire. It makes one appreciate gas furnaces.

When we got back home work began on the plane. I spent two solid days taking about 400 screws out of the two wings Walt bought and which we picked up in Pittsburgh in May when he was home for a short stay. This year Walt got the plywood sides on and I helped him pound dozens of tiny nails in the wood before he put the glue on. In order to get measurements for drilling we put the wings on and it was just great to see the plane with wings spread out in our backyard. I wonder what some pilot flying over must have thought. The FAA inspector OK'd the plane, so Walt can cover the top of it next year. It may be another year or two before it is flying, but fly it will!

Mom's eye got continually worse and in October she had an operation to remove the cataract from the left eye. We breathed a sigh of relief when it was over because we thought for once she got through an operation without any complications but, alas, they found that the retina was detached, probably because of her diabetic condition. On December 10$^{th}$ mom has to go in for another operation on the retina. They may take the cataract from her right eye while she is there. Her failing sight and Pinkie's failing health meant I have had this huge house to take care of, and I've also had to learn to cook. Pinkie does some of the cooking, but I did the Thanksgiving dinner, turkey and all, and it was delicious! I decided to try my luck at Christmas cookies and found a recipe for Springerle, which are flavored with anise. If I carried one of those in my purse I would be arrested for carrying a concealed weapon – they are so hard! I'll try another batch and see what happens.

Even Susie had an operation this year. The Vet found a tumor and said we could add three years to her life if she had a hysterectomy. Despite her 11 years we decided to take a chance and she came through well. The Vet sent her home the same day because she is such a people dog he felt she wouldn't recover as well at the hospital. She is fine now and we hope we'll have her another 11 years!

I hope you will all forgive me for not keeping in touch as often through the year as I used to, but that does not mean I don't think about you. I do hope the holidays will be happy ones, and if I could wish anything for you in the coming year, it would be the joy of lasting friendship, the peace one finds in the majestic beauty of nature, and the hope that comes with having faith in a loving God. This year I attended several services in which Catholics and Protestants worshipped together. I came away feeling that if God could bring about such changes in attitude, He can bring about changes in our world which needs His love so badly. May whatever changes that occur in your life this coming year be only the most pleasant kind!

With all my love to all of you, Alida

# 19<sup>th</sup> Christmas Letter, December 1, 1968 (At Home)

My dear family and friends,

   With Thanksgiving past, it is time to think of my 19<sup>th</sup> annual Christmas letter to you. In some ways 1968 seems like a lost year, and yet I feel I accomplished a great deal.

   When I wrote last year mom was recuperating from a cataract operation. When the cataract was removed, they discovered a detached retina. Early in December she had the retina operation and had a very bad time, but she got home in time so we could spend a quiet Christmas together. On January 8<sup>th</sup> I peeked in at Pinkie before going to work and discovered she was very sick. The doctor came, diagnosed pneumonia, and prepared me for the worst! I stayed home and that night mom came down with the same illness. I was forced to put charts on their doors so I could know who got what medicine, and when! After being home two days I got a licensed practical nurse in for seven days, and I took over when I got home at night. They both pulled through, and I could breathe again! Then, because mom lost vision in the first eye, the doctor said it was time to have the other cataract removed. So, the end of February found her returning to the hospital. One positive thing came out of all of this: I got some practice cooking and baking, and so far we have not starved. Weekends became one round of shopping, cooking, cleaning, and gardening, but I'm just grateful the good Lord kept me well so I could look after mom and Pinkie. I gave up all church activity and finally hired a woman to clean every other week. She is a delightful person who is always bringing us goodies to eat.

   By June, when Walt came home, I was glad to be able to get to Canada for a week, and friends checked on mom and Pinkie. At the Sportsman Show last spring, I picked up folders on fishing camps. One camp seemed rather primitive, but I sent the folder to Walt anyway, hoping he would not pick that one. He did! Obabika is a small lake next to Temagami where we were last year (80 miles north of North Bay). It WAS primitive! After traveling over 600 miles by car and boat, when we got to the cabin Walt said, "Is it alright?" What could I say but, "Of course!" The one-room cabin had two beds, the frames of which were logs. Our "shower" was a basin and a bucket of water which Walt filled in the lake, and we had a wood-burning stove to heat it on. For light there was a Coleman lantern, and bathroom facilities were in a specially made enclosure — better known as an outhouse! This was fine, unless a trip was necessary in the middle of a rainy night. Then, wearing a raincoat, boots, umbrella, pajamas, and thermal underwear, created a big nuisance.

   After a few days we were used to the slight inconvenience which was nothing compared to the joy of being in this absolutely beautiful place. We found ourselves relaxing in its tranquility. There was no TV, no telephone, and a radio we didn't listen to for fear it would mar the peaceful atmosphere. It was as if there was no outside world to worry about while in that sheltered spot. The camp's capacity is 16, but there were only four others there, other than Mr. and Mrs. Younger, the camp owners, and the girl who cleaned the cabins.

Three of the fellows were school teachers, and the other was an attendance officer. Walt and I joined them one day, and we had a nice time and a delicious shore lunch. I must admit I liked the odds, but the fellows were all too young and too married. The fish were not biting, but the black flies were, and I came home looking like a disaster area, with welts all over my neck — and a very sunburned nose! I was ashamed to be seen by anyone, and you can bet I have bought several head nets in preparation for next year's trip. It was with tears in my eyes that I said goodbye to Obabika, for I hated to leave this Shangri-la and return to the reality and turmoil of the outside world. May June come soon again!

While we were in Canada, Susie had an operation to remove a growth that formed in the incision after her hysterectomy last year. The Vet also pulled eight of her teeth. The day after the stitches were removed she had a stroke. I got her to the Vet who said he would give her several shots. I told him to give me one also, because I couldn't stop crying! For several days we carried her in and out of the house, and Pinkie sat up with her the first night. Right now she is as good as new and doesn't act like a pooch that was 12-years-old on July 25$^{th}$.

Beginning August 19$^{th}$, I took the last three weeks of my vacation and spent those helping Walt with the plane, entertaining, and getting some things done around here. The wings on the plane needed to be covered, the engine overhauled, controls connected, and the plane painted. If all goes well it should be finished and flying this summer. I'm hoping to have Christmas cards made next year with a picture of the plane so you can all see it.

This past summer I dabbled in gardening again, and a friend helped me get vegetables planted. We had tomatoes, green beans, parsley, carrots, radishes, and green peppers. I planted Zinnias in between and in back of the vegetables, and it was a rather pretty combination. I wouldn't worry about the yard as much, but Pinkie always had it looking nice and now that she can't do it, I would hate to have her looking out at a mess. She is dreaming of getting out there next spring, and I hope for her sake she can. We just learned that she will be going to the hospital January 6$^{th}$ for a second cataract operation. Here we go again!

As for work, I am still at Legal Aid and am thoroughly enjoying working with the lawyers. They have all been so wonderful to me, and it is partly because of their cooperation that this project has been so successful. I am totally on my own, and though technically I am still employed by Family Service, I get there for only an occasional staff meeting. The project is due to end in April, but Legal Aid would like to keep the service because it is so helpful to their clients.

May Christmas be a joyous time for you and yours, and may you find in Christ throughout the New Year the same strength, courage, and faith that sustained me this past year. More than ever I believe the words of Scripture: "I will never leave thee, nor forsake thee." (Hebrews 13:5)

With all my love to all of you, Alida

# 20<sup>th</sup> Christmas Letter, November 16, 1969 (At Home)

My dear family and friends,

After last year's Christmas letter a young friend of mine, Tom Eaton, said he wished I could write a happy letter because he felt it was time I had a break from family illnesses and housework. Let me warn you: this has not been a happy year! However, I'm beginning to feel that happiness is coming to the end of a year and being able to say, "Thank God I managed to survive despite the problems, and thank God for the simple little things and wonderful people that eased the burdens."

Last year I reported that my aunt, Pinkie, was scheduled to have a cataract operation in January. The operation was a success but all the emotional strain at age 84 was just too much for her. She became quite confused while in the hospital, and after she came home she must have had a stroke. She became increasingly difficult to care for and by March we had to place her in St. John's psychiatric ward for evaluation. The doctor discovered there was brain damage and felt we had no alternative but to place her in a nursing home. The weeks ahead were the most traumatic I've ever experienced; even now I can hardly bear to think about them. It was bad enough to probate Pinkie, but looking at eight nursing homes in order to choose a desirable one, and then actually taking her there was sheer torture!

The only thing that eased the strain of those first five months of '69 was, after several weeks of getting no sleep, I hired a Negro homemaker named Mattie. She was with us 10 days and nights prior to our getting Pinkie into St. John's. She is a truly fine person and was a source of strength for me, and knowing someone was looking after things at home allowed me to go to work with peace of mind. Pinkie entered the Good Samaritan Nursing Home on April 22<sup>nd</sup>, and though she was confused, she mentioned home often enough that I knew she missed us, Susie, and her home. Visiting her was more torture, knowing we had to leave her there. It was almost a relief for us when on July 11<sup>th</sup> death freed her from the bondage of illness. As if our sorrow wasn't great enough, the day after the funeral, Susie, who had been ill several weeks, had a convulsion. For the next several weeks we visited the Vet many times, for suddenly everything seems to be wrong with our 14-year-old dog. It was a low blow when on August 1<sup>st</sup> Susie joined Pinkie. At least I like to think they are together. Needless to say the house is very lonesome without them.

We were lucky the July 4<sup>th</sup> storm didn't do more damage. It was frightening, and we learned to live by candlelight several nights. The top of my beautiful tree in the front yard came down, but luckily fell in the neighbor's drive, so neither house was damaged. I cried as I helped clean up the mess because I always loved that tree. Hopefully new growth will cover up its wounds.

Two-and-a-half-years of Florida heat proved too much for our relatives, the Krieths, and they decided to return. They were due back on July 12<sup>th</sup>, but little did they know they were coming to a funeral. They asked if they could stay with us several weeks until they found an apartment. It was seven weeks before Aunt Mil and cousin Genevra left us, and it was fortunate that mom had someone with her during the day for the first few weeks after Pinkie's death. I had taken a week of vacation in June to go to Western Reserve for a course in Family Therapy. The week after the Krieths moved out I took my second week of vacation, worked around the house, and got Pinkie's things in order. The week of September 8<sup>th</sup> we were delighted to have our friend Jeanne, and her daughter Jill, visit us from Canada. It was so good having a little child in the house for that week; the place seemed very much alive again!

On September 11<sup>th</sup> Walt came home for his vacation. He got little done on the plane this year, for as soon as he unpacked his bags we began to tear down our old garage. In its place we now have a 2½ car brick garage that is prettier than our house — and heated, too! While the men worked on the garage, Walt and I retreated to the peace and quiet of Canada for one week. My 48<sup>th</sup> birthday was the most beautiful I ever experienced, for we traveled toward North Bay on October 4<sup>th</sup>, and nature's gift to me was a breathtaking panorama of fall colors at their height. It was quite cold the week we were there, but we were rewarded by bringing home a 16-pound lake trout which was hooked on my line but reeled in by Walt. To prove our fish story we are thinking of having it mounted.

The week after we got home from Canada we worked like beavers in the house, tearing down old cupboards in the basement, cleaning the fruit cellar, etc., and my last week of "vacation" was soon gone. We insulated the attic and then thought we could sit back and forget the house, but, alas, a hot water pipe burst under the tub and we had our own Niagara Falls in the kitchen. We are now in the process of remodeling the bathroom, and come spring we will do the kitchen — I think!

Mom has her good and bad days. Her eyes are not good and she is often unsteady on her feet. I worry about her being alone all day when Walt is gone a few weeks from now, but Jimmy, next door, will check on her during the day if need be. Walt will leave after Thanksgiving, so the holidays will find mom and me alone.

On July 1<sup>st</sup> I joined the staff of Legal Aid. It was very hard to leave Family Service after 10 years, and I still have a great deal of affection for that agency. When the Foundation grant ended, Legal Aid asked me to stay as their employee. Having started this project from scratch, I hated to give it up so I decided to stay. I wish everyone could have the beautiful view of the lake and mall that I have from my office. I haven't attended church for several years because I had my hands full at home; but as I look at that view my faith is renewed each day!

One of the happier things that occurred was that my Negro secretary, Neisha, was expecting her first child. On April 4<sup>th</sup> her baby girl arrived and she was named Alida Renee — after me! My middle name is Henriette, but Renee was always my favorite French name. This is my first namesake other than the baby in Thailand who may have been given my name. In these days of racial strife I feel it is a real compliment to have a black child named after me. My lawyer's secretary is thinking of naming her child Alida if it is a girl, so there will be a few more Alidas in this city.

Our yard never looked lovelier than it did this summer, thanks to friends who worked hard to make it a thing of beauty, and our grass responded well to all the Scotts products. New rose bushes, small spruce, plus many other different shrubs, beds of petunias, and snapdragons, made it colorful. We also planted a red maple, which I always wanted.

All my friends have meant more than ever this year. Jim, who is like another brother, and his mother, Mabel, have been a comfort to us. Good thing I didn't have all the yard work on top of everything else this year. A friend from CEI whom I've known for many years entered my life again in July. Bob lifted my spirits by taking me dining and dancing, and you know how I love to dance! Members of my church were so kind at the time of Pinkie's death, and my pastor comforted me throughout her illness. Wish I could mention each friend by name but space does not permit. I must mention Bob Bowers, without whose guidance and legal counsel I would have been totally lost.

A happy year? No! Can I count my blessings? Yes! I thank God for the strength to get through all the traumas, for my own continued health, and for the many kindnesses that made life bearable.

And so I end this 20th Christmas letter with the hope and prayer that each of you and yours had a good year, that the holidays will be happy ones, and the year ahead full of many joyous times. Above all, may you come to the end of each year feeling that no matter what happened, God has guided and blessed you as He has for me this year!

With all my love to all of you, Alida

Chapter Five

**Ten Christmas Letters
From 1970 to 1979**

# 21st Christmas Letter, November 11, 1970 (At Home)

My dear family and friends,

As I write this 21th Christmas letter the holidays seem so distant for some reason. I've read pros and cons about Christmas letters, but so many of you have asked me to keep you on my list that I intend to keep up the tradition as long as I can. To me Christmas is not only a religious time, but a time of remembering and of feeling close to people in a deeply personal way. Material gifts mean less each year and of prime importance become the feelings of warmth, appreciation, and love, when shared with family and friends. If my letters bring us a bit closer and help to express my feelings for each of you, then they have served their purpose.

At the end of my last letter I told you we were remodeling our bathroom, which was to take two weeks. Three months and many headaches later it was finished and looks lovely. We had enough frustration by then so decided plans for the kitchen could wait, but we did get new orange shag carpeting which brightened up the house.

The week before Christmas Walt was told a ship was available, and because shipping was so slow he decided to take it. He wished he had stayed home for the holidays when he found a miserable crate left over from World War II. He sailed for Bremerhaven, Germany where a flu bug landed him in the hospital for eight days. He was glad to get off the ship and was flown home, arriving January 15th. His next ship was fairly new, air-conditioned, and for the first time he journeyed to Australia where he found the people very friendly. He left home April 6th, was home again June 15th, and remained until October 6th. So, he didn't work much last year. The ship was to be laid up anyway for 20 days, so he decided to take the summer off to finish the "Puddle Jumper," which is what he calls the plane. I helped him as much as possible and we did get the wings covered; in fact, the plane is almost complete except for having the engine overhauled.

We didn't take our usual week's vacation in Canada, but in June I flew to London, Ontario for two days to visit Jeanne and Spike. One reason I went was because one of my kids, Marcia, now 12, had been ill, and I thought she would enjoy the flight because she wants to be an airline stewardess. She was thrilled! It was her first trip without her parents and she got a bit homesick, but she was better prepared for her first trip to camp the next month. Over Labor Day weekend friends of Walt's who have an island in Lake Temagami, where we have fished several times, invited us to fly up with them. We flew in a four-passenger plane to Sudbury where we transferred to a pontoon plane so we could land at the island. The Kesters, our hosts, followed in their plane. It was a crazy, fun-filled, relaxing weekend which did me a lot of good. As always, the beauty of Temagami refreshed my soul.

As for the family, mom's eyes are not good. She now has a spot on the retina of her one good eye. In February she began having severe heart pains, which a heart specialist seems to have under control now. Walt left on April 6th and on April 8th my Aunt Helen died in Florida. Mom was in no shape to be left alone, so I had to make some long distance decisions. Aunt Helen had sent me her will before entering the hospital for a minor operation, so I knew she wanted me to take care of things. Thank God she had picked a kind, conscientious lawyer, George Gilbert. With his help and that of our friend, Jack

Shakespeare in Miami, I was able to get all the arrangements made without having to travel to Florida. I will never forget their kindness.

In August my aunt, uncle and cousin who had returned from Florida just a year earlier, decided they could no longer adjust to Cleveland winters and returned to the warmth of Florida. We miss them but Ohio Bell makes distance seem less great. Mom and I feel very much alone at times as the house is so quiet with Pinkie and Susie gone and Walt away. I have given up all activities because I don't like leaving mom alone. I worry about her being home alone all day while I'm at work.

I am still with Legal Aid, enjoy my clients, and am glad for the chance to meet so many fine lawyers. I wish I could save more marriages, but I am finding more people don't seem to go into marriage with the old determination to stay together "until death do us part." I also feel I am battling some sociological problems which will take time to change. I must confess I don't have all the answers. I wish I did! To relax a little and keep her company, I signed up for a 12-week Slimnastic course with my friend, Dorothy. Two hours of exercise with a 15-minute rest is a big dose. If we survive and have a good figure it will be a miracle! I have a suspicion the orthopedists sponsor these groups to drum up business.

At the end of every year I think of all those who have been so kind, and I am very grateful. Just to mention a few, Al has continued to keep my yard looking lovely. My new young friends, Chad and Diane, continue to bring life into our home. They are in their 20's and we have bridged the generation gap nicely. It is such a pleasure having someone young and full of life around to offset all the problems of aging which I have faced this year. I'm glad they feel at home here. One person who has been a Godsend through the years is our Doctor Joe. For 42 years he has worked miracles in our lives, and I think of him as part of the family. Doctor Rossen has always been there when we needed him most. I certainly have needed him the last few years, and he never failed me.

The years are slipping by and all "my kids" are working, in college, or Junior High. As I look toward a New Year, I pray, for their sake, that somehow we will find a solution to all our domestic and foreign problems. Some things we are powerless to change as individuals, but each of us can try harder to fight pollution and conserve the beauty of our nation and our world. This year, more than ever, I feel there can be no peace on Earth until man once more takes stock of himself and his relationship to nature. We ARE part of nature! If we allow any part of nature to become extinct, if we upset the balance by permitting erosion and pollution, then we are hurting ourselves. I hope you will join with me in taking another look at all the wonders of nature and never again take them for granted. They have been given to us by God not only to enjoy but to care for in a responsible way.

May each of you and yours find abundant joy in the New Year and, if peace on Earth seems like a far off dream with the world as it is, then try to find peace in some moment each day, and let the spirit of Christmas be a daily blessing as you give love to others and as you appreciate what others give to you.

With all my love to all of you, Alida

# 22<sup>nd</sup> Christmas Letter, November 22, 1971 (At Home)

My dear family and friends,

A very long and beautiful fall ended abruptly this weekend with snow which makes one realize the holidays are near. The weather may be cool, but the greetings this letter brings are as warm and sincere as ever.

The year started off again with illness. Mom was in the hospital two weeks in February with a heart condition. In March a flu bug clobbered me, keeping me home two weeks and coughing two months. May was a sad month because I lost my Santa Claus — my Uncle Henry who played Santa so convincingly when we were little. With his death our immediate family got even smaller!

To brighten up the scene Walt arrived home July 6<sup>th</sup>, determined to finish and fly his plane. Later that month Marcia and I flew to Canada again for two days, and that was about all the vacation I had. When I got home I discovered Walt had torn down the kitchen cupboards. After our bathroom plumbing went kaput two years ago and the plumber put his foot through the kitchen ceiling, we had no choice but to fix that before it fell on us. So, we decided we might as well do a little more! As usual a two week job became a two month project, and we will finally have the curtains up Thanksgiving.

In the midst of all the work and our tripping over pots, pans, and dishes, mom slipped coming down the stairs one night on August 14<sup>th</sup> and was taken to the hospital in an ambulance. That was the beginning of 13 solid weeks of nightly visits and emotional strain. Labor Day weekend we were called because she had a heart attack and was in critical condition. She was not expected to live, but she did! After five weeks in the hospital and eight weeks in a Medicare facility where she got therapy, we were able to bring her home November 15<sup>th</sup>. We truly have something for which to be thankful this Thanksgiving. She is doing fairly well but I will need to have someone with her during the day while I'm at work.

The yard was very pretty this summer and our roses were unbelievably tall and full of blooms. Near the lilacs I planted tomatoes and the vines found this a perfect place to climb. Have you ever seen tomatoes hanging from a lilac bush? It really was a funny sight!

For us this was the year of the airplane. The last major job of overhauling the engine was completed thanks to our friend, Bill, who spent many hours working on it. The neighborhood youngsters came running at the first sound that jolted the street. On September 25<sup>th</sup> Walt took the plane to the Portage County Airport near Ravenna. The yard and garage seemed empty without it, but we were lucky to get hanger space in a sparsely populated area. On October 10<sup>th</sup> the plane moved under its own power for the first time when it was taxied slowly. On November 16<sup>th</sup> it looked great on the Portage County Airport runway when it was taxied at a high rate of speed.

November 4th the FAA inspected the plane and found it air-worthy. By then we feared we would run out of good weather, but luckily early November was almost like spring. Saturday, November 13th, was our lucky day. We saw the culmination of seven years of dreams, hopes, and hard work as Bill taxied down the runway. He skipped the usual small liftoffs and immediately took off! What a thrill it was to see the plane flying. What else could a woman do but cry with happiness, and I did have tears in my eyes. The people at the airport were thrilled and congratulated Walt. Unfortunately the 30-year-old champagne I took along to celebrate had decomposed into vinegar! But the plane went up and we didn't need champagne to make us happy. Thank God Walt had the joy of seeing his plane fly this year, and next year he can look forward to testing it on water. We took motion pictures and slides, and they prove what we could hardly believe — it flew! We have so many friends to thank for their help. Bill T., O'Neil, John G., and many others helped to bring this project to completion, and as a permanent "thank you" their names will be written as an adorning fixture within the plane.

We don't know when Walt will have to leave. He was supposed to ship out in September, but because of mom's illness he remained at home. Now he must wait for the dock strike to get settled; therefore, he may be home for Christmas. I certainly hope so! Last year his ship returned from Australia on Christmas day, and he flew home just in time for Christmas dinner. Fortunately for everyone, Walt was able to enjoy the holidays with us for several days.

As you can see, I do not have much to report this year, other than work at Legal Aid, my looking after the home, and my role as a general flunky and hostess for the airplane project. I took a refresher course in driving, but once again gave up when mom got sick. I was just too nervous to think about driving! I did reach the half century mark this year. From now on I am forgetting birthdays. It was a rough year, but we managed to get through it and that is what counts. My only relaxation was accompanying Walt to the airport on weekends. It is a tiny airport surrounded by woods, and it is just lovely there!

Though I have not returned to church, I still feel the love of my friends there, and the comfort of the faith has meant so much to me. I don't know how anyone gets through life without faith. May we all find again this Christmas season a new awareness of the love of God that will remain with us and sustain us throughout the coming year! May that love help us to be patient, kind, and loving toward others! Just today I received a letter from my friends, Somsri and Pote in Thailand. The envelope contained pictures of their three children, including four-year-old Alida! I am so grateful for the bonds of love and friend-ship that circle the world, for they have most certainly enriched my life! Whether near or far, each year my friends grow more dear.

With all my love to all of you, Alida

# 23rd Christmas Letter, November 9, 1972 (At Home)

My dear family and friends,

Please don't think I've gone off the deep end if I say I was "high" when I started writing this letter. To be consistent with the theme of my card this year, I began writing the letter on October 8th while in flight to Indiana to see "my other family." I took advantage of Walt being home and having Veterans Day off to visit the Reverend and Mrs. Garner. It was the first time in 20 years I've been in their home. The Garners have been an important part of my life since 1947 when I began attending daily noonday services he conducted at the Old Stone Church. Like anything sterling, time has only enhanced the beauty and value of that friendship. Happily, I can say that about my friendship with so many of you.

What can I say about a year in which I didn't do much? I can start with the end of 1971 when I took a two-week vacation at Christmas time. Walt was home so we got mom out a few times during the day to visit, and I was able to entertain a little and not have to worry about getting up the next morning. One night three of Walt's high school friends came over with their wives. It was the first time in 30 years they were all together. It was a very nice evening for everyone!

We weren't even able to get through January without illness striking. Mom began having serious problems because of her heart condition and the doctor felt it was necessary to insert a pacemaker. Walt absolutely had to leave on January 25th although mom's operation was scheduled for the 26th. Walt had taken two trips off in '71 when mom was hospitalized 13 weeks, and he had to get back to the ship. He flew in the 28th to check on her condition. This time mom was hospitalized for nine weeks. The only thing that eased the daily visits after a long day of work was a restaurant near the bus stop which served delicious home-cooked meals, thus sparing me the need to cook. I was also grateful for friends who picked me up many evenings to take me home. It was lonesome rattling around in the house alone! After mom returned home, a retired friend agreed to come and stay with her from 10:30 a.m. to 4:30 p.m. every day so I could go to work with some peace of mind. I thank God for Lee every day. She actually got mom to go for short walks down the street, which was encouraging.

In April my aunt came from Florida for a physical checkup and stayed with us awhile. I'm sure it cheered both her and mom to see each other again.

The end of July Walt came home, and August found mom back in the hospital for two weeks because she was so dizzy. The doctor changed her medicine and right now her condition is stabilized. I'm using these moments of calm to store up strength for whatever comes next!

The end of August I took a two-week vacation and just loafed. Labor Day weekend Walt and I were invited to a friend's cottage on an island in Lake Temagami where we have been before. It seemed unwise for both of us to be away at the same time. Because Walt had a fishing trip scheduled later that month, and because I was so tired, it was decided that I would go and Walt would look after mom. The last minute I learned that the other woman who was planning to go had cancelled, so there I was with three men and 14-year-old Tommy, flying in a private plane. How do you like those odds?

71

My trips with Walt had taught me how to rough it, so the fellows didn't have to worry about my being a helpless female, and they helped with the cooking and cleanup. Tommy taught me how to shoot his .22 caliber rifle, and we were all surprised when I hit the target after a few tries, which was a can bobbing in the water 40 feet away. I had never held a gun in my hand before. The beauty of Temagami left me refreshed as always, and my only regret was that I was there only a weekend and not a month.

I'm happy to report Walt has officially named his plane — Puddle Jumper! He has managed to get the necessary 50 hours flown so the FAA can certify it to go beyond the 25 mile radius it was restricted to while being tested. With all the rain we have had it was not easy to get the 50 hours, especially since he had to depend on two friends to fly the plane in their spare time. Walt has almost completed requirements for his own license, and maybe before he leaves early in December he can test the plane on water. Who knows, next year he may fly it to Canada — which is his dream!

For eight years my dream was to send a Christmas card with a picture of the plane in flight. When a friend of Walt's flew to the airport in his two-passenger plane, I suggested Walt go up and take some pictures. He declined and said, "You go!" I did! The pilot told me he would lower the canopy after we got up so I could take clearer pictures. It may not seem like much to some of you, but I'm not used to flying with nothing above me but the sky; nevertheless, there I was, and I was so busy pretending I was a photographer I wasn't even scared. George Plimpton has nothing on me — and to think I'm afraid to drive a car! The result of my efforts is my Christmas card and I'm proud of it. Walt has since painted a horizontal stripe on the sides of the fuselage and vertical stripes on the end of each wing to dress it up a bit. By the way, that isn't Santa at the controls, it is our friend and test pilot, Bill.

As for work, I've been very busy at Legal Aid and have had the rewarding experience of hearing from some former Family Service clients. One was in town recently and it was such a pleasure to see him after 10 years and to know he and his family are doing well. The Reverend Garner once said if his ministry made a difference in the life of only one person, he would feel it was worthwhile. I feel the same about my work!

I've gotten to Sunday worship service more often this year, and more and more realize how much I miss my church family. I also miss my old piano which I gave away two years ago when we got new carpeting. The black child I gave it to has gotten certificates for outstanding achievement in piano — which is wonderful! But I miss that old friend of mine and I'm looking around for a smaller one. That is my goal for 1973.

Here I am at the end of another year and another letter. Let us hope that the light of the Holy Spirit will guide each of us throughout the coming New Year, and let that light guide the leaders of every nation as well. Only then will we find peace and goodwill among the nations of the Earth.

With all my love to all of you, Alida

# 24<sup>th</sup> Christmas Letter, November 25, 1973 (At Home)

My dear family and friends,

A month from today is Christmas and I have made no preparations—except that I have the postage stamps! Which reminds me, last year someone mentioned how much my airplane card must have cost, and I kiddingly said that in '73 I would make up for it by sending only the postage stamp. If I don't get busy my joke will become a reality! Last year many of you wrote and asked me what that thing was on top of the plane? That is the engine! Because it is an amphibian and lands on water as well as on land, the engine must be located on top of the plane.

Our one big thrill in '73 came on September 16<sup>th</sup> when Walt and our friend, Baker, flew to Sandusky Bay for the first water test. I drove there with our neighbor, Eddie, as we needed a car to get Walt to a marina. There we met another friend, Chuck, who came to the bay in his cabin cruiser — just in case of a mishap! Thank God all of our precautions were unnecessary. The plane, piloted by Baker, landed and took off on the water just as Walt had dreamed. Later, Walt soloed it. We were hoping to get it to Canada for sure next year, but with the energy crisis things look bad for private flying. I feel sorry for all the home builders who have put so much work into their planes and may not be able to fly them.

I was determined to start this year with something happy for a change — and did! Early in January I went to a matinee of *Fiddler on the Roof*. We were early so I decided to look at pianos in a store next to the theater. Twenty minutes later I walked out the owner of a second-hand Baldwin console. For three years I had searched for a new piano, and now I am thoroughly enjoying it. In July I began taking lessons to improve my skill, and the teacher is pleased with my progress. Neither one of us expects me to be great, so I can relax and enjoy the lessons.

When I was 12-years-old I took some tap dancing lessons and loved them. For 40 years I said I was going to take more lessons. My friend, Elaine, learning of my "great ambition," found me a teacher. Diane is young and thought we were kidding until I produced an old pair of shoes with taps on them. She was shocked at how quickly I learned the steps. I now have regular tap shoes and can't wait for lessons to resume after the holidays. If the Lakewood Little Theater ever produces *No, No, Nanette*, I'll be ready. Ha! At least I'm having fun and we all need something to brighten our lives these days!

Mom had one of the best years she has had in a long time. She almost made it through all of '73 without being hospitalized, but yesterday she went in to have x-rays taken because of a pain in her side. The pacemaker has helped her tremendously! She takes 15 to 18 pills a day, which I put in nut cups every night so she gets the correct dosage. Unless Walt and I are home, Lee comes every day to help, and we are grateful for her assistance. In September my Aunt Mil came from Florida and stayed six weeks. One of those weeks she spent in the hospital for testing, but the rest of the time she and mom enjoyed being together.

No year goes by without some sadness. This year I lost my Aunt Margaret and Uncle Otto. They weren't blood relatives, but I grew up thinking of them as aunt and uncle and loved them dearly. Uncle Otto called Walt and me "Toledo" and "Sandusky," and our Christmas cards were always addressed that way. On August 30<sup>th</sup> I lost one of "my kids," Marcia, who would have been 15 years old October 1<sup>st</sup>.

You may recall I took her to Canada with me two years in a row. What I didn't say in the letters was that cancer had been diagnosed, and I wanted to be sure she had an airplane ride because at that time she dreamed of becoming an airline stewardess. Marcia also wanted to see Hawaii, so when the California vacation her parents had planned for her this year was cancelled, I decided to take her and her sister, Gayle, to Hawaii. Reservations were made for August 25$^{th}$ to September 2$^{nd}$, knowing a scheduled examination by her doctor might mean we could not go. The doctor's decision was negative, but I don't think even he knew how close death was. To ease her disappointment I was going to have a Hawaii night here at home, but death robbed her of that, too. I used to call her "Sweetie Pie," and she called me "Aunt Pizza" because we always had pizza when I visited them. I'm so grateful for the many happy times I had with her, and I'm even more grateful that years ago I learned that you should never put off doing the nice things you want to do for anyone because, if you wait, it just might be too late!

Walt has been working only six months a year. He got home the end of June and two days after he arrived two of his friends and I went with him to a fly-in in Baltimore. Our friend Russ had invited five men who built the same plane as Walt to a Volmer Fly-in. It was really a sight to see four amphibians moored in the Chesapeake Bay. Walt had to leave November 12$^{th}$ so I cooked the traditional Thanksgiving dinner before he left and defrosted the leftovers on the 22$^{nd}$. These eight rooms are terribly empty with both Walt and mom away!

Every year I thank God for supplying me with so many good friends, and each year He seems to add some new ones. For a number of years we have enjoyed our neighbors to the south, Dan and Dara, and we have so enjoyed watching Susie grow. It's good to have a child around. Our new neighbors Elaine and Bill have been good company and their young son, Bruce, helps me in the yard. God also seems to supply me with men to drive me around. I just can't force myself to drive alone and to do all the repairs that need to be done in a home. For the past year, our neighbor, Ed Richie, whom we have known since junior high days, has taken me to the store every Saturday. We all appreciated his kindness. He likes to get an early start, so he gets here at 7:30 a.m. and we're at the store by 8:00 a.m. With the gas shortage I may have to get my bike out. Maybe a tandem would be a good idea!

I am still with Legal Aid, trying to save marriages, and if that isn't possible then I try to help individuals find a new direction in life. The agency is doing a great job of making sure all segments of the community have access to legal help. The lawyers are very dedicated young men, and I enjoy working with them.

As I close this letter, I'm wondering what the New Year has in store for us. Watergate, pollution, crime, and the energy crisis all have been frightening. They certainly have made us keenly aware that we cannot take for granted our natural resources, the beauty of nature, nor the goodness of man. Maybe the energy crisis will slow us down and give us time to talk to one another again, and to meditate and renew our relationship with God. The words "Peace on Earth, Good will toward men," seem almost like an impossible dream this year. I believe we need to begin 1974 with the prayer that we will have the faith, wisdom, and courage to make these words a reality — in our lifetime. I couldn't stand to think about the problems of our nation and the world if I didn't believe that somehow God knows what He is doing and will once again bring order out of chaos. Our forefathers had great faith, and that faith enabled them to face and conquer many difficulties. We will, too! May renewed faith and hope be our greatest gift this Christmas season and give us strength in the year ahead.

With all my love to all of you, Alida

# 25<sup>th</sup> Christmas Letter, November 24, 1974 (At Home)

My dear family and friends,

It's hard to believe that this year I am celebrating the writing of my 25<sup>th</sup> Christmas letter. However, the early months of this year were uneventful. I continued piano and tap dancing lessons and thoroughly enjoy both. I hope the exercise helps the arthritis I'm getting in my right arm and hand, as well as my left hip. Tap dancing is so much fun! I wish I had started years ago. My teacher is amazed because I catch on quickly and, although I don't look like Ann Miller, I don't look like a baby elephant hopping around either. Susie, my favorite six-year-old neighbor, has been coming over once a week for a lesson since September, and she's doing well. If this keeps up my teacher will have a neighborhood dance studio in the basement.

In May I added voice lessons to my schedule in order to get my voice back in shape. In these years filled with illness at home I have become so isolated and have truly missed being a part of the church. In September I rejoined the choir after a long absence. It feels so good to be singing again and I'm glad to be serving my church even in this limited way.

Walt's stay at home was shorter this year. He was here from May 20<sup>th</sup> to September 25<sup>th</sup>. We had our Thanksgiving meal in September before he left. His plane is flying well but he didn't get it to Canada as he had hoped. He drove to the EAA National Fly-In in Wisconsin, but flew his plane to a local fly-in in Painesville where he got a trophy for making a spot landing. We laugh at that because there was such a crosswind he was just happy to get down, let alone find a spot on the runway. He also flew his plane, which he named the Puddle Jumper, to a state fly-in in Marion, Ohio.

Lee agreed to stay with mom a week in July so Walt and I could get to Canada for a week. I hadn't been away for more than just a day here and there for three years. We were only 15 minutes away from home, driving on the Shoreway to pick up Walt's friend, Frank O'Neil, when suddenly we saw a wrong-way driver speeding straight at us! Walt swerved in the nick of time! If anyone had been in the next lane that July 13<sup>th</sup> morning, we would have been in the hospital — or worse!

When we arrived I stayed at the cabin to rest and let the fellows do the fishing. One day I caught fish without ever going out — while they were in the hot sun all day and caught nothing. I made friends with Bill and Velma Rice in the next trailer. When Bill found out we had no fish for supper, he shared his catch with us. That was so nice of him. It was his 70<sup>th</sup> birthday so we played cards that night, and we played several other evenings as well. We visited the Dionne Museum in Callander, Ontario, and were amazed that those babies survived with their primitive equipment, and in an area which must have been very sparsely populated at that time. I went out in the boat just once, but a 15 mph northwest wind and high waves made me apprehensive to say the least. I kept my mouth shut as long as I could, but finally insisted on going back. By then Walt was drenched and raised no objection to my plea. I felt like kissing the shore when I set foot on it!

We almost adopted an abandoned kitten which found Walt in the garage. We looked after it three days, and it was so cute I hated to give it up. But I have enough to do without worrying about litter boxes, etc. My cousin Minerva said we could bring it to their farm, and I was glad to find it a good home.

I have been extremely busy at work and prefer it that way. All the Legal Aid offices will be moving to the building I'm in, so there will be some changes. As yet I don't know if I will lose my room and lovely view of the lake, which will kill old nature lover — me! Changes are never easy, but I've survived changes before. I just hope I can make it through nine more years, and then be able to afford to retire.

Mom was 80 on August 9th. I had an open house planned for her on the 11th, but at 3:30 that morning she suffered a mild stroke. Later in the morning she sufficiently improved, so I followed through with the open house. I dressed her and made her comfortable on the bed, and had the guests go upstairs to visit her. She enjoyed seeing everyone, and a few who couldn't come called to talk with her, so she had a nice day. I'm so glad she had that happy time because on October 19th, about a week after Walt left, she fell and fractured her hip. The first x-rays showed nothing and they insisted she sit in a chair, and also roll from side to side in bed. By the 28th she was out of her head with pain, so they re-x-rayed and found a fracture. She was operated on October 30th and a stainless steel ball was inserted. She has had a miserable time ever since. She is scared and so am I about what the future holds. On November 20th she entered St. Augustine Manor for the third time, and hopefully therapy will enable her to walk again. I thank God for Medicare, which keeps us from going to the poor house.

Though God has given me strength, I must admit after 41 years of family illnesses, at times I get discouraged. I told someone I'd like to go to an island in the Pacific, find a grass shack, get a bottle of sake (wine) and a beach boy, and forget to come back. Instead of doing that I treated my depression by buying new clothes. In between trips Walt flew in one night, saw mom a few hours and flew out the next day. It was a short visit, but it made mom happy! This will be my first holiday season with both mom and Walt away, and I hate the thought because my family has always meant so much to me.

Walt and I got in on the act this year and ended up getting x-rays. He had excruciating pains in his back after helping lift an airplane out of a ditch, and I slipped while cleaning tile in the shower and cracked my face on the ceramic soap holder. Neither of us broke anything, but the muscles in Walt's back hemorrhaged, causing severe pain. I had a real shiner, and still have a numb tooth. The night of the accident I stayed with my friend, Ruth Hinshaw, in case of complications. I'm lucky I have so many good friends.

Again, I thank God for my wonderful friends. They called to invite me to share Thanksgiving with them. They have also been so generous in picking me up at the hospital at night. Walter and I are both very grateful.

I'm sure we are all wondering what 1975 will bring. I'm so glad I can remember those peaceful, quiet years before the Great Depression. Those childhood days in Parma were so pleasant, when we kids played in fields full of buttercups and daisies. Everyone was honest, kind, and neighborly, and we more or less looked after one another if there was a family crisis. I may sound like the Bunkers, but more and more I feel "Those were the days!" I shutter every time I hear economists talk about the coming depression because I remember the horrors of the last one. None of us knows what is ahead, nor what we can do to cushion the blow if it comes. About all we can do is thank God for bringing us safely through another year and pray for courage to face whatever lies ahead. President Ford and I have one thing in common: a favorite *Bible* verse over which he had his hand when he was inaugurated. Perhaps it will have some special meaning to you:

Trust in the Lord with all thine heart;
And lean not unto thine own understanding.
In all thy way acknowledge Him,
And He shall direct thy paths. (Proverbs 3:5-6)

God bless you everyone, this season and always!

With all my love to all of you, Alida

# 26<sup>th</sup> Christmas Letter, November 16, 1975 (At Home)

My dear family and friends,

This year I'm celebrating the 26<sup>th</sup> year of writing this Christmas letter; that's 26 years of friendship and sharing a bit of my life with you. How grateful I have been for all of you. Some of us have been friends since the 1<sup>st</sup> grade; some of you were a part of my life for a brief time but you helped change the direction of it. Needless to say, you have all enriched and added meaning to my days. Despite all the negative things printed about mimeo'd Christmas letters, I have appreciated this convenient way of keeping in touch. Many of you have requested that I continue to send them, and I have decided that I would certainly do so.

Do you recall that I began writing Christmas letters in 1950 because I joined a church that year and got so busy I was unable to write individual letters? I knew you would never decipher my handwritten Christmas notes. Because I have been doing this for 26 years, allow me to reminisce a bit. On January 1<sup>st</sup>, 1940 I began my first job at Federal Reserve Bank at $60 a month. I worked there until 1946 when I went to the Illuminating Company. I did clerical work at both places. While working at the Illuminating Company I attended Noonday services at the Old Stone Church where I met the Reverend J. Herbert Garner and his family. He encouraged me to become a member of a neighborhood church. I wasn't sure which church I wanted to join, but I did become a member of the choir at the Lakewood Baptist Church because when in high school I had sung under its director, T. R. Evans. A year later, having found so much warmth and true Christian spirit in its members, I joined the church and my life has not been the same since.

Sunday school teaching led me to Green Lake for more training. There dedicated Christian women inspired me to go to college to prepare for some type of Christian service. I will always be grateful to the Baptist Women of Ohio, my church, and my family for helping me through undergraduate school. Though I was preparing to be a Director of Christian Education, a course in Casework in my junior year caused me to change my plans and I went on to get a Masters in Social Work. Six happy years of learning ended in 1959 when at the age of 38 I began a new career as a caseworker at the Family Service Association. I spent 10 years at FSA; the last 1½ years they lent me to The Legal Aid Society where I started a social service project. When the funding for this pilot project ended, Legal Aid asked me to join their staff, and I did in 1969. I am still with them, counseling people mostly from the inner city. I still pinch myself because it is hard to believe all this happened, but I am convinced God has guided me and worked so many miracles in my life.

Very briefly, let me tell you 1975 has been a fairly good year. Early in January mom came home from the extended care facility where she spent the 1974 holidays after fracturing her hip. I got plenty of exercise sprinting up and down the stairs for many weeks. But now, thank God, she can get up and down herself, though she has a lot of pain. Considering her lifetime health problems, she is fairly well at 81. Walt came home in June, and while he took over the household chores, I managed to get to Canada for about a week. On October 13<sup>th</sup> he left for New York where he took a five-week course in radar. He will ship out for Africa on November 21<sup>st</sup>, so he will not be home for the holidays. He will also miss the wedding of one of "my kids," Gayle Beth Roglin, on November 22nd. I'm looking forward to that happy occasion. Walt continues to fly his plane, and I have continued with piano, tap dancing, voice lessons, and the church choir — which is sheer joy!

As I look back over the last 26 years, I realize you have shared many joys and sorrows with me. In years gone by I have lost my dad, Aunt Pinkie, my Santa Claus, Uncle Henry, our family physician, Doctor Rossen, who I only knew as "Doctor Joe" for 47 years, and our loveable dog, Susie. It makes me sad to see our family dwindling. Walt and I will be the "Last of the Mohicans" in the Struze tribe, I'm afraid!

I seem to be ending 26 years where I began — getting back to church! After being active for many years I wasn't able to attend much or serve in any way for seven years because family illnesses pushed me into the roles of homemaker, gardener, nurse, etc. All this occurred while I was working everyday and running to doctors and hospitals with mom and Aunt Pinkie — sometimes 10 to 13 weeks at a time! With Walt absent from home so often, I never would have made it without faith and the help of all my friends! There were times when I got very depressed and I missed the good times I had at church. Joining the choir, after things settled down at home, got me back to church and the Fellowship class. The members of this class show concern for one another and have many good times together. They have elected me to be their president next year. I am the first single woman to have that post, as they usually have a husband and wife team. If I were a women's libber I suppose I would change the name to "Galship" or "Personship" class, but I don't go along with some of that nonsense, so the original name of "Fellowship" will remain. I may be biting off more than I can chew, but if I fall on my face, I'm sure someone will pick me up.

One cannot think of 26 years that have passed without feeling a bit sad, and wondering what the next 26 years will bring. If I am still here I will be 79 and only hope the words of Browning are correct: "Grow old along with me, the best is yet to be, the last for which the first was made…" Again, I am grateful for each of you and thankful that in these years your lives touched mine in so many different but meaningful ways. I sincerely hope that in some way I have added something good to your lives. I tell friends that when I die I want no eulogy. If I did not do anything worthwhile during my sojourn here, I do not deserve nice words when I'm gone. If something I did or said made someone's life a little easier or better, that person will know it — and that is eulogy enough! I've made my share of mistakes and hope I'll make fewer in the years ahead.

Despite all the international and national trauma surrounding us each day, I hope in the past year you have found many happy and bright moments, and that you will find many more in the year ahead. I love my country and all it stands for and pray that as we look forward to celebrating its birthday, we ask God to rekindle in us the faith, strength, and courage of our forefathers who brought our nation so far. I hope we can find a way to keep its beauty, goodness, and freedom from being tarnished by those who would ravage the landscape, from those who commit crimes, and from those who are more concerned about their own selfish needs rather than the good of the land and its people. As we think of the birthday of Christ, let us think about the birthday of our country and resolve to serve both of them more diligently and devotedly.

With all my love to all of you who have meant so much to me, Alida

# 27<sup>th</sup> Christmas Letter, November 19, 1976 (At Home)

My dear family and friends,

An announcer stating that there were only 30 more shopping days until Christmas jolted me into the realization that our bicentennial year was coming to an end. Wasn't it great to be able to share that memorable moment in history on July 4<sup>th</sup>? The end of the year means it is time for my annual letter, which many of you asked me to continue. Thanks for the many compliments on last year's 26<sup>th</sup> epistle.

In 1975 we managed to get past February without mom having some traumatic illness, but in '76 the jinx returned. She had just reached the point where she could get around well after fracturing her hip, but then in February she fell again and fractured a vertebra. The next four months were taken up with hospital visits, purchasing more equipment to make her comfortable and safe at home, mastering the technique of putting on her back brace (which I had to do before going to work), and finally having the reward of seeing her walk up and down the stairs again. For an 82-year-old woman, she has remarkable recuperative power! Recent falls haven't hurt her but they scared the daylights out of Walt and me. I thank God for the fact that somehow things always work out. Three days before mom fell, Walt came home after taking another course in New York. He was waiting for the ship to return in a few days, but luckily it was delayed because I had a two week bout with bronchitis and needed him to help me and visit mom. The day she was transferred to an extended care facility he left for New York.

The end of June Walt came home for his vacation. He put his plane up for sale. I hate to see it sold after all the hours he spent on it, and I put in many hours too. His plan to take a third course in October got scuttled when he fell roller skating and tore a tendon in his right arm. On October 6<sup>th</sup> he had an operation to repair the damage and sported a cast for a month. The doctor will tell him on December 4<sup>th</sup> whether or not he can go back to work. He can't lift anything heavy for three months.

Except for tap dancing, piano and voice lessons, none of which I have time to practice, I really haven't done much this year. So Walt would have a partner, I took some dancing lessons with him and learned to cha-cha. But I never go dancing so it doesn't do me much good. In August I spent five cold days at my favorite island retreat in Lake Temagami. The second night it was so cold in my cabin I might as well have been sleeping outside! The next three nights I slept with all my clothes on in front of the fireplace in the main cabin. The beauty is worth the discomfort. Last year I sent for leaflets regarding the preservation of our environment, which I forgot to enclose. Concern for our environment is still timely so I'm sending them this year.

My big expenditure in '76 was three caps on my front teeth. Our dentist, Doctor Morr, is such a great guy and hates to see his patients spend money. I had to talk him into doing the work and he did a good job. People tell me they never noticed the bad teeth, but I knew they were there! Now I feel like smiling again.

Choir is still a joy though I haven't found the nerve to do solo work as I did in my younger years and, besides, I am having problems with a constant sore and tight feeling in my throat. Being the President of

Fellowship class was no problem. Things went smoothly and everyone was so helpful. We have lost many members who retired and are forming a branch of our class in St. Petersburg. I have been asked to be President another year, and to ensure having some members left by '78, I will not allow Florida vacations. Even our pastor is leaving to take a position at our Baptist Assembly in Green Lake, Wisconsin. We will miss him and envy him working in such lovely surroundings.

As for work, I am now doing two jobs. One of our women had to quit because of illness and I was asked to be Director of Referral Service as well as Director of Social Service. I have enjoyed talking to attorneys who take clients not eligible for Legal Aid. I can't say enough nice things about so many of them who have been so kind and generous. Without the help of my secretary, Mary Schroeder, who is loyal and dependable, I could never handle both jobs. At this point she is more of a paraprofessional than a secretary. The end of May the agency is moving to a new location in a rather depressed part of downtown Cleveland. I will miss my view of the lake and the trees on the mall. Maybe I can find some way of beautifying the new location because I respond to my surroundings.

This year hasn't been very exciting; sometimes it was depressing; but I can count my blessings and am grateful for having my loved ones, my health, a job which enables me to help others, and I still have all of you as friends! My experiences again this year strengthened my faith. As bad as things were and as tired as I got, with God's help I got through it!

With all my love to all of you, Alida

# 28<sup>th</sup> Christmas Letter, November, 1977 (At Home)

My dear family and friends,

Several years ago my neighbors Dan, and Susie, who was then five, took me to the dentist for an emergency appointment. I waited with dread for what seemed like an eternity. Suddenly Susie broke the silence with, "My, time flies when you're having fun!" Dan, the receptionist, and I burst into laughter. Time flies whether you're having fun or not, and here it is time to pull together the year's happenings to share with you.

Walt wasn't home for Christmas '76 so mom and I were alone. Jim and Mabel next door usually come over but Mabel ended up in the hospital Christmas Day. Jim came over for a meal I saved for him. He deserves credit for looking after his mother all year. We're both going to apply for LPN licenses. Walt will be leaving after Thanksgiving so we'll be alone this Christmas too, and I hate the thought. I'll have to try to find someone who needs a family.

Critics of Christmas letters would shudder to learn that two of my friends asked if they could Xerox all my letters from 1950 to 1976. They were social workers, so I was glad when they told me they liked the content and weren't going to do a Freudian analysis of the letters. I felt complimented but my ego wasn't inflated to the point where I have thought of publishing them — not yet! Ha!

The first of the year illness jinx hit us again. In the worst three weeks of January, with temperatures reaching -55 with the wind-chill factor, and snow piled above the fence, I had bronchitis. It was depressing and frightening to be ill with blizzards outside while inside we had drapes and shades drawn to keep the cold out. In February of '76 mom fell three days after Walt arrived home, fracturing a vertebra. In February '77 mom fell three days after Walt arrived home, and this time she had contusions and again had to be hospitalized. The repetition was unbelievable! In May she had small strokes and was disoriented several weeks, snapped out of it, and had another in September. Her orthopedic doctor never spoke truer words than when he told me "Your mother is a walking medical textbook."

April brought nice surprises. It was no April fool joke when on April 1<sup>st</sup> at a Legal Aid party I was given one of the annual awards for outstanding service. It is always nice to know one's efforts are appreciated. The second surprise came Good Friday when my dear Thailand friend, Somsri, phoned from Columbus, which was one stop on a speaking tour across the country. I convinced her to spend Easter Sunday with us. How wonderful it was to see her, to meet her son, Man, and to get caught up on what has happened in the 18 years since I saw her last. I hope her daughter, Alida Kantamala, will get to America some day.

In New York Walt met a member of the Metropolitan Opera chorus and told her to contact me when she got to Cleveland. Walt was home when the opera arrived so we were able to entertain Dena, who is such a fine person. I autographed my 9<sup>th</sup> grade class picture "from the future finest, famous Metropolitan Opera singer." Dena is as close as I'll get to that Met! An old friend and neighbor I grew up with, Dan Zaffarano, surprised me at work with a brief visit. I hadn't seen Dan for 25 to 30 years. He is now a Professor of Physics at the University at Ames, Iowa. I'm always glad to make new friends, and grateful that old bonds of friendship can last so long.

For her May birthday Susie got a black spaniel she called Muffin. He would walk through the fence to see me, is too big for that now, but I enjoy the royal treatment I get when he sees me in the yard. I always think puppies are part of God's plan to cheer up the world.

The end of May Legal Aid moved its offices to a depressing section of town, away from stores, bakeries, and close to the lake where it will be cold this winter. Luckily we have a coffee shop downstairs run by Irv and Rose Irwin. They make the area seem friendlier, as do some of the early morning customers like Jeannie and Sam whom I see every day. I miss my former view of the lake, trees, and fountains. We planted two trees outside this building, which may one day peek into my window. Poor things look so alone out there but I'm praying others will follow suit to try to beautify this dismal street.

A pregnancy epidemic hit my piano and tap dance teachers so right now I'm only taking voice lessons to ease tense throat muscles. In January a doctor told me I should stop singing forever and do little talking. A specialist in Oberlin vehemently disagreed, told my voice teacher what to do, and gradually my voice is improving. Our choir director caught me in a weak moment and signed me up for a solo August 21$^{st}$. After not singing before an audience for 22 years, to say I was scared was an understatement, but I did it! Though my fear was evident, at least my voice was good that day.

After two years of being President of our church school class, I will be Vice President next year. I will also be on our Social Concerns Committee which meets once a month, so I'll continue to do what I can for my church.

In September, for the first time ever, Walt's ship sailed up the Great Lakes and stopped in Cleveland. At last I was able to see his radio shack and room, which are small. The dining room was pleasant with small tables covered with cloths. We took five of the men to dinner, then back home for cheesecake and coffee. They were well-educated, extremely nice men, contrary to what people think of sailors.

The saddest day this year was October 15$^{th}$ when Walt sold the Puddle Jumper to a man from Baltimore. I am glad it will get more use in the Chesapeake Bay, but when I saw it fly off into the blue for the last time, I cried! After all the years of watching it being built and spending many hours helping Walt, I felt as if part of me went with it. I'll also miss the quiet little airport where we kept it. Walt enjoys building more than flying, so he may build another plane.

I took one week of vacation in October and will probably take two more during the holidays. I missed my Canadian Shangri-La this year. In October Walt and I took a day to drive to the dairy farm of my "cousin" Minerva and her husband George in Lisbon. I've loved going there since I was a kid. Minerva is such a warm, kind, good person, and I love being on the farm surrounded by nature and not skyscrapers. On a box of stationary I have there is a beautiful pastoral scene with the words of Thoreau: "Heaven is under our feet as well as over our heads." How true!

The holidays will be different with no Bing Crosby singing *White Christmas* and no Guy Lombardo to bring in the New Year with *"Auld Lang Syne."* But we still have Christmas with its message of love and hope in Christ, and we still have New Years with its assurance that there are always new beginnings — and we still have each other. Thank God!

With all my love to all of you, Alida

# 29<sup>th</sup> Christmas Letter, November 25, 1978 (At Home)

My dear family and friends,

A month from today is Christmas and this letter should have been done by now. I've had a terrible time getting it written, probably because I had to share with you that my mother found peace and freedom from pain on June 28<sup>th</sup>. After a lifetime of illness, with the last seven years filled with nothing but pain and suffering, I could not wish her back even though it is hard to lose one's mother.

The first of the year jinx began on December 23<sup>rd</sup>, 1977, when I was sure mom had a stroke when I could not awaken her for hours. Christmas Day she stayed in her room. It was a sad Christmas, brightened a bit by my friend Beulah Carey coming for dinner. On December 26<sup>th</sup>, while I was downstairs, mom fell, fracturing her arm and shoulder. She was very disoriented! I took her to the hospital — and she never came home again! The doctor tried a cast but the arm didn't heal, so on January 9<sup>th</sup> he operated to insert a plate. While she was in intensive care, I spent four days in bed with bronchitis, and when I saw her on the 13<sup>th</sup> and 14<sup>th</sup>, I knew something was terribly wrong with her! On January 15<sup>th</sup> the doctor called to say mom had twisted her colon when she fell, and they would have to take her to surgery to prevent gangrene. Another week of tubes, bottles, and liquid diets!

After all the times I had nursed her back to health, when it came time for mom to be discharged I hoped I could bring her home again, but this time I was licked! It took two nurses to get mom from the wheelchair to the bed, so I had no alternative but to find a nursing home! February 2<sup>nd</sup>, the day I placed her, was the worst day of my life! I hated leaving her there just as I had hated leaving Aunt Pinkie in a nursing home nine years earlier. It was a good nursing home, within walking distance, and the nurses were all kind to mom. But it still wasn't like home!

From December 26<sup>th</sup> until June 28<sup>th</sup> my life consisted of working all day and going directly to the hospital or nursing home. Mom called for me constantly, and was content when I was with her. On March 4<sup>th</sup> she fell in the nursing home as she tried to get out of bed. Again she was in emergency for hours, and this time fractured a bone under her eye. Her face, which had just healed from the December fall, was horribly bruised, as was her hand. She could not be quieted!

It is impossible to understand why one person had to go through so much pain and suffering. In May she began to have trouble swallowing because of the congestion which had developed. The last two days of her life she could neither eat nor drink. It was painful watching her struggle. Luckily Walt had come home June 5<sup>th</sup>, and we were both with her before she died. I had rubbed her back after which she seemed to relax, stopped struggling, and went to sleep. We left not knowing that 10 minutes later when we got home the phone would ring, telling us to come back. Mom's years of suffering had ended! How grateful we are to all of you for your many kindnesses to mom through the years, and for your cards, flowers, and helpful deeds at the time of her death.

Suddenly, I have time on my hands, but after doing so little for the last seven to ten years, I don't know where or how to begin to get in the swing of things again. At times I get very frightened, but I trust that God, who brought me through so much, will help me find some new sense of direction.

Several weeks after mom's death the crew of *Montage* interviewed me for a special entitled "Families in Conflict." The program was about the abuse of children, spouses, and the elderly. They asked me to share how I got through years of illness without abusing my mother. It was a chance to tell others how much my faith helped me through many challenges. I also admitted how terribly hopeless and helpless I felt in the face of constant pain, and how tired I got at times. The program is being used for teaching purposes and may be repeated in January or February on Channel 3. I missed my TV debut in September, so I hope it will be aired again. I am also going to the Medical School at Case Western Reserve University to do a videotape about my experiences with doctors, hospitals, etc. to help train doctors in the new Family Medicine program. If all the years of illness can be used in some positive way, then it will give those years some meaning.

The end of August my Aunt Mil and cousin, Genevra, moved back to Cleveland from Florida. They weren't here a week when both ended up in the emergency room, and Aunt Mill was hospitalized for two weeks. Gene found an apartment, but after she moved in realized it was in terrible shape. I got her to a Legal Aid lawyer and wrote a letter to the Mayor's office. The landlord got the message and moved them into a different apartment. Aunt Mil is 82, in poor health, and has made good use of St. John's emergency room which is across the street from them. She cannot be left alone too long so Gene is going through what I did and I feel as if I'm reliving it.

On top of everything else our neighbor of 44 years, Mabel, died three months before mom, so Jim is now alone. Tom, who drove me to and from work for three years, moved to New Jersey. So I'm back to waiting for buses this winter. Mary, who did my cleaning and loved mom so much she went to the nursing home every night to feed her, had a stroke. My secretary, Mary, was hit by a car Labor Day weekend and has been out of work since with a fractured arm and pelvis. On November 4th Walt came home with a cast on his fractured wrist which was the result of someone trying to rob him in Africa. Someone said God only gives you what you have the strength to take. My reply was "I wish He would cut it out already." The year 1979 just has to be better than 1978!

I did get to my Canadian retreat for four days in July, and planned to take two weeks off in October. But with Mary being ill, I have only been able to take a day now and then. I've continued my singing lessons and choir for relaxation. One bright moment came in August when I had a baby shower for "my kid" Gayle. We probably wouldn't have been so relaxed had we known that the very next day she would give birth to her first child, Rodney.

As I thought of the holidays, I felt I would like to forget them this year. Then I realized how much I have to be thankful for and how much the spirit of Christmas has been with me all year. At Thanksgiving time I thank God for parents who adopted me and gave me a good home. They truly loved my brother, who was not adopted, and me. I'm grateful that my Aunt Pinkie taught me to love nature; from dad I learned patience, and mom set an example which taught me to be generous to, and thoughtful of, others. From them as well as from Aunt Mil and Uncle Henry I learned the meaning of the word love. What greater gifts could anyone be given? If the true meaning of Christmas is loving, sharing, and knowing God is with us, then I surely had Christmas all year, for I found strength in my faith, and love of family and friends sustained me.

With all my love to all of you, Alida

# 30<sup>th</sup> Christmas Letter, November 26, 1979 (At Home)

My dear family and friends,

It has been such an uneventful, depressing year I was tempted not to write a letter this year, but decided I would continue the tradition at least through this year which marks 30 years of keeping in touch this way. My life was wrapped up in family illnesses for so long it is hard to know where to begin again, and I've found nothing that interests me to fill the void. I need some fun and laughter but don't know where to find it, and the thought of traveling alone doesn't appeal to me. Church activities and choir have been about my only sources of satisfaction.

Early in the year I made a videotape with Doctor Medalie, head of the CWRU Medical School's Family Medicine program. I was glad to put years of trauma to good use in helping train new doctors who will hopefully begin to think of the effects of illness not only on the patient but also on the family members who have to cope with it.

In July the Lakewood High class of '39 celebrated its 40<sup>th</sup> reunion, and it was a lovely event. I led the singing of the alma mater which in itself is nothing, but it made me happy to sing for one of our guests, T. R. Evans, who directed the a cappella choir at LHS for many years. They don't come any better than T. R., and my happiest memories of high school are of the hours I spent singing under his direction.

My aunt, who moved back to Cleveland a few months after mom's death, has been continually ill. In August she had several strokes, broke her arm in October and had another stroke the day she was to leave the hospital. I can understand how frustrating it is for my cousin Genevra who cares for her. Also in August our friend, John Calson, had a severe heart attack. His friend Bill and I visited him frequently because he had no family, and we made the funeral arrangements when he died Labor Day after a month of coronary care. Illness still haunts!

I almost bought a '79 Plymouth Volare, but when our friend John died I decided to buy his '72 Buick Skylark — which is in excellent shape! Because I never used the license I got in '63 I took a refresher course and Jim, my "other brother" next door, has braved helping me get some practice. I'm gaining confidence slowly, but if I don't get over my fear this time, I will give up driving forever and ease the gas shortage!

Currently, I'm not taking voice, tap, or piano lessons. I was in a "Gong Show" at church, so I took a few tap lessons to brush up on steps I had forgotten after not dancing for a year. We planned to continue the lessons but Diane got pregnant again. Teaching me seems to have that effect on her! My voice teacher is doing graduate work but got me to the point where I sang a duet at church this summer with Steve Morse, an attorney from work. Our voices blend nicely and it was a joy singing with him.

Walt came home September 28<sup>th</sup>, and I believe he may retire. I envy him! It would be nice to be home and do things leisurely. I was hoping to retire at 62 and will start a protest march if they raise the early

Social Security retirement age from 62 to 65. Who knows, maybe I would be bored if I retired. I am still at Legal Aid and enjoy my contact with clients and attorneys.

I hate doing this in a Christmas letter, but what better way to send out an SOS to the person in the Cleveland area to whom I lent one of my favorite books over a year ago. The book is *All Creatures Great and Small*, by James Herriot. It may not have my name in it, but if you remember borrowing it, I'll never tell who returned it to me!

I must admit I am approaching the holidays with a feeling of sadness rather than joy. This year, more than last, I feel the loss of so many in my family and can't help remembering happier times when we were all together. At least I'm glad for nice memories! Events in the world don't make one feel joyous either. I wish the love we sing and talk about at this season was more active in the world. This weekend I saw a Christmas card with the simple but profound message: God Still Cares! I was grateful for that unexpected message of hope — which is the eternal message of Christmas! Whatever Christmas means to you, I pray you will have a blessed day and a year ahead that fulfills your needs if not your dreams. God bless you all.

With all my love to all of you, Alida

Chapter Six

**Ten Christmas Letters
From 1980 to 1989**

# 31<sup>st</sup> Christmas Letter, November 25, 1980 (At Home)

My dear family and friends,

Happy 31<sup>st</sup> Anniversary to us! It is hard for me to believe that 31 years ago I wrote my first Christmas letter. In these years we have all experienced many changes; some good, some bad, some glad, some sad, but change is inevitable. Perhaps we all wish we could turn back the hands of time and do some things differently, but if we had it to do all over we would probably do the very same things. One nice tradition came out of this letter; "my kid" next door, Susie, looks forward to helping me put stamps and stickers on the letters and we enjoy that time together.

I'm sorry for causing confusion by stapling that little slip to last year's letter announcing Emily Alida was born November 18<sup>th</sup>. In my letter I told you that just as I resumed taking tap dance lessons my teacher got pregnant with her second child. The letter was already printed when the baby arrived, and I was so pleased that Diane named her daughter Emily Alida I could not wait until this year to tell you. The result of that slip was that I got some cards addressed to Emily Alida Struze, and received birthday cards in November instead of October. It was nice having an extended birthday and I got a few chuckles out of the confusion.

Walt retired in January and says he doesn't miss the ship. He keeps himself busy with assorted activities, including making gourmet meals. It seems as if no matter what he throws into a pot it comes out good! To fill his leisure time he bought a Wurlitzer organ which he is learning to play. We now have a corner in the parlor with a Baldwin piano, an organ, and two amateur musicians who will NEVER be asked to audition for Lawrence Welk.

In June Walt, our friends Frank and Mary O'Neil, and I traveled to Camp Mac Mac on Lake Nipissing in Ontario, Canada. We had a two-bedroom cabin with one faucet (cold water), a wood-burning stove on which we kept a tea kettle going all the time, and an outdoor toilet. A portable commode we took came in handy at night. Fishing wasn't the greatest, but we managed to have four or five fish dinners, and had plenty of other food for variety. We were told this was the coldest month of June they ever had, and we believed it! Mary and I were glad Frank and Walt got up to build a fire and make us a hot cup of coffee before we braved getting out of the warm sleeping bags and into cold clothing.

The closest thing to adventure came with a storm which brought gale-force winds which lasted 24 hours. The noise of the tall pines and the angry lake went on all night and made one realize that nature still has the upper hand. We had plenty of firewood and a deck of cards, so while we waited out the storm Walt and I learned the fundamentals of pinochle. As always, I loved being there and hated to leave. The little inconveniences are a small price to pay for a week away from the city with only the sounds of nature for listening pleasure, and the peace and beauty of Northern Canada to quiet one's soul. Five jovial fellows from Canada had a cabin near ours, and we enjoyed their company and humor. I spent a second week of vacation doing things around the house and joining friends for lunch. I'll take more vacation around the holidays.

Believe it or not, as of December 6$^{th}$, 1979, when I did my first solo trip, I have been driving a little — at least enough to get to church and back! Sometimes I venture a bit farther. Since I had the rust removed, my '72 Buick looks like a new car. One Sunday my friend Beulah Carey and I drove to Lisbon, Ohio. She drove to Ravenna and I took over for the remaining 30 miles on secondary roads. I decided she was a trusting, brave soul when I discovered that instead of watching the road while I drove, she had taken a nap! I have to admit I really don't enjoy driving, but I'm glad I found the courage to do a little.

After a lifetime of illness, which paralleled my mother's medical history, my Aunt Mil, whom Walt and I nicknamed "Body" when we were little, died on October 19$^{th}$. She and my cousin returned to Cleveland two months after mom died, and hospital visits started all over again. At least she was in her hometown the last two years of her life. I will always remember the bushels of cookies she made at Christmas, and she gave almost all of them away as gifts. My cousin Genevra has returned to Florida, hoping, after a long period of looking after her parents, to find a job and start life anew.

I never realized how long it would take to get over years and years of coping with family illness. The effects of those years are still with me, and I have not been able to shake some of the depressed feelings one gets when emotionally drained. Now that I have the time to do things I don't seem to be able to get moving to find something to give life new meaning. Thank God for my church! I am still in choir, have taught an adult class every four months, and next year may take on the duties of Church School Superintendent, which will be a new challenge. One thing I still would like to do is some writing — if I ever get an electric typewriter. An article I wrote about a Workshop on Aging, which we had at church, will be published in the January '81 edition of the *Baptist Leader*.

It has been a joy keeping in touch with all of you for 31 years. The gifts of friendship and love are good for all seasons, but somehow seem special at Christmas time! Especially now, since almost all of my family is gone, I welcome even more the warmth and kindness of so many of you who have been so caring through the years. About the only skill I've ever had is loving others, and you can be sure my loving thoughts are often with you and will continue to be with you whether I continue this letter or not. I pray that the blessings of Christmas will be with you and yours and spill over into the New Year.

With all my love to all of you, Alida

# 32nd Christmas Letter, November 25, 1981 (At Home)

My dear family and friends,

It is hard to believe a month from today is Christmas. Every January 2nd I jolt those around me by saying, "The next thing we know it will be Christmas." The years really do go by that fast! At this time last year I thought I would discontinue my annual letter but, to paraphrase an old song, you have gotten to be a habit with me. It wouldn't seem like Christmas to me if I didn't write the letter, so I've decided to continue until I can't, especially since so many of you requested I do so.

This year started out with a big surprise. In my last letter I mentioned wanting to buy an electric typewriter. Shortly after Christmas my friend, Irene, told me not to buy one because she had one she insisted I accept. As if that wasn't enough, she gave me a chair to go with it. Because I couldn't type fast enough on it, with her permission, I traded it in on a secondhand IBM. I haven't done much writing, but did get several letters to the editor printed and have sent an article to *The Plain Dealer*, which wasn't accepted.

July brought an unexpected trip to California with my friend Beulah Carey. We met at the Federal Reserve Bank in 1941. I sang at her wedding, and "my first kid" was her son, Neal, who now lives in Mission Viejo. The trip was triggered by the fact that her youngest son, Drew, wanted his family there when he graduated from the Marine boot camp in San Diego. It was an impressive ceremony. We got to San Diego a day early so we could visit the fabulous zoo. Would you believe that in that mass of people we bumped into the fellow who occupied the third seat in our row on the plane? When we got off the plane we kiddingly told him we would meet him at the zoo, never believing that could happen. Neal and his wife Dora drove us from San Diego to their home which is 60 miles away. I stayed there about four days and spent another four with my social work friend, Barbara Moore, and her family who live in Newport Beach. Barbara, her children, and I took a boat tour of the Newport Islands to see the million dollar homes of movie stars. It was fun getting reacquainted with Andy, Julie, and Steven, who were glad to see what "Aunt Alida" looked like. They were little when I saw them last, which was 10 years ago.

I was glad to meet Neal's wife and children; they helped to make our first trip west a memorable one. We saw places we never would have gotten to if Neal and Dora had not taken their vacation time to take us sightseeing. We drove past San Clemente, stopped at Dana Point, which has a replica of one of the pilgrim ships, took a boat ride to Catalina Island, and spent five to six hours at Disneyland, which was one of the most well-run, well-organized places I've ever seen. One day we drove 75 miles to Ensenada, Mexico where we browsed and bought in the many gift shops. Neal felt a trip to Ensenada would not be complete without our visiting the famous American bar — Hussong's Cantina! It was a long, narrow room with a bar on each side, and reminded me of a western movie setting. I have never seen so many people in one place in my life — all standing and talking! The noise was deafening and there was no air-conditioning, so we didn't stay long, but we can say we were there. Another day we drove through the Cleveland National Forest to an elevation of 6,000 feet, where we saw evidence of recent forest fires. From there we drove through the desert to Palm Springs. Now I know how hot the desert can be!

Two weeks after I got home from California, Walt and I were invited to go to my beloved Temagami. I hadn't been there for several years and missed it. The weather was perfect; warm enough for us to bathe in the lake. The serenity and quiet beauty of nature are God's tranquilizers. How I love that place! As our amphibian approached the island, we saw Cindy on top of the diving board platform, dressed in something white and pointing to the plane. We knew she was saying, "The plane, the plane!" As we stepped on land Bill handed each of us a drink to make sure we arrived at our "Canadian Fantasy Island" in style.

In October I turned 60 and don't mind saying so because I feel great! My doctor tells me I should live to be 100. I told him not to wish that on me, but I do thank God everyday for His gift of health. The end of October my friend, Mary Lou, and I took a seven-week course in Home and Business Computers. It was enough to convince me computers are not for me, but now I know a little more about them.

As Church School Superintendent, I have been kept busy making sure there is a full staff of teachers. Top priority this first year was cleaning every cupboard and closet to get rid of old material. I understand someone said they would hire me to do their basement. My next goal is to have some Workers' Conferences for continued sharing and training. The Lord has blessed the church with teachers who are treasures. Some of them have volunteered to teach four to five months at a time in Nursery and Kindergarten, which is ideal for the children to have the same teachers. The enthusiasm of all the teachers makes my job easier and one can feel it spreading and generating more of the same. No wonder our church school is growing. We now have many members from Romania and the latest group of new Americans is three families from Laos who just started their own class on Sunday morning. Those from other lands have enriched our lives as they share their cultures with us. I'm glad our church not only has gone into all the world by supporting missions, but that we have taken in the world by welcoming and, with love, helping these new friends become settled in their new land.

This year I experimented with ways to help beautify America. Flowers I planted around the trees in front of our office on West 6th brightened one spot on a very gloomy street and brought positive responses. I hope local merchants will follow suit. I volunteered to be on the Keep Lakewood Beautiful Committee, which is a program to counteract litter. When two 10-year-old neighbors, Neil and Katie Ostromek, asked me if I had anything they could do to keep busy and earn a little money, with their mother's permission I asked them if they would like to pick up litter from the lawns from the corner to my house once a day. They jumped at the chance! What a joy it is to get off the bus at night and see a tidy street. I am sending an article about their efforts to our local paper hoping it will be printed and that the idea might catch on.

Are you as tired of the commercialization of Christmas as I am? I wish we would all start giving gifts of kindness and service, because in these days when we are confronted with economic concerns, fear of nuclear war, and so many social problems, material gifts mean very little. In the midst of so much anxiety and fear the Christmas message of Peace, Hope, and Love shines as brightly as the Star of Bethlehem. The greatest gift we have is the assurance that no matter what happens, God's love and grace will be with us. I pray that you and yours will have a blessed Christmas. In the New Year let's all resolve to be more active in spreading the true message of Christmas. God be with you all. Shalom!

With all my love to all of you, Alida

# 33<sup>rd</sup> Christmas Letter, November 12, 1982 (At Home)

My dear family and friends,

Long before Halloween the stores were heralding the coming of Christmas. Every year I resent this commercialization of Christmas, especially when they start the sales pitch so early and bypass the real meaning and message of the season. In my church we are encouraging people to spend their money on food and clothing for the needy instead of purchasing frivolous things. A gift now and then is undeniably a welcome sign of someone's caring, but in the long run I feel it is the consistent concern and generosity over an extended period of time that enhances one's life. That's why I love writing this letter and getting your notes.

Those of you in Florida and California who once knew the beauty of our fall season must surely get a bit homesick for Ohio in October. This year the color seemed to last longer than it normally does, and warm temperatures lulled us into forgetting that snow is just around the corner. No matter how many times I experience the beauty of fall foliage, I am as thrilled as I was the first time.

Before we know it spring, with all its loveliness, will be here again. It was a miracle that the tulips I planted in front of our building on West 6<sup>th</sup> Street came up and survived all the traffic. Not one tulip was picked! I think people were so amazed to see those tiny gardens around each tree, on an otherwise dismal street, that they wanted to preserve them. Absolute strangers would come up as I watered the flowers to tell me how much brighter it made their morning. When the tulips died I planted geraniums and white petunias, surrounded with tiny white picket fences. The people in the building across the street caught on and set up window boxes on the sidewalk level filled with the same flowers. Walt thought that I ought to be committed for planting flowers on West 6<sup>th</sup>, but he cooperated by making signs which read "Please Keep Off — Tulips Growing." The picket fences near the street took a beating but, being a persistent soul, I kept buying more. My desire to keep the world beautiful extended to my being on the Keep Lakewood Beautiful Committee. Our efforts to keep Lakewood free of litter seem to be paying off.

The Legal Aid Society (you read about it as Legal Services Corporation in the newspapers) is still in operation despite severe budget cuts and the President's efforts to abolish it. We have had to close offices, lay off secretaries, and make other modifications, but we are doing all we can to make sure the disadvantaged get as good legal representation as anyone else because that is one of their basic rights. Cases we cannot handle I refer to private attorneys who have been generous beyond description despite the fact that the economy has also clobbered them. I have been doing more referral work than social work, but love the public relations aspect of this kind of service, as well as enjoying the warm, friendly relationships I have formed with so many attorneys.

There was no long vacation this year, but I got to my oasis in Canada for a week. As luck would have it, the weather was perfect the week I was there. It was sandwiched in between a week of cold weather and one that was cold and rainy. I declared my birthday a holiday and took a day of vacation to celebrate the start of my 61<sup>st</sup> year of life! I took a day here and there around other holidays to give me extra time. Walt and I went to a flea market in Hartsville, Ohio (near Akron) a few times and that was a nice change.

My one dream is to find someone who could take three to four weeks to tour the country with me so I could see the beauty I have been trying to preserve with contributions to all the environmental agencies such as the Sierra Club. Any takers?

There are always church activities to keep one busy. I am still Church School Superintendent and sing in the choir. I still love to sing though I can't sing the high notes I could at age 16. This fall we had a retreat from Friday night through Sunday afternoon, which was a nice experience. We have many young adults in the church who have had no group to identify with. At the retreat we decided to concentrate this year on helping them get a group started, which promises to be a lot of fun. We older adults will do all we can to give them whatever support they want. Being part of a church family means helping fulfill the needs of others in the family, but we hope as this group moves along it will also be the beginning of an outreach to other young adults in the community.

Except for some letters to the editor, mostly about the environment, I have not done much writing, and except for driving to church, I have not done much driving. I tell people my car is computerized so it knows its way to church and back. I'm admittedly a coward when it comes to driving, but at least I manage to do some.

Some of you who get this letter are my old BMTS friends. I'm looking forward to seeing many of you when the American Baptist Convention will be held in Cleveland June 14th through the 18th. I don't like going to conventions so I'm glad we will be the host city this year.

It is always fun to see people after many years. This past summer my friend, Grace Astikian, with whom I worked at the Federal Reserve Bank in the '40's, was in Cleveland, and we enjoyed a brief visit. Another day of renewed acquaintances and memories was my "cousin" Margaret's 40th wedding anniversary. Her brother, Fred, and I were the only bridesmaid-usher combination, but the rest of the men in the wedding party were there. The open house at her daughter's, with two grandchildren running around, made one realize how much time had gone by.

And so another year has almost gone and another Christmas letter will be added to my annual diary. Most of us can come to the end of '82 saying "Thank God" for a job, health, and the ability to share what God has so graciously provided. There are many others who will not be so fortunate. The only gift they may get this year is the thoughtfulness and sharing of someone else. The only good thing about these tough economic times is that we are being forced to get our priorities in order again.

I believe God would be glad if we would use the Christmas season to ponder and appreciate the many gifts He has given us: love, joy, beauty, and life itself! One of my favorite people and authors is Leo Buscaglia, whose TV lectures are found in his books, *Love: What Life Is All About, Personhood: The Art of Being Fully Human,* and *Living, Loving & Learning.*

God bless all of you and yours as we celebrate the birth of one who came to bring the message of love and peace to the world. May each of us in our own way be a bearer of that message in the New Year!

With all my love to all of you, Alida

# 34<sup>th</sup> Christmas Letter, November 1, 1983 (At Home)

My dear family and friends,

This has been a year full of unexpected but nice happenings. Maybe it was getting my ears pierced early in the year that started the ball rolling. I might have backed down but my teenage neighbor, Susan, went with me and I didn't dare look like a coward. The clerk laughed when I presented myself and said, "Let's get the deed done." She had never heard it called that before. Sorry I didn't do this years ago because I've enjoyed the earrings.

In the spring I learned that an article I had submitted to the *Baptist Leader* months before was going to be printed in the August issue. It was a tribute to patients in the nursing home who in their own way helped me while mom was there. I'll never win the Pulitzer Prize, but it's good to see one's thoughts in print and I hope my sharing will help someone else.

In April the agency asked me to go to a conference in Detroit. As long as I was so close, I decided to visit my friend, Lillian Panek, with whom I worked at Family Service. When I arrived in Grand Rapids, she surprised me with the news that the next day we were going to Holland, Michigan for the last day of the Tulip Festival which I had always wanted to attend. I had picked the right weekend for my visit and enjoyed the rows and rows of tulips in the parks and at the nursery. We also visited the Gerald R. Ford Museum, which was worth seeing.

After returning from Michigan, I attended rehearsals for a mass choir which sang at the American Baptist Convention in May. I looked forward to seeing college friends whom I had not seen since 1957. Marilyn Owens Amerson came from California, and it was a pleasure to show her some of downtown Cleveland and have her spend a night with me. My freshman roommate, Ruby McDonald Shepherd, came from Washington, and we were happy to see each other. On Friday night I stayed at the Bond Court Hotel so I could entertain any BMTS alumni who wished to come, and was delighted with the grand turnout. We sang college songs, reminisced, snacked, and enjoyed every minute. I was glad Jean Counts Hansen of my class was able to join us at the breakfast Saturday morning, On Sunday, seven alumni, including Martha Keucher, worshiped at my church and we had dinner together. It was a great weekend!

The biggest surprise of the year was when I said "Yes" before I could say "No" when Ginny Noyes, a member of my church, asked me to go to Europe with her and her parents. I hate traveling alone because I like to share the experience with someone so I decided not to pass up this opportunity, especially since I would see eight countries in 13 days. Despite the usual anxiety about what to pack, I managed to take the right amount of apparel. We were only allowed one suitcase and a carry-on-bag. The suitcase on wheels with a pull strap which I bought for the trip was a terrific help. We arrived in London July 17<sup>th</sup> and, without sleep, Ginny and I took a six-hour walking tour of the city, which included St. Paul's Cathedral where Prince Charles and Di were married.

The next day we crossed the English Channel by boat and picked up our tour bus in Ostend, Belgium. From there we visited Amsterdam and Volendam in Holland; in Germany we stopped in Cologne, Nuremberg, and Bonn where Beethoven was born, and saw the Olympic Village in Munich as we drove by. From Germany we went to Austria, stayed overnight at Hallein where Franz Gruber, composer of *Silent Night*, is buried. The next day we went to Salzburg, and from there to Vienna; then to Venice, Italy, which was a unique treat. From Italy we went to Lake Lugano and Lake Lucerne in Switzerland, and we ended the trip in Paris after which we went back to Ostend and London, arriving home July 31$^{st}$. We were thrilled with the beauty of the Austrian and Swiss country sides, awed by the splendor of the Alps and excited by the four-stage cable car ride to the top of Mt. Titlis where at 10,000 feet we ate lunch. We rode on the canals in Amsterdam and Venice, cruised partway down the Rhine River and around Lake Lucerne and were entertained many evenings.

By the time we left Europe we had seen enough castles, cathedrals, and palaces with all their 24-carat gold to last a lifetime. We marveled at how these structures were built so many years ago and were a bit disturbed by all the opulence. Best of all, many countries were represented on our bus: Malaysia, Hong Kong, England, Canada, the Island of Mauritius, Sri Lanka, Japan, Italy, Austria, and one-third of the tourists were from all over America. Our tour guide, Tina, and driver, Nino, made the tour a memorable one. We were an international, interracial, interfaith, and intergenerational group (ages 10 through 83). We may or may not see each other again but I'm sure we are all glad we shared this happy interlude and will remember one another with affection. In the 13 days we had no rain and just a few hot days which made the ice cold Swiss water taste better than all the European wine. The only anxious moments we had were when the French detained us for four hours at the border claiming the bus papers were not in order, which was not true. It was a helpless feeling wondering what they would do with us, but we chalked it up to adventure. I had a great time and am so glad I took the trip.

The end of August found me at my Canadian oasis in Temagami for four days. To me it is the most beautiful of all places on Earth and I still cry when I leave. The second day I was there Tommy, my friend's son, got an electric shock and fell off a roof on which he was working. It is a miracle that he was not killed and that the circular saw in his hand did not cut him. A fractured vertebra is healing; God must have something special in mind for him. Before the month of August concluded I had recruited teachers for the beginning of our new church school year and was looking forward to September when choir, committee meetings, and other church activities would keep us busy.

Columbus Day weekend my neighbor, Jim, drove me to Washington, D.C. to see friends. It was so good to spend a few hours with Reverend Herbert and Peg Garner who were so kind to me when he was a minister at the Old Stone Church. Ruby and Ollie Shepherd invited us to stay with them and gave us a grand tour of Georgetown and Washington by day and night. I saw Washington in 1950 but had forgotten how beautiful it is. On Monday we drove to Baltimore for a quick visit with the Fatzingers. Russ built two airplanes, and by 7:30 that night we were home. The leaves in some spots were beautiful and my car had a good run.

Being a nature lover, the one cause I would march for is the protection of our environment so there will be something left for the children of the world. I support a number of groups, such as the Sierra Club, which are trying to protect our land and endangered species. Let me share two quotes, both of which come from those who respected our land — the Indian Americans. Chief Standing Bear said, "Man's heart away from nature grows hard; a lack of respect for growing, living things soon leads to a lack of respect for humans, too." Chief Seattle is quoted saying, "What is man without the beast? If all the beasts were gone, man would die from great loneliness of spirit, for whatever happens to the beasts also happens to the man."

At work I am busier than ever making referrals to attorneys willing to take volunteer cases Legal Aid cannot handle, and I still do some casework. The response of the attorneys has been heartwarming and I am going to send a letter to the editor to thank them for their generosity.

As I come to the end of my 34th Christmas letter, I pray that you will have a meaningful Christmas and New Year filled with hope. In these days of uncertainty it is good to know that God still loves us. I pray, too, that people all over the world will find a way to care about one another as did the 52 strangers who got on a bus at Ostend and 13 days later said goodbye as friends. In this season and always may you and yours have the joy of giving and receiving the greatest of all lasting gifts — love!

With all my love to all of you, Alida

# 35<sup>th</sup> Christmas Letter, October 27, 1984 (At Home)

My dear family and friends,

If it weren't for the fact that leaves are falling and I've planted bulbs, I would never believe it is time to write my 35<sup>th</sup> annual Christmas letter. On January 1<sup>st</sup> of every year I jolt someone by saying, "Before we know it, it will be Christmas." That is exactly how fast the year goes by.

Shortly after the holidays last year Walt took off for two months in Florida in an RV he bought. He got back the end of March so he avoided the worst of winter. He is enjoying his retirement. He plays tennis, golf, does some gourmet cooking, and is involved with ham radio.

I've been very busy at work and church. Since the Reagan budget cuts, we are all under more pressure at Legal Aid because the needs in the community have gotten greater. My little garden outside the building didn't do too well this year. Next year I'll try marigolds instead of geraniums. The rather dismal street on which I work is coming alive as the old buildings are being restored and turned into living quarters. Being Church School Superintendent means never-ending responsibility, but I'm grateful to the many wonderful teachers we have. This year we treated our teachers to an evening out at a party center with a magician for entertainment. We had a great time! The anti-church trend of the '60's may be reversing itself because it has been good to see more young people joining the church and assuming leadership roles. I'm still in choir and am taking lessons to try to get my voice focused.

In May our Pastor Noyes allowed me to celebrate 50 years of friendship. It occurred to me to do this when I realized we have lived in this house 50 years, which means I have known some friends that long. I spoke a few words during the worship service about how much my friends have meant to me. After the service we had a coffee hour and everyone was invited — provided they gave a friend a hug! I will always treasure the memory of the warm, friendly spirit at that coffee hour. "A friend is one who knows all about you and likes you anyway." — Christi Mary Warner

My letters to the editor continue to be published and I seem to be a regular contributor. Palm Sunday a letter I wrote about a group of us who met on the bus and now meet every other month to dine out was published. In July Channel 3 did a segment about the group. A reporter and two cameramen rode home with us and at 7:00 p.m. Tom Sweeny and two other cameramen came to cover the picnic at my home. In September I went to a public hearing held by RTA, and for some reason they chose my speech to air on TV. That's as close as I'll ever get to being an entertainer!

Never dreamed I would go overseas two years in a row, but on July 16<sup>th</sup> I was heading for Scandinavia with Wilma, an attorney at Legal Aid, her sister May, and Betty, one of my bus friends. We arrived in Oslo July 17<sup>th</sup> and liked this clean city. From there we went to Bergen, a picturesque city with red-roofed homes dotting the mountains everywhere we looked. Then we had the thrill of a ferry ride on the beautiful fjords, which for me was the best part of the trip. The combination of majestic mountains and water was an aesthetic treat with every turn of the ferry bringing a new scene. As I traveled through this almost pristine land of mountains and lakes, I felt as if I had traveled back in time to the beginning of the planet when it was quiet, peaceful, and uncluttered. A goat or sheep which we would take for granted any other time brought shouts of joy when we saw them high in the mountains. The harshness of the mountains is softened by the beauty of many waterfalls. There are 100,000 lakes in Norway, but one never finds a water fountain at rest stops, which we found amusing. At Lom we visited a Stave church. Stave refers to the wooden columns which support these all wood churches. After 800 years these churches are still in excellent condition!

After Norway, Sweden and Denmark seemed flat and rather bland. We stayed at a brand new hotel in Stockholm and our room was tops! The water there is so clean that people fish from a bridge across from the City Hall and catch salmon. We saw old Stockholm and will never forget the gold room in the City Hall where the walls are totally covered with 23.5-carat gold mosaic. It is in that room that the Nobel Prize for literature is presented. From Stockholm we drove the length of Sweden to Helsingborg, where we took a ferry to Denmark. We spent several days in Copenhagen shopping and sightseeing with a local guide. We saw Kronborg Castle, the setting for *Hamlet*, but missed the famous mermaid because some inebriated jerks had sawed off her arm and she was being repaired. We just saw the rocks on which she sits.

We ended our tour by dining at a lovely restaurant in Tivoli Gardens, which reminded me of our Euclid Beach Park, but with more flowers. We loved our overnight stays in Lofthus and Balestrand in the fjords area and throughout the trip visited palaces and churches. The Scandinavian churches were more beautiful, warm, homey, and made one feel more worshipful than the mammoth, cold cathedrals in Europe. One thing we'll never forget is the delicious fish. We had trout with sliced almonds, white fish in wine sauce, as well as salmon and halibut dinners. Huge buffet tables for breakfast had a variety of meat and cheese, along with regular breakfast food, but to my delight they also had pickled herring which I ate in large quantity while I had the chance. For one who would rather dance than eat, the frosting on the cake of this trip is the memory I will always cherish of the dances I had with our tour guide who was such an excellent dancer. I will always remember him telling someone that some women are like pushing trucks around, but he thought I was like a sports car. That compliment meant a lot to me!

On October 13th the Lakewood High Class of 1939 celebrated its 45th anniversary, and we had a lovely time with over 200 attending. It was so good to see old friends and teachers. We are already looking forward to the 50th. As I write this letter I look forward to the November wedding of "my kid," Ted Hinshaw. It has been such a joy to watch all my friends' children grow and start their own families. My life has been so much richer because of all of them, and now "Great-Aunt Alida" is watching still another generation start on life's journey.

My dream for next year is to visit the Banff beginning in Portland and going on from there. I figure I had better travel while I'm still able and working. Just from the little I have traveled I am convinced that no matter where one goes there is beauty which God gave us to enjoy and cherish. It infuriates me when I hear that there are those who would turn some of our national parks into nuclear waste dumps. I hope you all fight these movements with letters to your senators.

As we approach Christmas, I do pray that no matter what happens in this crazy world, you will find peace within yourself, that you will be a blessing and comfort to others. I pray your faith will strengthen and sustain you. May the Christmas message of unselfishness and joy be with you always!

With all my love to all of you, Alida

# 36<sup>th</sup> Christmas Letter, October 31, 1985 (At Home)

My dear family and friends,

After 36 years I guess it is safe to say this letter has become a tradition. I have used the same salutation every year. As I typed it this year I realized that at this point in my life it is sad to realize that I have more friends than family. Except for my brother, Walt, a few cousins I seldom see, and one aunt in North Carolina, I have no family. Happily, through the years I have amassed a terrific "family" of adult friends, and I have children of all ages with a "son," Barry, in England and a "daughter," Mayumi, in Japan. It seems God keeps putting people in my life to love, and I love to love all of you!

This has been a rather low-key year, and as I look back I'm ashamed of all the time I have wasted. I hope next year I will do more writing or learn something new. One of my greatest joys in '85 was being "grandma" to four- (now five-) year-old Casey whom I first met on the bus in the morning. His dad walked two long blocks to take him to the nursery school across from where I work. After a while I offered to escort Casey to save his dad the walk. Many mornings Casey would con me into buying him breakfast, and I always had to have two treats so he could share one with other children at snack time. Customers in the coffee shop were surprised when they discovered Casey wasn't my grandchild. He enjoyed helping me water the plants in my office and make coffee while we waited for the school to open. I always chuckle when I recall the first day I took him to school and thought they would take his things off. As I turned to leave Casey said, "You didn't take my coat off!" Then he gave me a quick lesson in proper mothering by instructing me to put his gloves in the pockets of his coat, put his cap in one sleeve, his scarf in another, and hang his coat on the hook below his name. I was glad when spring came and there were no more boots to take off and shoes to put on, but I loved every minute I spent with Casey. I always got a goodbye kiss and he would watch as I crossed the street and wave before I entered the building. I was shattered when he went to live with his mother in another city, but his dad either has me over or brings Casey and his brother, Aaron, to visit me when they are in town.

Although I miss counseling with clients due to lack of time, I continue to enjoy my association with the attorneys in private practice. In each of the last two years they have taken 1,400 volunteer cases. The only way I can thank them is to send another letter to the editor which I have written. When Legal Aid moved to West 6<sup>th</sup> it was a miserable street. This year two warehouses were renovated just south of us and the apartments are very nice. That represents only the beginning of the plans for our street. I kiddingly say I started the beautification of West 6<sup>th</sup> when I planted the first flowers. I know it isn't so, but it boosts my ego! This year I planted orange and yellow marigolds with ageratum around the border. It was simple but colorful. I've planted some new tulip and daffodil bulbs as well as delphinium, which will hopefully survive to brighten the area next spring. Many of the merchants have left the area and I miss them. Irv, who owned the coffee shop, sold it to a nice young couple who have great plans for the restaurant, but Irv will not be forgotten.

As one gets older it seems no year goes by without some personal loss. This year an old friend died of a heart attack, and Leona Vetter, who was 88 years young, succumbed to a stroke. I will forever be grateful to Lee because without her I could not have gotten through the last seven years of mom's life.

Lee came every weekday which enabled me to get to work with some peace of mind. If there was ever a saint, Lee was one — even if she liked to go to the race track, which she thoroughly enjoyed.

Walt and I have chalked up 51 years in our home, which these days is a record. He has become an expert in Chinese cooking, which I thoroughly enjoy. When winter comes he will be off to somewhere warm until spring.

Late in July I got to my oasis in Temagami for a few days. While there, friends introduced me to the beautiful music of Zamfir. The tones of the pan flute reminded me of the loons and in that lovely setting the music enhanced nature and vice versa.

Great things are happening at church with church school enrollment increasing, more young people taking leadership positions, more people joining, and a general upbeat feeling. Choir, meetings, and being Church School Superintendent keep me busy. I'm planning an appreciation dinner for our church school teachers at a party center November 11th because they deserve a real treat. We celebrated our 80th birthday this year. "My kids" on the street, Matt and Neil, have started to attend church school and enjoy being there. The teachers are grateful for Neil's help in Kindergarten, second hour.

One of my dreams came true the end of June when the four of us who traveled to Europe three years ago took off for Seattle where we joined a tour to Vancouver and the Canadian Rockies. Ginny's cousins in Seattle and Vancouver insisted on giving us a grand tour by night. Both cities impressed us as places we would like to live. Buildings were surrounded by flowers and the streets were without litter. Obviously, the local people care about the appearance of their communities. In Vernon we were amazed at the gigantic petunias. The scenery en route to Banff and Jasper was all I dreamed it would be — and more! I tried to compare it to the beauty of Norway but it was impossible. Each place has its own unique way of testifying that God did touch this Earth with beauty. We loved driving onto the Athabasca Glacier in the Canadian Rockies and tasting the pure water and we followed that with a rubber raft ride down the Athabasca River.

About 20 of us ended the ride with very wet bottoms. Mine was blue because my slacks faded. The Fourth of July we were surprised to find the bus decorated with red, white, and blue streamers and an American flag with appropriate music being played. For lunch our tour guide planned a picnic in a wooded area with a decorated sheet cake for dessert. The Canadian beef was excellent but I'll never forget the salmon at Ivar's on the Seattle waterfront and the trout I had in Banff. They were superb! The highlight of the trip for me was not Lake Louise with its chateau, where we had an excellent buffet lunch, but rather the serene elegance of Lake Moraine.

Our flight from Seattle to San Francisco, where we got our plane to Cleveland, took us over the crater of Mt. St. Helen. We could see a plume of smoke rising and were glad the volcano remained quiet while we flew over it. This was another nature lover's trip and I would love to go back but next time would include Portland and Victoria. God willing, next year I will see the Grand Canyon and visit friends in Phoenix. I would also like to take a quick trip to see my friend, Hollie, who deserted Cleveland for the warmth of Florida. She is already tired of taking visitors to Epcot, but promised to take me.

In September I saw the first Christmas tree in Higbee's. It seems the stores celebrate Christmas earlier every year. At least they used to wait until Halloween was over. I wish we could convince people that Christmas is not a one day celebration preceded by so much activity one is exhausted when it arrives. Christmas is an attitude in response to faith which challenges us to celebrate the birth of Christ EVERDAY as we reach out and share what we have with others in whatever way we can and as generously as we can. The real joy of Christmas is knowing we have tried to make life a bit more livable for someone.

I love you all for having made my life more livable by sharing yourselves with me. I wish you a blessed Christmas and pray that in the New Year each day will be a little Christmas as others share with you and as you share with those around you.

With all my love to all of you, Alida

# 37<sup>th</sup> Christmas Letter, November 7, 1986 (At Home)

My dear family and friends,

Like "Old Man River," the years keep rolling along and here we are at the end of another. No matter what has happened throughout the year, we can look back and thank God that we are alive and well and have had the privilege of experiencing all that life has to offer. Speaking of experiences, I've had a variety of them this year.

On January 31<sup>st</sup>, I was an outpatient at St. John's Hospital. The doctor had removed a tiny cyst from my head. I was on a hospital cart waiting to be released when suddenly everything in the room shook. The nurse scurried to call the custodian thinking a boiler had blown. Someone said it felt like an earthquake. It was! I was glad when the shaking stopped since I was in no position to make a hasty retreat with my clothing secure in a locker down the hall and a hospital gown and flimsy slippers the only thing between me and nudity. I suppose I could have made a sari out of the blanket but am grateful that wasn't necessary. I'm also glad the doctor wasn't operating on me when the shaking started.

In March I lost my dear friend, Reverend Garner, whose wife preceded him in death a year or two earlier. It was so nice of his daughter, Peg, to insist on paying my way to Washington, D.C. so I could be with her and Jim at the memorial service. The Garners, whom I call "my other family," made a difference in my life. The only way I can repay them for their love and goodness is to pass it on to others. It was over 30 years since I had seen Peg and Jim and I was so glad to be with them. The trouble with getting older is that one finds final goodbyes coming more frequently. I lost several other friends and "my kid" John Thomas this year. Another earthquake of sorts hit me in May when Walt got married. I'm glad Walt and Ceil are happy but it was a jolt, after so many years of having family around, to find myself alone. Change is never easy for anyone but it's another of life's experiences and, hopefully, out of the change we will find that God has something new in store for us.

Memorial Day weekend I traveled to Toronto with Ginny and her parents, Ben and Edith Bowers. This was our third trip together. We picked the perfect weekend because the lilacs — acres of all varieties — were in full bloom. What a beautiful sight that was and the fragrance was better than any perfume. It was a short trip but we enjoyed the sights and all the good food Toronto had to offer. I knew the years had rolled by when "my kid," Susan, who lives next door, graduated from high school and enrolled in Baldwin Wallace University. Earlier in the year I was delighted when she invited me to see her induction into the National Honor Society. Ever since she was a tiny tot she has helped me mail out this letter. It's one of those sweet traditions that one treasures.

The people in my life have always been very important to me. I was happy to have dinner with Ruby and Ollie Shepherd when I was in Washington, and in August Hollie came from Florida to be with her sister for a week. She spent a weekend with me which we both enjoyed. The RTA bus group has been together at least three years, and we still have dinner together every other month. Five people from the morning bus I take will join us this month. My Casey, whom I told you about in last year's letter, is now in the 1<sup>st</sup> grade and doing well. I had him with me one weekend. My neighbor, Jim, helped entertain him and the two of them had a great time.

I was beginning to think my dream of seeing the Grand Canyon would be just that because I couldn't find anyone who was able to go with me. At a bus group dinner someone suggested I ask Mary Davis. In the next minute I asked her, she said she would love to go, and the trip was in the making. On September 13th we flew to Phoenix where I spent two days with "my kids," Tom and Doug Whitmer. I was happy to see Tom's wife and children after many years. The fellows took me to breakfast on Sunday and then drove me all over Phoenix. On Monday Doug helped me pick out turquoise jewelry and introduced me to some good Mexican food. In Phoenix I also saw Park and Frances Rushford and Jack and Janet Fuget but am sorry I missed seeing Jack Blaha. There is nothing as great as lasting friendships.

On September 15th the tour bus left Scottsdale, Arizona for Oak Creek Canyon where we took a jeep ride, and we also saw the red rock of Sedona. By that afternoon my dream of seeing the Grand Canyon came true! As young people say today, "It was awesome!" We took a half-hour helicopter ride the next day. When the copter crossed the rim and we were enveloped by the beauty of the Canyon, I had tears in my eyes. I wish everyone could see the Grand Canyon sometime in their life. From there we journeyed to Lake Powell and spent the night in Page.

Then we went through Navaho country to Zion National Park in Utah. Just before making a very, very steep descent to the park valley, the bus driver announced there was a loss of air in the brakes. The nearest repair station was 80 miles away. We were lucky that another driver disobeyed the rules and came back for us after discharging his passengers. Thank God our driver was alert or I might not be here to write this letter. When I looked up at the towering peaks of Zion, I felt like an ant. All I could think of were the words, "What is man that thou art mindful of him?" From Zion we went to Bryce National Park where the unusual rock formations made me feel as if I was on another planet. On Sunday we said goodbye to Bryce, made a quick stop in St. George, Utah to see an old Mormon home and a Mormon Temple, and then we headed for Las Vegas. After all the natural beauty we had seen I would have preferred skipping the superficial splendor of that town. Of course we tried the slot machines but when we each lost $20.00 we quit. We stayed an extra day to see the Hoover Dam and that was worth seeing, but Vegas is on my list of places I would not choose to revisit. Mary and I thoroughly enjoyed the others who were on the tour as well as Sigrid, the tour guide and Ronnie, our driver.

I don't mind admitting that on October 4th, I made it to Medicare. I celebrated my 65th birthday in fine style. From October 3rd through the 7th I was taken to dinner every night and several more times during the month. It was wonderful and "weightful!" Retire? I think I'll work until I get a signal from my body that it is time to quit. I would miss the daily contact with people. Last year I assigned 1,400 volunteer cases to private attorneys. I'm surprised they call back knowing what I want but they have all been so nice to me and so good about taking free cases.

Every so often someone asks me who the "kids" are I talk about. Never having had any of my own, I've "adopted" the children that have come into my life. What a joy they have been and I'm grateful to their parents for allowing me to share and love their children. Somewhere I saw a title, "Jesus is the Reason for the Season." I like those words which remind us that Jesus taught us to love and share all year. "My kids," as I lovingly call them, have put a little bit of Christmas into each day for me, and I pray that the spirit of Christmas will be part of each of your days in 1987.

With all my love to all of you, Alida

# 38th Christmas Letter, November 1, 1987 (At Home)

My dear family and friends,

It seems as if I sent my 1986 letter just a few weeks ago. The years have a way of sailing by as one gets older. Remember when it seemed like an eternity before Easter, Halloween, and Christmas would come? It also seemed like an eternity before school was over and summer vacation would begin. The anticipation of those events when we were young made time go slowly; the busyness of adult life with schedules and deadlines to meet makes time go far too fast.

This has been another busy year for me with many unexpected and pleasurable happenings as well as the routine items. I'm still working, will be Church School Superintendent another year, and am still in choir. The bus group continues to meet every other month. We're in our fourth year — which is remarkable! You don't mind getting on the bus morning and night when you know you will be greeted by friends.

A spur of the moment trip to Greensboro, North Carolina started the year off right. My Aunt Jane celebrated her 87th birthday on January 19th and, because we had that day off, I decided to keep my promise to visit her. It also gave me a chance to get reacquainted with my cousin Carl and his wife, Elma. It's fun to do things once in a while without a lot of planning and fuss.

In May the American Baptist Biennial Convention was held in Pittsburgh. It was so close to home I was able to attend the BMTS breakfast. It was great seeing some friends I had not seen for 30 years. Only wish more of the class of '57 had been there for our reunion. My friend Ruth Hinshaw drove my car to give it a run, and we shared a room with her sister Esther Young. It was a weekend full of memories.

Spring found me on my knees planting flowers in front of our building on West 6th Street. This may be the last year because next spring there will be new sidewalks and possibly grates around the trees. Maybe I'll plant flowers in large pots. To watch a dull, drab street turn into a thing of beauty has been a real joy. My efforts to beautify the street were featured in a column in our Cleveland paper. It was rewarding to have one's efforts recognized, but I'm the first to admit that while I had the vision, it took someone with money to get things moving. So many great things are happening in Cleveland, comedians are going to have to find another city to be the brunt of jokes.

In July I looked forward to having Hollie with me for several weeks. When she returned to Florida I began preparations for an August trip to the American Baptist Assembly in Green Lake, Wisconsin where I attended the Christian Education Conference. It was good to return to that beautiful place which the Winnebago Indians once thought of as their holy site. After 30 years it was a joy to meet some old friends and make new ones. I came home feeling relaxed, refreshed, and renewed.

In September we had an anniversary celebration honoring our pastor, Bill Noyes, who has been with us 10 years. It was my pleasure to write and deliver the testimonial on behalf of the congregation. A big change came for Walt and Ceil, who, after much sorting, selling, and packing, moved to Florida and a new home about the middle of September.

By October I was ready for a real rest so decided to keep my promise to spend a week with Hollie in Orlando, Florida. The first 2½ days it rained, so we shopped, saw *The Princess Bride*, which is a delightful fantasy worth seeing, and we visited Fort Christmas and an alligator farm. For a while it appeared that Hurricane Floyd was going to give me a real Florida welcome but it veered in another direction. We spent a day at the Kennedy Space Center which I've always wanted to see. October proved to be an excellent time to visit Epcot because fewer tourists made lines shorter. We were able to get through all the exhibits in one day. The creativity in all of them made one marvel at the inventiveness of mere humans. The grounds were beautifully landscaped and meticulously clean. It was worth the price of admission, and I would love to go back when they complete the Norway exhibit. On Friday we drove to Cocoa Beach where we walked a long way and picked up shells as the waves washed them in. For a while we just sat and listened to the roar of the ocean. It was a restful and enjoyable week.

My main accomplishment this year was redecorating the house. The living room looks totally different thanks to my dear friend, Amelia Grey, who is an interior decorator. Her decorating is warm and homey, not outlandish like some. She helped me select drapes and a couch, then added a few other items, rearranged some old things and gave the place a new look. I have always loved our house with its beautiful light oak wood, and feel as if I have dressed up an old lady and made her look lovely. I met Amelia in 1939 when she was a substitute music teacher for a cappella choir at Lakewood High. When I decided to enter an interscholastic solo contest, despite having no training, she offered to coach me because she liked my high B-flat, soprano voice. I cried all the way home because I was the only soprano from Lakewood High to get a first rating. That was the happiest memory I have of those Depression years. Every year since '39, on May 13th I have phoned or sent a card to thank her, and on the 25th and 50th anniversaries I sent her 25 red roses. What made all she has done for me so special is that she has done it with so much love. Amelia and John are an amazing couple. They are still very active and looking forward to the future at a time when many people would be twiddling their thumbs.

"My kids" still bring me much joy. Ted and his wife Bobbi made me a "great-aunt," and Drew Carey has been chosen to be on *Star Search*. I'm sure Drew is going to go places in the entertainment field. He is on stage at the *Comedy Club* in various cities and also does comedy writing. His two-minute segment will be taped November 14th and aired nationally later. My "English son," Barry, phoned recently to let me know he will be here to visit his American daughter at Christmas time and may spend a day or two with his "American mother," as he calls me. It has been almost a year since I saw Casey, but I phone him when I can and hope he can spend a weekend with me sometime soon.

When I think of Christmas I will always remember last year when the teenage son of a member of our bus group called and asked if he could help decorate the house. When he finished I had lights around windows and doorways and on the mantel. He was so full of enthusiasm he made my Christmas merrier. That is the real spirit of Christmas: giving of oneself to make life a bit happier and joyous for another. David did that for me. The gift he gave didn't cost a cent. It just took a little time and a lot of caring. What a great example he set for all of us to follow at Christmas and throughout the coming year.

May God's richest blessings be yours as you celebrate Christmas or Hanukkah and be with you in all of 1988.

With all my love to all of you, Alida

# 39<sup>th</sup> Christmas Letter, October 25, 1988 (At Home)

My dear family and friends,

Two months from today is Christmas so it is time for me to get this letter written. It has been such an uneventful year I wondered if I should write a Christmas letter. I finally decided to write this 39<sup>th</sup> letter because some of you have said it wouldn't be Christmas without getting the letter. For me it is a way of keeping in touch with all of you and a way of sending loving greetings at this special time of year.

I didn't do any traveling this year but had the joy of entertaining a lot of travelers. Early in January I got a call from a friend in Chicago asking if I would let his wife stay with me during a period of recuperation from a serious illness. While visiting in Lakewood she was hospitalized for six weeks. I feel if God put someone in your path to care for, you should help. I was glad to give Dorothy a quiet place to recuperate. She was with me three weeks.

In April Barry, my "English son," came for a week to see his daughter, Veronica, now eight-years-old, and she went to England with him for the summer. When he brought her home in August he was with me for several weeks and this time his friend, Christina, came with him. They are planning to marry next year. Barry is trying to get custody of Veronica and it was important that Christina be interviewed. Barry will be back at Christmas for a short time and I will be glad not to be alone for the holidays.

Walt arrived the end of September for two weeks. He packed things he had left behind when he and Ceil moved to Florida. He was home to help me celebrate my birthday. He treated me to dinner one night, and on my birthday I entertained mutual friends for dinner and had neighbors in for dessert. Walt left on Tuesday and on Thursday my friend, Rita Boroviak, came to stay for five days. She attended her 50<sup>th</sup> class reunion. Mine is next year. We have known each other since 1941 when we worked at the Federal Reserve Bank. She has been in Florida for six years so I gave her the grand tour of the Galleria, the new harbor, the Warehouse District, and the Flats. She was amazed at what has happened here. More improvements are on the way with two new office towers taller than the Terminal, which is too bad, along with three hotels, the Rock and Roll Hall of Fame, which I wish was a Big-Band Hall of Fame, and a totally new Terminal concourse with theaters, shops, etc. We have had promises, promises before, but this time things are really happening. Rita has missed the fall colors so she enjoyed a ride through our Metropolitan Park. With both Walt and Rita gone the house seemed very empty.

Another special visitor was Casey, the little boy I used to take to nursery school across from Legal Aid. His folks came from Columbus to visit relatives and I had Casey, now eight-years-old, over night. Jim, my neighbor, took us to visit several merchants who were so fond of him, and then we went to the Natural History Museum to see the dinosaur exhibit. They are life-sized creatures which moved and made sounds. He loved it and I loved having him with me.

Yes, I am still working. I need people around and believe I would get terribly depressed being home. I am sure I will know when the time is right to retire. Yes, I am still Church School Superintendent and still in choir. That keeps me busy!

The only place I went to this year was Lisbon, Ohio one Sunday to see Minerva, George, and their family. About six years ago I started growing a Colorado Spruce tree from a twig a nursery sent me. It was about a foot tall when I took it to Lisbon where it could grow better in a wide open space on the farm. It is now about six feet tall, just beautiful, and houses bird nests in its branches. Every year I take pictures of the "Alida" tree as we call it.

My interest in environmental causes has not waned and I continue to support every group I can. Toxic wastes, the greenhouse problem, acid rain, and other serious problems have been with us so long. It infuriates me to think the politicians have allowed it to continue until it is almost too late. God created man to be a good steward of His natural resources, but instead we are destroying them. Sometimes we forget we are all part of nature, and when that is destroyed — so are we! Teddy Roosevelt said, "The nation behaves well if it treats the natural resources as an asset which it must turn over to the next generation increased and not impaired in value."

Last year I told you that one of "my kids," Drew Carey, was on *Star Search*. We are now waiting anxiously for him to appear on Johnny Carson's show, possibly in November. He has been seen on 10-second Ohio Lottery commercials. I'm proud of him, but I'm proud of all "my kids" and the things they have accomplished. In October I was invited to the 40th wedding anniversary of Bianca and Bob Wiegand. Bianca, her brothers Frank and Dan, and cousin Lea, lived across the street when we moved into this house 54 years ago. The five of us had a wonderful reunion at the anniversary and I met some of their children I had never seen. What a warm, wonderful evening it was!

It was getting more and more difficult for the bus group to get together with jobs and residences changing. Although we had a lot of fun while it lasted, we no longer meet for dinner, but we are still friends. On my way to work in the morning I got acquainted with a few of the fellows who are renovating a building on West 6th Street. When Lennie learned that I love fresh fish he saw to it that I got perch and walleye once a week. I have some frozen to enjoy this winter. To repay that kindness I buy cookies for the fellows. Friendship has its rewards.

Murphy's Law was in operation when I had a new lawn planted three weeks before the drought and sprinkling ban hit. Prior to the ban I had to water the new lawn two hours a day for three weeks. I'm sure that saved the lawn and my 75-year-old maple tree. The lawn looks good but the water bill looked like the national debt. If hell is as hot as last summer I am going to try to be good.

As I think about Christmas and gifts one could buy, it occurs to me that a small tree, a shrub, or order of bulbs would be a lasting gift that would also beautify the environment. At Christmas we celebrate the everlasting gift of God's love for us. I pray that as Christians look at the child in the manger or as our Jewish friends at Hanukkah light candles for eight days we will all remember how much our faith has meant to us. I hope we will also take seriously the fact that those of us living on the Earth have been entrusted to care for it and all the creatures living on it. What better way is there to praise God than to honor, respect, and protect all His creation?

Martin L. Davey wrote, "Trees are necessary to our life and our contentment. They give us something infinitely fine to bless and to enrich our lives. We need only to open our eyes to see them in their great beauty and their incomparable value, and be happier because we are permitted to live among them.

Trees add joy and blessing to our lives in proportion to our capacity to feel their presence and comprehend their beauty." I would say "Amen" to that!

May you and yours be immersed in the peace, joy, and love of this season and experience it throughout the coming year.

With all my love to all of you, Alida

# 40<sup>th</sup> Christmas Letter, November 8, 1989 (At Home)

My dear family and friends,

"Oh, the comfort, the inexpressible comfort of feeling safe with a person: having neither to weigh thoughts nor measure words, but pour them all right out just as they are, chaff and grain together, knowing that a faithful hand will take and sift them, keep what is worth having, and with the breath of kindness blow the rest away." — John Oliver Hobbes

The above lovely quote, which was displayed in a Travelers Aid office where I worked as a student in 1958, expresses the epitome of loving communication. This 40<sup>th</sup> Christmas letter almost didn't get written because there didn't seem much to write about, but sharing what I did this year is, after all, secondary to communicating with you so you know I am still thinking of you.

Last Christmas was enjoyable because Barry, my "English son," and his six-year-old daughter, Veronica, were with me. It was fun having a child for the holiday week, especially one who was such a joy to have that I hated to see her leave. Barry returned to England New Year's Eve and early in '89 he and Christina got married. Veronica spent the summer with them and was there when her half-brother, Michael, was born. Barry invited me to visit them this Christmas but, as much as I would like to see them and the baby, I decided to stay home. I've learned that Casey, who now lives with his father in Florida, may be in Columbus for Christmas and I hope to see him and his brother, Aaron.

We had roller coaster weather all year. In January we had some days so warm it felt like spring, and the snow we had during the winter didn't last too long. We thought summer would never come because the cool days and continuous rain in the spring more than made up for the heat and drought of the previous summer. Planting was delayed, but the spring flowers lasted a long time because of the coolness. When the flowers faded I dug up every bulb in the yard knowing I would hate myself in the fall when they had to be replanted. Jim Wagner, a young man I would see at breakfast in our diner, volunteered to help and spent five hours digging one Saturday. In three days I spent 12 hours replanting about 200 bulbs. I have no idea what is planted where, so, I will be in for a big surprise come spring, and I can't wait to see what I did!

The year 1989 could be summed up as the year of work. At the end of '88, as Coordinator, I began planning for a citywide workshop held in my church in April. Then it was time to plan for Easter. In the meantime there were committee meetings for the Lakewood High Class of '39's 50<sup>th</sup> reunion the end of June. There were other church meetings, choir rehearsals, and Church School Superintendent duties, plus working everyday at Legal Aid.

The 50<sup>th</sup> reunion was worth the year's work. On Friday night a get-together we thought would attract about 50 was attended by 150. Saturday morning we needed three Lolly Trolleys for a tour of Cleveland, and that was followed by a brown bag lunch at the high school, along with a tour of the school. Our new swimming pool is impressive. Saturday evening's dinner and dance was super with only big-band music for dancing. I have labeled ballroom dancing "Olympic" (up close and personal) as compared to the "calisthenics" of the rock era. Young people have no idea what they are missing in not learning ballroom dancing which is a real art form when done well. I would rather dance than eat, as many of you know. The 298 who attended were delighted with what the committee had planned and requested a 55th reunion. We might settle for just meeting somewhere for dinner in five years. By then we'll all be in our 70's! Can't be!

Did I take any trips this year? Only those I took to the dentist for crown work. That is expensive but at least the money we put in our mouths we CAN take with us. Day trips included a day at Put-in-Bay with my neighbor, Jim, and "my kid," Matt, who is 10, which was all the more enjoyable because Matt is always so full of enthusiasm when you take him places. Those of you who remember Euclid Beach Park would have loved the exhibit of memorabilia at the Cleveland Health Museum. My friend Elaine and I had our picture taken with "Laughing Sal" who once stood in front of the Fun House, and Jim had his taken next to Flying Turns car #1. Large crowds proved that people still have fond memories and much affection for that park. I spent my 68th birthday in Lisbon, Ohio, and the last warm fall day Jim suggested a ride to Mohican State Park, and we also got to Millersburg. The leaves were beyond their peak, but just being away from the city was refreshing.

Every year is full of some "Hellos" and "Goodbyes." New friends on the morning and evening buses make the rides anything but boring. The diner in our building is closed temporarily but I enjoyed the friends I made there. Karen, who made a reputation for baking delicious bread, invited me to her wedding, which was one of the most simple, lovely, affordable ones I've attended. She wore a dress dating to 1925, a gardenia in her dark hair, and came down the aisle with her two nieces who carried the rings. My pastor came in with the groom and acted as usher at the end of a meaningful ceremony. Forty attended a reception at the couple's home and the next day they had a cookout for other friends. The goodbye I dreaded for years came when Dr. Morr, my dentist, retired. It's hard to believe anyone would look forward to seeing their dentist every six months, but he was always so full of jokes — and I trusted him! I hope he enjoys his retirement. I no longer mind going to dentists.

People ask me when I'm going to retire. All I can say is that work is more or less therapy for me, and I still feel good, so we'll see. In October a new panel of attorneys was formed to help clients with AIDS. It is too soon to know how much more work this will require, but I might just have to work until I'm 80! I'm kidding of course. Another letter to the editor commending volunteer attorneys made *The Plain Dealer* in November.

I've been baking up a storm since Inez, who does my dry cleaning, gave me a starter and recipe for Amish Friendship bread. I've lost track of how many loaves I've made and given away just so I could keep the starter going because no one has the recipe for that. I'm experimenting with freezing some starter. If that works I won't have to open a bakery.

This has been a year of tragedies caused by nature and others caused by man. Drugs, homelessness, the deplorable state of education, lack of concern for the environment, and so many other problems make one wonder if greed and the lust for power have replaced kindness, concern, and caring. (Loving, caring, and sharing are so easy and so healing.) Thank God for Christmas with its reminder to get our priorities in order to love one another. Christmas is like a flower planted by God, and it blossoms only when it is cultivated by man. May the message of Christmas reach your heart and mine and guide us in the year ahead. Shalom!

   With all my love to all of you, Alida

Chapter Seven

**Ten Christmas Letters
From 1990 to 1999**

# 41$^{st}$ Christmas Letter, November, 1990 (At Home)

My dear family and friends,

Little did I think when I wrote the first Christmas letter in 1950 that it would be continued for more than 40 years! Forty-one years! Where did they go? I have been asked why I started the letter. Let me answer that briefly and recap a few things about those 41 years.

When I graduated in '39 it was hard to find work because of the Great Depression. I thought I had made it when I started at the Federal Reserve Bank January 1$^{st}$, 1940, at $60 a month. When World War II began, those not called by Uncle Sam worked until 8:00 or 9:00 at night, all day Saturday and one-half day on Sunday. My contribution to the war effort was writing 10 to 15 letters a week to those in the service, and I also wrote to other friends. In 1946 I began working at the Illuminating Company and finally had weekends to myself. I love to sing, so in 1948 I joined the choir at Lakewood Baptist Church because I knew the Director from my high school days. In 1950 I joined the church and got so involved in church activities along with all the other things I was doing that I could not write as many letters to family and friends but didn't want to lose contact — thus the Christmas letter was created!

I never dreamed in 1950 that three years later I would quit work after 14 years and go to college at age 32, which was not common in those days. I expected to be a Director of Christian Education, but life is full of detours and surprises. Possibly because people would come to me when they needed someone to listen; a course in casework made me feel I had found what I was searching for and this inspired me to go on for a Master's degree in Social Work. In '59 I began a new career at Family Service which eventually led to my starting a pilot social service project at The Legal Aid Society in '67. I am still there but now doing the referral work. Who knows, I might follow the example of Mrs. Baker who is still working at age 91. She has a shop in the Old Arcade.

Through these 41 years I have shared sorrow and happiness with you. I miss my parents and aunts and uncles who have died, and I'm grateful for the love and values they gave me. With all of them gone, and Walt married and living in Florida, I feel very much alone at times. One reason I love the house I've lived in for 56 years is because it is so full of memories. Your friendship and my faith sustained me through years of family illness and nursing home placements. However, there were happy events to share with you, such as trips to Europe, Scandinavia, and my beloved Temagami. I also shared seven years of being the helper when Walt built his amphibian, my tap dancing lessons (I wish I had continued them); the experiences I had at church where I'm still active, and all the other ordinary happenings in life. You also shared my love of nature and my hope that we would all do our best to protect the environment for the sake of the next generation.

I've lost count of how many children I've borrowed from friends throughout years. My life would have been empty without all "my kids." Neal Carey, my very first kid, who lives in California, visited his mother for a week in November and I was so glad to see him. When the Rosettes moved next door Dora was expecting. Twenty-two years later I am looking forward to attending Susan's wedding December 29$^{th}$. It has been so nice to watch her grow. We began a tradition when she was quite young; she would help me put stamps on my Christmas letters. They are all doing well and I am proud of them.

This year began with my "cousin," Minerva, asking me to let her granddaughter stay with me until she could find a place to live. Peggy knew nothing about Cleveland when she took a job at CWRU doing Alzheimer's research. I had never met Peggy, but said she could come for two weeks. It took awhile for her to get adjusted and find a place. She was with me three months and I missed her when she moved to an apartment in Lakewood. I had another temporary guest — a cat I saved from kitty heaven because friends who had to move could not locate a home for their Miss Kitty. On the morning bus I mentioned needing a home for a cat and a man who had not been on the bus before nor since offered to take her. I swear God put him there that morning because it isn't easy finding a home for a cat. He asked me to keep her until after he got back from reserve training. Much to my relief, he called as soon as he got back. I like dogs better than cats but she was well-trained and I was beginning to get attached to her.

I can't resist telling you about Charlie the squirrel. My neighbor, Jim, gave him the name. Not only does he come for the nuts we give him, but now he brings two or three of his friends along. They are so secure they will take the nuts out of my hand and eat them just a foot away. One night when I got off the bus I thought I saw Charlie. I knew it was him because he got up on his hindquarters when I called him. He followed me down the street and waited at the side door until I got in and got the nuts. The nature lover in me enjoys this trusting relationship with Charlie and his friends.

I had one of the nicest surprises ever this year! At the annual meeting of the Cleveland Academy of Trial Attorneys I was given a Distinguished Service Award. I have given out awards to attorneys at Legal Aid annual meetings but never, in my wildest imagination, did I ever expect to get this special recognition. It was especially nice because it came from attorneys I appreciate and respect because of their kindness and generosity to our clients. I really would miss my contact with them if I retired.

In early November, on a spring-like day, I discovered two places in Ohio I didn't know existed and I'm sure you would love. The Warther Museum in Dover houses magnificent carvings of trains and a mill done by Mooney Warther. Carvers in Oberammergau named him the "Master Carver of the World" because they recognized his genius. He could not find knives to suit him so he made his own, and Warther knives are still being made and can be purchased today. Not far from Dover is the town of Wilmot, and there one finds Alpine Alpa, which is a bit of Switzerland with excellent food. Swiss imports such as cuckoo clocks as well as Amish wares are available and at certain hours one can see the cheese factory in operation. It was so refreshing being in the country on winding, hilly roads. At the crest of some hills one gets a panoramic view of four to five Amish farms. Ohio does have a lot of beauty!

Another year is coming to a close as is my 41$^{st}$ Christmas letter. I don't know if there will be a 42$^{nd}$. Just in case there isn't, let me thank you all for letting me share 41 years of my life with you. I'm glad you have been a part of my life and thank you for having enriched it in your own special way.

At Christmas we give gifts while remembering the gifts given to the Christ child who was God's gift to us. At Hanukkah gifts are given in remembrance of God's gift of the tiny bit of oil found in the temple to light lamps which miraculously lasted eight days. Your love and friendship have been lifetime gifts to me, and I pray that my love and friendship have added something to your life. I close this 41$^{st}$ Christmas letter with a favorite quote from an unknown author: "For friendship is a gift apart, a lighted candle in the heart." I'm sure that light will glow forever. God bless you and yours in 1991 and all the years ahead!

With all my love to all of you, Alida

# 42<sup>nd</sup> Christmas Letter, November 26, 1991 (At Home)

My dear family and friends,

Last year I hinted that there might not be a 42$^{nd}$ Christmas letter. I got so many notes asking me not to stop writing the letter, so here it is, back by popular demand! I probably would have written one anyway because it wouldn't seem like Christmas if I didn't keep in touch with all of you. This has been such a WONDERFUL year I would like to repeat it!

The early part of the year was routine except for a January article about me in the *Cleveland Bar Journal* titled, "Meet the Lady Who Loves Lawyers." That title tickled me. As a matter of fact, I do love the lawyers on the referral panel who do so much for Legal Aid Society clients.

Early in April Bobbi Hinshaw, the wife of one of "my kids," and I took a weekend trip to Valley Forge to see the American Baptist Headquarters. While there we visited the Valley Forge National Park — which we enjoyed. Later that month at church we had the annual Appreciation Dinner for our church school teachers. My neighbor, Dan Rosette, was a guest speaker. He is a walking encyclopedia on American Indians. Everyone was fascinated by his presentation, so I might ask him to share more in '92.

The year was made special by visitors. Hollie stayed with me a week on her way back to Florida from Oregon. While she was here Harold Strauss flew in from Texas to attend ceremonies at B.W. where Lois Garber got her Master's degree. Lois invited me to have tea with her and her dad at the Ritz Carlton and Hollie joined us. It was a lovely afternoon. At the end of June, Walt and Ceil came north to get away from the extreme Florida heat. Unfortunately the two weeks they were here we had a heat wave and this house isn't air-conditioned. They enjoyed visits with friends and family and on July 4$^{th}$ we had a cookout here. They left the next day and were happy to leave behind all the orange barrels they saw everywhere because of road construction. In September Tom Whitmer flew in from Phoenix and that was a pleasant surprise. He is another one of "my kids" and I enjoyed the dinner we had together. They were all impressed with improvements in Cleveland — especially Tower City.

Speaking of "my kids," Drew Carey was at the Improv Comedy Club in the Flats this summer and will be the headliner New Year's Eve. Drew is making the rounds of TV shows. He made *The Tonight Show* November 8$^{th}$. He was so great Johnny Carson called him over to chat and invited him to return to the show. On December 7$^{th}$ he will be in HBO's annual "Young Comedians Special."

When plans for a vacation seemed to be in jeopardy, I ordered new carpeting. Then Wilma Sevcik and I decided we would travel after all. Between getting everything ready for the September quarter of church school, new carpeting installed, and packing, I could not wait to get on the plane to rest. August 21$^{st}$ eight of us flew to Las Vegas to join a tour of the National Parks. In Vegas I was glad to see my cousin Genevra and her friend Midge even though it was only for a few hours. The tour began at the Hoover Dam and then to the Grand Canyon, Bryce, and Zion. We flew over the Canyon and Monument Valley before heading for Salt Lake City where we visited Temple Square and Brigham Young's home.

Jackson Hole, Wyoming was a real western town. Prior to leaving there we rafted down the Snake River for two hours while enjoying the beauty of the Grand Tetons. Then it was on to Yellowstone where we were surprised to see a buffalo standing in the middle of the parking lot of Old Faithful Inn. We saw the geyser do its thing three times and the next day visited all the geological wonders in Yellowstone. The bus had to stop twice to let buffalos cross the road. One doesn't fool with those creatures! In Cody we saw the fabulous Buffalo Bill Museum. Near Spearfish we were awed by the Devils Tower National Monument, which is the solidified cone of a volcano. In Deadwood a visit to Mt. Moriah Cemetery, where Wild Bill Hickok and Calamity Jane are buried, was livened up by a city tour guide who was a real comedian. Next we went to Keystone and the Borglum Museum. A film showing all the work it took to create Mt. Rushmore made me appreciate Borglum's genius all the more. Our farewell party was at the Westin Hotel in Denver. We couldn't thank Gayle, our tour guide, and Dean, our bus driver, enough for such a lovely tour. I would encourage everyone to take that Globus Gateway tour. It renewed my commitment to help organizations who are trying to protect nature for future generations.

I also came home wishing we had kept the promises we made to American Indians. We promised that no white man would set foot in one part of South Dakota. Then gold was discovered and the promise was forgotten.

Nothing could top that trip, I thought, but then came my 70th birthday. On the morning of October 4th Lyonel, my boss, surprised me with a dozen yellow roses from the staff. As if that wasn't enough, that afternoon they had a party in a conference room all decorated with birthday balloons. Thank God I only had to blow out seven and not 70 candles on a delicious cake which we enjoyed along with fruit punch. The staff really put one over on me and they will never know how much I appreciated their thoughtfulness. Two days later I had another glorious party. I was going to have a party at my home but my friend Marilu Simon insisted on planning one for me. Other than giving her names of friends, I had no idea what was planned. A party room at the Winton Place on the Gold Coast was a lovely setting. At 2:00 p.m. some came for a clam bake that was catered and at 4:00 p.m. others came for cake and coffee. A "roast" read by Ginny Noyes summed up the 70 years of my life.

Remember Casey, the four-year-old I took to nursery school for several months in 1985? He now lives with his mother in Columbus. Imagine my surprise when I walked in the room and saw him and then spotted his dad and Scott who flew in from Florida just to make sure he got to the party. What a precious gift! There were friends there from every area of my life: work, church, neighbors, former clients, and the bus. Prior to the party I had phone calls from two of "my kids" in California, Neal and Drew Carey. Dorothy Smith, whom I've known since the 1st grade, Sonia, also from California, and Barry in England, also called. I have never felt so enveloped by love and friendship as I did that day and am glad I could experience such a gathering of people I love while I was alive to enjoy them. George Collingwood, Beulah's husband, videotaped the party so I can enjoy it over and over. Thanks to all of you who sent cards. I enjoyed them all. In case you are wondering; Yes, I'm going to keep working a while longer. It's healthier for me.

I close this 42nd Christmas letter wishing that each of you, sometime in your life, will have the rich and joyous experience I had surrounded by loving friends, and I pray that next year will be as great for all of you as this year was for me!

With all my love to all of you, Alida

# 43<sup>rd</sup> Christmas Letter, November, 1992 (At Home)

My dear family and friends,

Christmas brings back memories of childhood and I'm sure you have memories of days when life was more sweet and simple. I long for the sound of the frogs in the pond across the street from us in Parma and wish I could hear them once again. Do you wonder as I do, where all the butterflies have gone?

There is still a lot of beauty in our world which we must protect. I saw a lot of beauty while on my first vacation of the year. I visited Walt and Ceil the end of February. Their home is lovely and I enjoyed eating meals while looking at the canal and trees that lined it. They had my week well-planned. We saw the Edison Home/Museum and Ford homes; the lovely city of Naples with its Tin City full of stores; and Sanibel Island with its bird refuge. There we ate at the Bubble Room which was filled with memories, pictures of old movie stars, and under the glass of the tables such things as celluloid dolls! There was a day of shopping and a Sunday afternoon boat ride to the Sanibel area. Ceil kept me well-fed, and one night we dined with ex-Clevelanders Mary and Frank O'Neil. After a week with Walt I spent three days in Punta Gorda with Bill and Cindy Kester (my friends who have the island I love in Canada). We visited Fisherman's Village, an animal refuge, and Boca Grande where we walked the beach and looked for shells. Their son Tommie and his wife Brenda were there, which was a special treat. I'm glad their daughter Laurie and her family live in Cleveland. Florida is beautiful and Cape Coral has a leisurely way of life, but I'll still take the north – snow and all!

I got home from Florida March 7<sup>th</sup> and did my spring cleaning. On March 25<sup>th</sup> my "English son," Barry, came to see his daughter, Veronica, and he spent 18 days with me. Veronica came on weekends, which I loved. The house was empty when Barry left, but I was busy planning a party for "my kid," Matt Nelan. He started going to my church when he was six or seven, and was baptized on Palm Sunday. That day I had a party to share his special day with church school teachers and other friends who have been a part of his life and loved him. I'm proud, too, of his brother, Neil, who is in his third year of college. It has been a real joy to watch all "my kids" grow into fine young people.

The most memorable thing about the next few months was the first shiner of my life, which I got when I tripped on a sidewalk one morning in July. I fell so hard the plastic lens in my glasses shattered, but the x-rays proved the bones in my face were okay. I thank God everyday for my good health, but am saddened by the illnesses of so many friends, including that of Hollie who moved to Portland, Oregon because the Florida humidity exacerbated her breathing problems. It was difficult to endure the deaths of John Grey in June and Minerva Moser on November 2<sup>nd</sup>. Minerva was a very special person in my life since childhood — and I'll miss her! There were happy times this year with three weddings and the Golden wedding anniversary of Margaret and Al Ellsworth on October 3<sup>rd</sup>. Fred Eilert and I were usher and bridesmaid 50 years ago and the only two from the wedding party that were present that evening.

On October 4<sup>th</sup> I celebrated my 71<sup>st</sup> birthday. I didn't have the gala celebration I had for my 70<sup>th</sup>, but treated myself to a week's tour of Washington, D.C., Williamsburg, and Charlottesville, Virginia. Ginny Noyes from church went with me. This might be our last trip together because she is retiring and hopes to return to her home in Maine. On Monday, October 5<sup>th</sup>, we arrived in Mt. Vernon about 2:00 p.m., spent hours there and then went to Hogate's on the river for a delicious fish diner. We then toured the city and visited the illuminated monuments of Lincoln and Jefferson and the Vietnam Memorial. Tuesday we got into the White House by 8:00 a.m. thanks to a letter from some authority. It was good to see it during this bicentennial year. Having a Washington guide and a bus to transport us made it possible for us to tour the FBI Building, Ford Theater, Kennedy Center for the Performing Arts, the Capitol, National Cathedral, and Smithsonian Institute. At the end of that busy day we boarded the Spirit of Washington for a dinner cruise on the Potomac.

Our first stop on Wednesday was at Arlington Cemetery where we saw the changing of the guard at the tomb of the unknowns and the graves of Jack and Robert Kennedy. Then we went on to Williamsburg where a southern-style meal at King's Arm Tavern was topped with delectable pecan pie. We had about five hours to browse and to get the feeling of what it was like to live in colonial times. Ginny and I took pictures of each other with our head in the stocks and were glad it was only a picture. Thursday we drove to Charlottesville where we toured Carter's Grove and saw what slave quarters were like. A lunch of fried chicken at Michie's Tavern will never be forgotten. Our last stop was at Monticello where we were impressed with the inventiveness of Thomas Jefferson. Except for a little rain when we started home Friday morning, the weather was perfect and as we traveled through the mountains we were treated to miles of gorgeous fall colors. It was truly a wonderful week!

Homes always need some repair and this was the year of the basement. With all the rain we had, more and more water was seeping in so I had part of the basement waterproofed from the inside. This gave me a good reason to get rid of things that were useless, including the old incinerator and wash tubs. There is something very therapeutic about getting rid of such stuff. It is so clean and empty now that it is a pleasure to go down to use the Nordic Track I bought for exercise. My brain is also getting some exercise trying to figure out the computer I bought which is used only for letter writing. I doubt if I will ever master all of the intricacies of that technological Dracula!

Some things remained the same this year. I'm still working and loving my job and my attorneys. This is my eleventh year as Church School Superintendent and choir is still part of my life. If only I could sing as I did when I was younger.

It has been a good year for many of us, but we can never forget that for others it was a disaster. With so much fighting all over the world and so many natural disasters which left people hungry and homeless, the message of peace and hope is needed more than ever this week. We hear the word "love" over and over again at Christmas time and must remember to put it into practice all year. This thought which I found on a calendar seems appropriate: Whoever has a heart full of love always has something to give!

As we celebrate the gift of God's love at Christmas and Hanukkah, may we know that no matter what is happening He stills cares about us. I pray that in the coming year we, and our government, will find new ways of helping those in need at home as well as around the world. I pray, too, that you will support those who are trying to protect and preserve all the beauty and wonders of nature. The following words in the Euclid Beach video are worth remembering: One of the saddest lessons of history is how little we treasure what we have until we have it no more.

With all my love to all of you, Alida

# 44<sup>th</sup> Christmas Letter, October, 1993 (At Home)

My dear family and friends,

I now begin my 44<sup>th</sup> Christmas letter. Do you suppose I might make the book of *Guinness World Records* some day? This year got off to a very sad start with the death of my good friend Hollie Cole. I miss her weekly letters and I'm sure the mailman does too because she always drew clever pictures all over the envelopes. I'm glad I saved many of them. In March my friend Ruth lost her husband, Earl, and later in the year Lee Trivison, a classmate of my brother, Walt, died of a heart attack. Death is part of life but it is never easy to accept. Thank God for memories which ease the loss.

In February I flew to Florida for 10 days, dividing my time between Cindy and Bill Kester in Punta Gorda and Walt and Ceil in Cape Coral. It was an enjoyable stay but I'm glad I missed their terribly hot summer. A short time after I got home Walt informed me that x-rays located a small, operable tumor in his lung. Surgery was followed by 31 radiation treatments to kill cancer cells. The radiation caused some inflammation in the lungs which resulted in involuntary coughing which seems to be subsiding. We are glad the worst is over and pray for only the best for Walt in the future.

A decision to get new kitchen and bathroom paper mushroomed, as often happens, into other projects both inside and outside the house. Except for some minor things, the home I've lived in for 59 years is in good shape. I believe old houses, like older people, should be given tender, loving care.

The big news of the year was "Drew News," as I call it. "My kid," Drew Carey, is making great strides in his career. It was a real thrill to see his name on the marquee of the State Theater when he filmed a *Showtime* special. He has been invited to appear at events with big name comedians and he will soon finish taping 13 segments of a show, *The Good Life*, which will be a replacement show in October or November on NBC. I was invited to go to LA with his folks in November to see him tape the last segment, but because I had already made plans for a trip to Maine, I had to decline with regret.

I got a new passport so I could go to England, but that trip was cancelled when I had to have tests for some discomfort. A small hiatal hernia was discovered but is under control as long as I watch acid and caffeine intake. It's a sign of age!

To keep my social work license another two years I had to take five continuing education courses this fall and they have been excellent. On my 72<sup>nd</sup> birthday the course was on Dying and Hospice Care. I told someone that as a Girl Scout I took the motto "Always Be Prepared" very seriously, but this was ridiculous. The course was not morbid but inspiring. I have never seen such dedicated people as was the team of hospice workers who shared their experiences with us.

On October 8<sup>th</sup> I traveled to Maine for a week. I've always wanted to see the fall leaves in New England, and combined that with a visit to Ginny Noyes who now lives in Ocean Park — just two blocks from the ocean! She had the week planned with our first stop at the Fryeburg Fair where we spent two hours walking around and three to four hours trying to get out of the parking lot! We went to Freeport where L.L. Bean and other outlet stores lure hundreds of shoppers. A two-day trip to the White Mountains was a joy with brilliant fall leaves decorating the landscape.

The first day we ate lunch at a campground amid stately pines with birds our only company. It was heavenly! Later we walked up endless steps to the top of The Flame, a natural gourge, and hiked back to the main building through the forest, which is a two-mile walk amid the beauty of nature. The second day we went as far as Mt. Washington, whose snow-capped peak we had seen for miles. Another day we went to Kennebunkport. That night we had clams and lobster, and I received my first lesson in how to tear a whole lobster apart. An added treat was a visit with Helen and Clint Condict who live near Ginny. He was an associate pastor at my church in the 1950's and I haven't seen them in all these years. I came home refreshed from my communion with nature. Nature is vitamins for the soul, and I'm grateful to Ginny for such a grand visit.

Yes, I'm still working and probably will until the good Lord shoves me in some other direction. I would miss my contact with people and I still enjoy what I'm doing, so we'll see what happens! After 12 years as Superintendent of the church school I am going to step down so that someone else can take over while I'm still able to help. I will be the Assistant. I feel sad giving up this job which has been such a major part of my life all these years. I purchased a tree for the church which is planted next to one dedicated to a former Superintendent, so we now have "Superintendent's Row" as I call it.

One of the best things about Christmas is communicating with friends and learning what has happened to all of you during the year. The following quote by John Oliver Hobbes expresses what I feel is the epitome of friendship: "Oh, the comfort, the inexpressible comfort of feeling safe with a person; having neither to weigh thoughts nor measure words, but pour them all right out just as they are, chaff and grain together, knowing that a faithful hand will take and sift them, keep what is worth having, and with the breadth of kindness blow the rest away."

Real friendship surmounts time and distance as evidenced by the fact that I still hear from Dorothy Smith in California; we were in the 1st grade together 66 years ago!

I pray for each of you that the year ahead will be filled with many precious moments, good health, and the joy you will find in some new venture or adventure. May God grant you courage when you need it, and may your faith give peace and comfort in times of stress and uncertainty. I know we are all wishing and praying that the peace we sing about during the holidays will be prevalent in all the world. What a gift to humanity that would be!

God bless you and yours as you celebrate Christmas and Hanukkah.

With all my love to all of you, Alida

# 45<sup>th</sup> Christmas Letter, November, 1994 (At Home)

My dear family and friends,

The words "love" and "giving" are often found on lips, cards, and letters during the holidays. They are simple but profound words. It is so easy to think about loving and giving at Christmas time, but also very easy to forget as we carry on the business of life throughout the rest of the year. By now I usually have this Christmas letter written and almost ready to be mailed. This year it has been difficult to get started, probably because the year was a mixture of joy and sadness. This is letter number 45.

Last year ended with a number of us from church attending the wedding of Chris Todd who grew up in the church. It was the most beautiful and lavish affair I've ever attended and I'm sure those of us who went will never forget it. The hospitality equaled the beauty, which made for a memorable trip to Grosse Pointe, Michigan.

January was a lost month. We had the coldest day in the history of Cleveland when the temperature was 20 degrees below zero. For once my timing was right because I picked the worst of the winter to be home 2½ weeks with a stubborn virus. Thanks to Christa, one of my RTA bus friends, and her son, Tim, who got up extra early in order to take us, I got a ride to work the rest of winter. That was great!

For many years my "English son," Barry, wanted me to visit him in England. He is remarried and has two boys, Michael, five, and Matthew, two. I never dreamed I would find the courage to travel overseas alone, but on May 9<sup>th</sup> I boarded a plane for London where Barry met me. We drove to Portsmouth where we took a ferry to the Isle of Wight. It was good to be with Barry and Christina and a joy to get to know Michael and Matthew. A book about a monkey was a real hit with Matthew and I was glad I bought it for him. After reading it to him a dozen times a day, Dida, as he called me, had it memorized. We went to places of interest on the Isle and I enjoyed all the lovely scenery. A seven-hour flight can be tiring, but I was fortunate to have very nice seat partners which made the time go faster.

Before going to England and when I returned on the 19<sup>th</sup>, I phoned my brother, Walt. My intuition told me I MUST call him in Florida Memorial Day, May 30<sup>th</sup>. Thank God I did! On the 31<sup>st</sup>, "my kid," Ted, drove me to North Royalton to the visitation for my cousin, Donny, who died. As we drove down State Road in Parma on the way home I suddenly had the urge to see my childhood home and asked Ted to turn down Russell Avenue. Then we went to the end of the street to see the school Walt and I attended. Walt went to Thoreau Park five years and I went six years. I shared with Ted things Walt and I did as kids, and how sad we were when we lost the home during the Great Depression. When I got out of the car I thanked Ted for letting me have such happy memories.

Two hours later Ceil, Walt's wife, called to tell me Walt had been killed instantly in an auto accident at 6:15 p.m. I would like to think he was with me on that memory trip a few hours after his death. He had not been well since the lung cancer operation and was concerned about a reoccurrence. If he had to die, I'm sure he would prefer it to be instant. The Reverend William Noyes officiated at his funeral and I will always be grateful to all those, who in so many ways, gave Ceil and me the love and support we needed.

122

On a happier note, I have so many fond memories, such as spending many hours helping Walt when he built the Volmer amphibian in our garage. As big a coward as I am when it comes to driving, I flew in the plane when it had flown only three hours because I trusted Walt's craftsmanship! I will always be grateful to him for introducing me to the REAL Canada. We went to fishing camps 80 miles above North Bay and stayed in some very primitive places. I wouldn't have done that for anyone else in the world! The enduring memories of enchanting scenery and steadfast companionship outweighed the hardships.

Walt was a very creative person. He could paint, sew, repair anything, and loved to cook. He built two guitars which turned out beautifully. In later years he learned to play the organ, refused to obey timing, but thoroughly enjoyed playing the music anyway he chose. I loved my brother and would do anything for him. One time he conned me into letting him make a plaster mask of my face. I was fine until he told me he was going to cover my nose and I would have to breathe through a straw. That was the end of that bit of creativity!

No matter what happens, life goes on. In July the Lakewood High class of '39 had its 55th reunion, which was well attended. God willing, we will have a 60th. In August I celebrated my 25th year with The Legal Aid Society, though I went there two years earlier while employed by Family Service to start the pilot social service project. I'm still working because I need to be with people and would miss my friends on the bus, at work, in the coffee shop, and the private attorneys I talk to during the day. I believe work is keeping me healthy so I might as well continue until the good Lord shoves me elsewhere.

Church is still an important part of my life. Singing was the one great joy of my life. While I can't sing solos anymore (wish I could), I enjoy being part of the choir. After 12 years as Church School Super-intendent I felt someone else should be trained in case anything happened to me. Never dreamed how much a part of my life that job was until I gave it up and had more time on my hands than I knew what to do with. I was Assistant to Keith this year. Next year I will be on another board but, because Christian Education has been part of my life for 44 years, I will do what I can to help Keith.

In October Lakewood High offered a tour to Fallingwater, south of Pittsburgh. Designed by Frank Lloyd Wright, it is a lovely home and I'm so glad it was given to the Western Pennsylvania Nature Conservatory so developers can never destroy the natural beauty surrounding this house. It was such a beautiful fall day; we all enjoyed the colorful trees which were all the more beautiful with the sun shining on them. A week later friends drove me to my favorite farm in Hanoverton, Ohio, where in 1979 I planted a one-foot Colorado spruce I had started from a sprig in my yard. It is now 10 to 12-feet tall and perfectly shaped. I told them not to let the White House know about it. Our planet would certainly not be as pleasant to live on if it were not for the trees which cool, purify, and decorate it. And to think some people cut them down as fast as they can is disheartening!

Are you acquainted with Leo Buscaglia? I love his philosophy. He believes in letting people know we love them by giving them a hug or doing something nice for them. We all need to know someone cares about us. As I approach Christmas, it is with sorrow that I, the adopted one, am the last of my immediate family. I'm grateful that as I grew up I was surrounded with love. During my childhood we didn't have a lot of the latest things, but I had a dad who went to work even when he didn't feel good — and he did hard sheet metal work! If he was late for supper it was because he was so tired he fell asleep on the streetcar. I had a mother who worked hard for us. She loved to cook and bake. Best of all she taught

Walt and me to be on time for school, and that discipline continued for both of us. I had an aunt who lived with us and taught me to love nature, and urged Walt and me to go to college. And I had a brother whose philosophy was far different from mine, but I loved him and admired his skills. He didn't care about sending cards, but he never forgot my birthday. I'm glad I let them know that I loved them when I could.

May Christmas and Hanukkah be happy and meaningful for you, and filled with heartwarming memories which will last forever — and may God bless you in the New Year!

With all my love to all of you, Alida

# 46<sup>th</sup> Christmas Letter, November 19, 1995 (At Home)

My dear family and friends,

Wouldn't it be nice if all the leaders in the world would start thinking about peace instead of war? What if everyone would start thinking about helping other people instead of hurting them? I've decided to stress love in this 46<sup>th</sup> letter because I'm so tired of conflict and hate, and I believe you may feel the same way as I do!

Some things I've loved haven't changed. For 61 years I've lived in this home with its beautiful light oak wood, all the memories it holds of my family, sheltered by my dear old maple tree. After 28 years of working at The Legal Aid Society, I still enjoy what I'm doing and love talking with private attorneys who are so kind and generous in taking free cases. I celebrated 45 years as a member of the Lakewood Baptist Church where I am now a deacon, and lend what is left of my voice to the choir. Because Christian Education is my first love, I help Keith, who succeeded me as Superintendent, by looking after the Crib Room and doing other things without getting in the way. I love my church which made such a difference in my life!

I love unexpected happenings. In May a choir from Sioux Falls College stopped at our church en route to Washington, D.C. Five of the young women stayed with me and I enjoyed having them. Later in the year a young woman who needed a quiet place to study for state exams stayed with me a short time.

I love all of "my kids" and can't imagine what life would have been like without all of them. They all make me feel so proud! Drew Carey worked hard as a standup comic. His dream came true this year when NBC liked the pilot he produced and initially gave his sitcom 13 weeks of television airtime — then extended it to 20 weeks! I'm sure he has a bright future.

I love all the other people who keep streaming into my life. I've met the nicest people on both the morning and evening Madison bus ride. Last year the evening group got together at Christmas and we'll do the same this year with a few new people. If one of us isn't on the bus we check to make sure the person is OK. Every morning I have breakfast in the diner in my building called "Checkers." Since we moved into the building in '77 I've known five owners and they have all been so nice. When I have flowers in bloom I take some to the diner and place them near the cash register. I have made some lasting friendships with both staff and customers. The current owner, Taras, was in major work all through school with Drew Carey. It's a small world! When I wasn't there by 7:00 a.m. one morning the cook and one of the customers went outside to look for me. The world is full of so many wonderful people if we just take time to get to know them.

The trouble with getting older is that you have to say that final "goodbye" more often to people who you care about. This year I lost my former dentist, Doctor Morr. When I was a young girl he would tell jokes and tap dance and I've never feared a dentist since then. The loss of Al Ellsworth and Bunny Rossen, widow of our dear Doctor Joe, left an empty place in my life.

Did I go anywhere this year? There were two trips to Hanoverton, Ohio to my favorite farm to see "my kids" and the beautiful Colorado Spruce that is now almost 16-feet tall. The end of June I attended the Alumni breakfast of my undergraduate college, which is now part of Colgate-Rochester Divinity School. It was worth traveling 700 miles round trip to see former classmates and roommates at breakfast. We had lunch at the Divinity School and I was glad to see the campus and memorabilia from BMTS. My friend, Ruth Hinshaw, and her sister, Esther, drove because I'm still "that little old lady who drives to church and back – in good weather!"

On August 22$^{nd}$ Ginny Noyes and I flew to Anchorage, Alaska for an 18-day love fest with nature. There was not one hitch in all those days. We figured we were on 15 different vehicles, including three boats, a cruise ship for three days and four nights, two trains, a number of buses, a tram which took us to the top of Mount Alyeska, planes, a ferry, a hydrofoil, and cabs. We cruised the Chena and Yukon Rivers, the Lynn Canal, and the inside passage to Glacier Bay.

We were lucky to have good weather, except for one or two days when it rained a bit. The food was excellent and we competed with the polar bears to see who could eat the most salmon. We met many nice people but Bev, Laura June, Helen, Ginny, and I became a five-some and had fun together, sometimes playing Golf, which is a new card game. In Anchorage there were hanging baskets everywhere and all the flowers were huge. There we saw the Portage Glacier, and then we boarded a train to Denali National Park which is the size of Massachusetts. A bus took us through the park and the scenery was awesome! It made me wish "America the Beautiful" was our national anthem. In Fairbanks we took a paddle wheel boat to an Indian village where we were told how Indians lived. We also saw Susan Butcher and her Iditarod sled dogs, and we petted a couple of them. She named her baby after one of the dogs that saved her life. Then we journeyed to Tok where our bags had to be out by 5:00 a.m. and departure was at 6:00 a.m. On our way to Eagle we stopped for coffee in a remote place called Chicken, so named because they couldn't spell Ptarmigan. A sign on a big empty drum read, "Welcome to Downtown Chicken." The town consisted of three old buildings side by side, along with an outhouse!

From Eagle we entered British Columbia. Our first stop was in Dawson City, which had one paved street. The rest were dirt roads along with various boardwalks. They try to keep it the way it was during the Yukon gold rush. We saw the hilarious Gaslight Follies and were glad to stay two nights. En route to Whitehorse we saw the Yukon Wildlife Game Preserve, and in the city I saw the Yukon Legal Aid Society. We rode the White Pass & Yukon R.R. from the top of the mountain down to Skagway, which had more gift shops than homes. From Skagway we went to Juneau for a night. The next day we saw their lovely museum, and at 1:00 p.m. we boarded the beautiful Holland America cruise ship named Statendam. We were able to rest a bit after the long journey, and the huge glaciers at Glacier Bay were spectacular! Ginny is still laughing because as we rushed to comply with the compulsory life boat drill, the strap on my life jacket got caught in the cabin door and I couldn't get to my key. She rescued me! The tour ended in Vancouver, but we took a ferry and went to Victoria where we had high tea at the Empress, visited the Butchart Gardens, and saw the B.C. Royal Museum. We had dinner with Ginny's foster son. On September 1$^{st}$ we took a hydrofoil to Seattle where Ginny's cousin, Meredith, treated us to dinner at the Painted Table, and also took us to see a play. The next day we reluctantly headed home to reality.

I came home even more convinced that we must protect our environment. As Chief Seattle said, "Man did not weave the web of life. He is merely a strand in it. Whatever he does to the web, he does to himself." One reason President Clinton would veto the budget is because a bill was tacked on allowing gas and oil development in the Arctic Wildlife Refuge. This would pose a threat to herds of caribou which use the area as a calving ground, and it would hurt the way of life of the Gwich'in Indians. I have made many calls to those in the Senate and House of Representatives to let them know I want something left for future generations. I love my country and I don't want one bit of its beauty destroyed!

A surprise visit from Gayle and Larry Tidwell and their baby, Garrett Scott, made my 74th birthday special. Gayle is the daughter of my late friend, Hollie, and now Gayle is one of "my kids." She calls me "Grandma." I think Hollie would like that!

The greatest gift I could wish for you is that God has enriched your life as he has mine with so many loving and caring friends and acquaintances. Love flavors life with goodness and hope. You have done that for me.

May your celebration of Christmas or Hanukkah be joyous for you and may love abide in your life throughout the coming the New Year!

With all my love to all of you, Alida

# 47<sup>th</sup> Christmas Letter, November, 1996 (At Home)

My dear family and friends,

This year started off uneventfully. I've continued to work because I like being around people. They are my vitamins! At Lakewood Baptist Church I've remained in choir, worked on the Historical files — which was a challenge, and asked the Trustees to put me in charge of keeping all nooks and crannies tidy. I've enjoyed getting rid of things no longer useable. Sometimes I think I must have been a cleaning lady in another life!

The big news early in the year was DREW NEWS. We were happy when "my kid," Drew Carey, had his television show renewed. He treated his writers, other staff, and cast member, Christa Miller, to a weekend in Cleveland so they could enjoy our revitalized city. His mom and I were delighted to be included for dinner at Sammy's and impressed with the quality of everyone working on the show. Drew will be the Grand Marshall in Cleveland's Bicentennial Thanksgiving Day Parade. He will make a guest appearance on *Lois and Clark*, and will emcee the *Cable Ace Awards* show November 16<sup>th</sup>.

In August my regular eye exam led to cataract surgery on the 19<sup>th</sup>. My plan to go back to work in two days proved unrealistic, so I was off one week. The other eye will also need surgery, but at least I'll know what to expect. August and September were filled with showers and weddings, which kept me busy.

Every year there are losses we must endure. On Christmas Day last year one of my childhood friends, Fred Van Horn, passed away. I have many happy memories of those days in the early '30's in Parma, and Fred was a part of them. When I came home from vacation, a letter from my physician, Dr. Carlos, announced his retirement and that, too, was sad news. He has been such a kind, warm, caring doctor it will be hard to get used to someone else, but he deserves some rest and joy in retirement.

Vacation...that magical word! Hawaii was on my list of places I wanted to see, and see it I did! That was a good way to celebrate my 75<sup>th</sup> birthday. Your Man Tours organized a wonderful tour from October 8<sup>th</sup> to the 23<sup>rd</sup>, and my friend of 62 years, Ruth Hinshaw, went with me. This was her first tour and it was fun sharing it with her. Let me share some with you!

"Just hang loose, just have fun, sip on a drink, or lie in the sun. Don't try to fight it, there ain't no use; cause when you're in Hawaii you should just hang loose." They kept telling us to "hang loose" and we did. It was relaxing to dress casually, enjoy the weather, drink in all the beauty and forget everything else. It was a long flight to Oahu and we had four flights between islands without one hitch. Our escort, Cousin Richard, (everyone is cousin in Hawaii) was dependable, full of fun, and a talented singer. It was good to have Ronnie Barrett from Radio Station WRMR with us and a pleasure to get to know him. There were about 52 in our group — all great people!

A special bonus early in the trip was having lunch with Larry Grean at a hotel on the beach at Waikiki. Larry is a prosecuting attorney in Honolulu and I had not seen him since he was a law clerk at Legal Aid 28 years ago, though we did keep in touch at Christmas. While dining we looked at the ocean with all its hues, and little birds walked around the tables and sometimes hopped upon them. I worked with Ed

Wake at Family Service, but lost track of him when he moved to Hawaii 30 years ago. Luckily he was in the phone book, so we had a brief but happy reunion. Seeing those two friends and talking with Lisa Caraulia, a young woman who grew up in my church, made the trip even more delightful.

On Oahu we went to a dinner show and were entertained by the Society of Seven, which is seven very talented men with beautiful voices, but are also very funny. Seeing a film of Pearl Harbor being bombed and then going to the Arizona Memorial brought back many memories of World War II. Oil is still leaking in drops from the ship after 50 years; they say it is the tears of the men who are buried in this sunken ship. We took the fresh flowers from the leis we got when we arrived in Oahu and threw them in the ocean in memory of the men who perished in the attack. We also visited the Polynesian Cultural Center which was a full day of sampling the cultures of Samoa, Tahiti, Fiji, New Zealand, and Marquesas.

On Maui we took the Hana Tour which tested the expertise of our driver, Gigi. She had to drive around 619 curves over 18 miles of rough road on a day-long ride! Gigi was fun to be with as she had an infectious laugh which reminded us of the robotic "Laughing Sal" at old Euclid Beach Park in Cleveland, Ohio. That day we saw the grave of Charles Lindberg. It is in the graveyard of a very tiny church in the wilderness on the island he loved.

We flew to Hilo, Hawaii where we saw the Macadamia Nut Factory and, of course, bought some. An unforgettable experience was a walk through the rain forest to see the Akaka Falls. I was amazed at the density and wondered how anyone could have the audacity to destroy rain forests all over the world for the sake of money. After Hilo we drove to Kona on the other side of the island where we stayed three days. We visited an orchid nursery, saw black sand beach (pulverized lava), and visited the Volcanic National Park. We took a ride on the Nautilus, which is a kind of submarine, to see fish and coral. On Captain Bean's dinner sail young men and women danced hulas on the low tables we sat at, and by the end of the evening many of us were dancing on them too. It was a fun evening!

The last island was Kauai where we traveled down the Wailua River to a Fern Grotto which defies description it was so beautiful. It rained the day we went to the Waimea Canyon, but stopped when we got there. So, we saw some of it, but a little sunlight would have illuminated our view. We had a few more hours to shop after that trip, before donning our muumuu's, adding flowered earrings and a flower in our hair, and finally heading for the Luau. That was a lovely way to end two happy weeks! I would like to go back to Hawaii in two years if I can. Want to come along?

I will never forget all the beauty of God's creation that I saw. I'm sure when our charges come in we will not forget the Hilo Hattie and ABC stores which tempt visitors with t-shirts and every souvenir imaginable. Of course at every rest stop we were lured with guava jelly, Kona coffee, and other goodies. Our luggage got so heavy we gave in and mailed a box home.

As we approach Christmas, Hanukkah, and the New Year, I hope we will all try to "hang loose" and enjoy each moment of the precious time we have on this planet. We can't change all the trouble in the world, but our faith will help us get through whatever lies ahead. So, just "hang loose." I wish you and yours Aloha (Love), Mele Kalikimaka (Merry Christmas) and a Hau'oli Makahiki Hou (Happy New Year) and every good thing in 1997.

With all my love to all of you, Alida

# 48<sup>th</sup> Christmas Letter, November 7, 1997 (At Home)

My dear family and friends,

This has been a WOW year full of surprises and enjoyment. The world may be a mess but I have had a feeling of contentment, peace, and joy! The first surprise came early in the year with a phone call from Nadine Petranek. I spoke with her briefly at dinner one night in Hawaii but we didn't exchange names. I sent a Christmas letter to her friend, Maxine, who was in our group and she told Nadine she got a letter from Alida. The name triggered memories and Nadine asked what my last name was. Would you believe, it turned out her parents were neighbors of my folks in the '20's and Nadine, then eight, was looking out her bedroom window the day I was brought home when I was adopted. I visited her and gave her some pictures I had of her father holding me, and one picture of her and me together. Amazing!

In February my dream of being in show business came true when Drew Carey let me be an extra on his show. His mother, Beulah, and I went to California, first visiting his brother and his family in Oceanside for a few days. On February 11<sup>th</sup> we took a train to L.A. where Drew had a limo waiting for us, along with a room at the Mondrian Hotel. Our bellman, Chad Bartulis, had attended St. Edward's High School in Lakewood, and was delighted to learn that we were from Cleveland. He couldn't do enough for us. He, like many others in L.A., is hoping for that one big break. On Tuesday we visited the set and it was determined I would be in two scenes in the Warsaw Bar. I was sent to wardrobe to find out what to wear. My call time was 1:00 p.m. Wednesday, but it was about 8:00 p.m. before I went on with no rehearsals. I felt as if I had been doing this all my life. When young I loved being in plays, could sing and dance, and always wanted to be on stage. God had other plans for me. In one scene Drew came up to me at the bar and said, "Fran, do you remember when you caught your husband in bed with another man? What did you hit him over the head with? Buzz beer!" I am still being called "Fran." It was a treat to meet the cast and most of the crew. They are all such nice people, they love working with Drew because he is good to everyone, and there is a feeling of camaraderie on the set. It tickles me that Mimi, with her blue eyes, told me I had beautiful eyes. On Thursday we were taken to Drew's dressing room on the Jay Leno set. I looked up and there was Jay, and then Kevin came in. It was fun meeting them. We had a tour of the Warner lot and Mann's Theatre where I saw all the foot and hand prints of the stars. It was a once-in-a-life-time experience, but I told Drew if he ever needs a grandma on the show I'll take the first plane to L.A. The headline in *The Plain Dealer* read, "Aunt Alida Makes TV Debut at 75." It was a debut with only re-runs!

May brought more joy when I attended the BMTS alumni breakfast in Indianapolis. It was a mini-vacation for Bobbi Hinshaw, wife of one of "my kids," who kindly drove me there. I saw classmates I hadn't seen for 40 years. I was 32 as a freshman, and most in my class were 18. They kiddingly called me Grandma Struze, and I loved it! Those young girls have grown into such lovely women; it was worth the trip to see them.

Cataract surgery in July was successful and the laser treatment in October cleared up some blurriness. I'm glad both eyes are done. Every day I thank God for the good health I've had and continue to work because it is my belief that work keeps me healthy. Besides, I would miss "my attorneys" (I wish the ones I know would get more publicity), the friends I've made on the bus and in the coffee shop, and the people I work with. Like most of us, I should get more exercise. I bought a Nordic Track but the only thing getting exercise are my eyes looking at it. Activities at Lakewood Baptist Church keep me busy. I'm still in choir, have enjoyed being on the Board of Deacons, but will probably be on another board now that my three-year term is over. It sounds crazy but I enjoy keeping all the nooks and crannies tidy. There is no such things as "sacred junk" when I'm around.

Some of you have asked me about the bus group that would meet every other month, along with one of the RTA drivers. The first group was disbanded because some moved or got other jobs. There is a new group which started out with four of us, but we keep picking up more passengers for the group. We meet at my home during the holidays for an evening of eating and chatting. Christa calls me her "bus mother" and she and her husband, Richard, even treat me like their mother. They even pick me up at work at night when they can.

Another surprise came when Reindle's, whom I met in Hawaii, invited me to join them for an autumn leaf tour of the New England states and Montreal the first of October. The tour included Valley Forge, Philadelphia with all its history, and there we visited the Norman Rockwell Museum. In Rhode Island we toured the Vanderbilt Marble Mansion. We went on to Massachusetts where we stopped at Concord, Lexington, and Salem. In Gloucester we were treated to a lobster dinner. All the instructions on how to eat lobster were useless. We just pulled, tugged, and cracked until we got to the meat. It was a bit messy, but delicious! It was a treat to get on the Mayflower II (How did 128 people survive the journey on that little ship?) and Old Ironsides. We visited the Old North Church and that day I celebrated my 76th birthday. In New Hampshire we took a tram to the top of the Franconia Notch, and nearby saw the Old Man of the Mountain. There wasn't much leaf color except some yellow, but Vermont made up for it. We oohed and aahed at the vivid red and orange colors. It was both an exhilarating and spiritual experience viewing all that beauty. Did you ever think about how barren this Earth would be without trees? We must do all we can to protect all of God's creation. Of course we stopped to buy and sample some maple syrup, and then we had a long ride to Quebec City (pronounced "Qebec." The "u" is silent.) We toured the city, stopped to view or buy copper items, and saw the Shrine of St. Anne de Beaupre. We had lunch in Old Quebec and visited many shops along cobblestoned streets. We went on to Montreal where we had another tour of that city and saw the Basilica de Notre Dame. It was the most ornate church I have ever seen with all its 24-carat gold. As a place of worship, it was almost too lavish for my taste. We ended the tour at Niagara Falls. It was a delightful 10 days with good friends and more memories to treasure.

Sadly, when I got to Quebec, I had a message that my "cousin," Fred Eilert, had died after months of illness. Many of you know that I would rather do ballroom dancing than eat. After Fred's wife died, if he needed someone to accompany him to a wedding, he would ask me. We danced so well together that at one wedding the band leader told us how much the band members enjoyed watching us. Years ago when our parents and two other couples would visit every Saturday night, Fred, his sister, Margaret, and my brother and I would play together. Margaret and I are the only survivors and we're grateful for many fond memories.

As my 48th Christmas letter closes, I wish you all a joyous Christmas, Hanukkah, and New Year!

With all my love to all of you, Alida

# 49<sup>th</sup> Christmas Letter, November, 1998 (At Home)

My dear family and friends,

I come to Christmas every year wishing I could take a butter knife and spread the message of love, joy, hope, and peace around the globe. Too bad we can't send up a satellite that would release a love potion as it circles the Earth. So much for my Christmas dream!

This has been a rather different year, very busy but not exciting. So many people asked me where I was going to travel this year that I feel that I should apologize for not going anywhere! In previous years my travels have taken me to every place I ever really wanted to see, so I didn't have any strong desire to travel this year. It has been years since I visited my friends on their island in Lake Temagami, Ontario, and every year I think I will go back to that beautiful place but have not gotten there. I hate making them travel an hour by boat and another hour by car to pick me up in North Bay, even though they are so gracious when they do it. Maybe next year! One thing I do want to see before I can't travel are the redwoods in California.

Did you ever see a year go by as swiftly as this one? It seems as if every month had three days, the first, fifteenth, and last! It may have been because we had such a wonderful mild winter. When we're waiting for the cold and snow to go away it seems to take forever. Last winter I wore my boots only twice and my neighbor, Jim, used the snow blower only twice, and once it wasn't really necessary. I told him he must have gotten lonesome for it because most winters he is out there many times. The months were gone before you could make plans to do anything even if you wanted to travel.

At least I got to Grove City, Ohio. Some of you may remember my meeting Casey and his dad on the Madison bus in the morning. His dad would get off the bus to take Casey, then three, to a nursery school that was across the street from Legal Aid. After I got to know them, I offered to take Casey so his dad could stay on the bus and go right to work. Casey would have a second breakfast with me in the coffee shop and then help me make coffee and water plants in my office. That went on for about six to nine months and it was a real joy for me. Eventually Casey went to live with his mother and stepfather, and the separation was a jolt for both Casey and me. I kept in touch with him through the years. Early this year he phoned insisting I make no plans for June 4<sup>th</sup> because he wanted me at his high school graduation. Nothing would have kept me from being there! He is a great kid, but now I have to look up because he is over six feet tall. He is living with his dad in Florida and going to a college there. It was good to see his folks and his brother, Aaron, who has finished college and is doing very well.

In place of a vacation I made improvements on my home in which I've lived 64½ years! The last words my aunt said to me were, "Take care of the house," and I have. She willed the house to my brother and me, and when Walt died I became the owner. This year I got three new windows on the back porch, nine glass block windows in the basement, and kitchen linoleum. Next year I may have the house sided with vinyl. There goes another vacation! Why don't you move into a smaller place, people keep asking? I may have to someday, but I love my home which is so full of memories. It has beautiful light oak wood and other features you would never find in new homes. I have wonderful neighbors, stores are close, my church is near, and for one who only drives to church and back, I'm near a bus line, so don't count on my address changing!

Questions, questions! Another one I get all the time is, "When are you going to retire?" I don't know! I love what I am doing, and can't imagine staying home all the time and I would miss all the people I come in contact with everyday. The bus group is still going strong and we keep picking up more people. The group will be at my home again this Christmas. I would miss the people I work with and all the attorneys I talk to everyday. At 77 my health is still good so I guess I'll be here until I get a signal from God that it is time to go.

Let me tell you about some of the attorneys I have come to know so well. Those who get in trouble get all the publicity. I can testify that there are many more who deserve our respect. The attorneys at Legal Aid are some of the most dedicated you will find. The demand for our service is so great we can't possibly fill every request. There are attorneys in private practice willing to take cases on a volunteer basis, and it is those I talk to and ask for help. I can't thank them enough for their kindness, generosity, and willingness to give something back to the community. I should mention that there are many judges out there that started their careers at Legal Aid. Among them you will find Jose Villenueva and Chris and Tim McMonagle. When Judge Burt Griffin was Executive Director of Legal Aid, he thought it would be helpful to have a social worker on the staff, so I thank him for my being at Legal Aid since 1967.

I'm so grateful to all my friends for sharing their children with me. "My kids" are all doing so well and now their children are going to college. Of course the most famous is Drew Carey, whose rise to stardom has been phenomenal since he appeared on *The Tonight Show* with Johnny Carson in 1991. He is a great person and has not forgotten his roots nor his family. He bought his mom, Beulah, a lovely townhouse and is generous with his brothers. Not every star remembers family and friends as he has. He renovated his childhood home and added a pool and garage. I guess he hopes to live there someday!

What did I do all year? I was busy but can't report anything spectacular. I'm Chairman of the Board of Christian Education at church, still sing in the choir, and enjoy being God's "Neatnik!" I had t-shirts made for three or four other "Neatniks" who help me keep things tidy. In October my friend, Rita, came to Cleveland for her 60th high school reunion and stayed with me. She, Beulah and I worked together at the Federal Reserve Bank in the 1940's. We took a Lolly Trolley ride and visited the totally new Terminal Tower, now called Tower City. She was amazed at all the changes in Cleveland. All of you who have not been here for a while should visit and see what has been done. If only we could spend some of the money on our schools; maybe that will happen!

My environmental message is that we, unfortunately, have forgotten that we are part of nature and not separate from it. When nature is being destroyed, we too, are destroyed. What will our children have if greedy oil companies, developers, and politicians have their way? I wish I could have been on the shuttle with John Glenn to see the beauty of our planet from space!

As we approach Christmas and Hanukkah, I pray that it will be time for us to reflect on all the good we have been given in life. The gift of life itself should be a source of constant wonder and gratitude, and we have so little time to give back some of what we have been given.

May the light of the Christmas and Hanukkah candles light your way through the next year, and may you find joy in the little things that sometimes get forgotten.

With all my love to all of you, Alida

# 50<sup>th</sup> Christmas Letter, November 2, 1999 (At Home)

"Each second we live is a new and unique moment of the universe, a moment that will never be again." — Pablo Casals

My dear family and friends,

This 50<sup>th</sup> Christmas letter will be the last before we greet the year 2000, the end of the 20<sup>th</sup> century. The 21<sup>st</sup>, according to what I have read, will not start until 2001. It does make one a bit philosophical as we face those two zeros and think about all the seconds we have lived, and hope we have used them wisely. Who would have thought a couple zeros would cause so much fear and cost so much to fix. It amazes me that with all the experts we have, the fact that the year 2000 was near has eluded them. I, for one, have faith that we are not going to have all the disasters some have predicted for January 1<sup>st</sup>, but if there is some incident I'm sure we will survive.

The early part of the year was uneventful but I decided to have my home, in which I have lived 65 years, sided. Did you ever try to pick out a color for such a big project? I wanted a shade of green, but with every estimate I was given the same samples of blue, beige, white, and other uninteresting colors from which to choose. A beige/pink was the only different color I saw and I toyed with the idea of using that with a white trim and cranberry sills. It did occur to me that in sunlight I might have a pink house and would have to include pink flamingos in my yard! Thanks to Tom Ostromek who lives across the street, that idea got scuttled when he said he wouldn't want to look at a Valentine all year! Finally, an architect friend, Drew Sondles, referred me to Home Environments. Joe and Larry, the contractors, worked hard to find me a lovely moss green, and I decided to use a cream trim with hunter green sills. We all know one thing leads to another. I had not thought about the roof but was told it was in bad shape and the shingles should be replaced before the house was sided. Why not? I'm glad I was at work when three layers, including the original slate, were ripped off, boards repaired and new shingles pounded on. What a mess, but now it looks nice! Then there was painting, installation of a sensor light, and I had the driveway pressure washed. Between the drought and work on the house, the lawn needed help. Rich Nowak dethatched it, put new soil down along with so much seed I think we fed all the pigeons and other birds in Lakewood. Needless to say, this was my "vacation" for the year and then some. Why, some wondered, would I go through all this at my age? To me my old home is like a family member or an old friend. If you love them you take care of them. By the way, my neighbors are happy with the new look.

Life is always full of surprises. A big one came when the former President of the Cleveland Bar Association, Barbara Smith, called to tell me I was to be given the Liberty Bell Award at the Law Day Luncheon. I'm still not sure why I was given this prestigious award which "is given to non-lawyers whose efforts have positively impacted the legal profession." I love what I'm doing, enjoy working with so many great attorneys, and the award was icing on the cake. Is it any wonder why I am still working? I keep reading about women who are working at 90! Who knows, I might become one of them!

Church activities are a big part of my life. I wasn't going back to choir, but would miss it so much I returned for, as I've said before, one more year. As Chairman of the Board of Christian Education I maintain a love for that area of church work. I thoroughly enjoy being God's "Neatnik" and now have five others helping me check cupboards and drawers, things custodians don't do. Next year I will celebrate being a member of Lakewood Baptist Church for 50 years. Joining my church totally changed my life and gave it a new direction for which I will ever be grateful.

My concern for the environment is constant. I worry about how much of God's creation we are destroying each day. A former Interior Secretary, Cecil Andrus, said, "In some places, such as the Arctic Refuge, the wildlife and natural values are so magnificent and so enduring that they transcend the value of any mineral that may lie beneath the surface." I wish we could put environmental ads instead of beer ads in stadiums and arenas.

In September I attended two class reunions. The first was my 60th from Lakewood High. We had a great time with about 165 at the dinner. The sister of Will Scott, Jane, was there as a guest. At 80 she is still writing a column about Rock and Roll bands for *The Plain Dealer*. When she learned that I knew Drew Carey she arranged to call me at home. Wonders never cease. I, known for loving big-band music, was the subject of a small paragraph in a Rock and Roll column. Two weeks after that reunion, I was again meeting old friends at the 40th from CWRU's School of Applied Social Sciences. We had a luncheon at the new school and dinner that evening. We had about half the class there and it was thrilling to hear of all they have accomplished. It was a pleasure to have classmate Karechepone George stay with me for three days. He arrived after a 24-hour trip from Madras, India, where he was head of the School of Social Work, to find his reservation had not reached the hotel. He was glad for a quiet place where he could rest and get over the jet lag.

My only vacation was the first week of October which I took to celebrate my 78th birthday and to clean the attic and get rid of stuff up there. It was too hot to do that when they completed the siding. I started on my birthday, got something in my eye and spent three hours that evening in emergency where they discovered a scratch. I left the hospital looking like a pirate with a patch over one eye. I took it easy for a few days and then finished cleaning the attic.

Because we got a new computer system at work, I invested in Windows 98 so I could practice at home. My neighbor, Tom Ollie, purchased and installed it for me. I wish you could see the professional setup I have. At least it looks like I know what I'm doing. I can write letters, but there are many things still to be mastered. If little children can learn I guess we adults can also, but it's a challenge! I haven't tried email or the Internet yet. Maybe someday!

Every year there are cards saying we should get together. Let's try to do that this year. Call me or send me your phone number. If we don't set a date we will never get together, and it would be so nice to see many of you. My friends and neighbors mean so much to me. With the death of my cousin, Genevieve, this year I have only two members of my immediate family left, Janice in Florida and Genevra in Las Vegas. I've created a family because some of my women friends are like sisters and Jim McGrath, who helps me in many ways, is like a brother. Jim has lived next door about 61 years.

In the Family Circus panel I saved, two children are shown and one says, "Yesterday's the past, tomorrow's the future, but today is a GIFT. That's why it's called the present." The world is full of misery and sorrow, but it is also filled with much happiness and joy. As we think of Christmas gifts, perhaps we should think about the gift we have been given of experiencing all of life. As we approach the year 2000 let's resolve to use each second and each day we have to try to make our corner of the world a bit better.

May God bless your celebration of Christmas and Hanukkah and may the joy of the season be with you the year ahead.

With all my love to all of you, Alida

Chapter Eight

**Ten Christmas Letters
From 2000 to 2009**

# 51<sup>st</sup> Christmas Letter, November 7, 2000 (At Home)

My dear family and friends,

It's hard to believe this is my 51<sup>st</sup> Christmas letter. I never dreamed it would go on so long nor that so many of you would encourage me to continue it. Some of you have said "It wouldn't be Christmas without your letter." Some of you have suggested I write a book. The thought entered my mind but I don't know who would be interested in what I've done. I began sending about 40 letters and now get 800 made. I only mail about 400 and hand out the rest and save a few.

On this anniversary it seems appropriate to briefly recap the years. After graduating from Lakewood High in '39 during the Depression years, my first real job was at the Federal Reserve Bank starting on January 1<sup>st</sup>, 1940. In '46 I went to the Illuminating Company. I wanted to go to college but at 28 was told I was too old to go; that was the attitude in the 50's. After being in the choir two years, I joined Lakewood Baptist in '50 and got so busy I couldn't write a lot of letters so decided to write a letter at Christmas and had it mimeographed (remember that ancient device?) At a Lab School for church school teachers at Green Lake I was inspired to become a Director of Christian Education, and at 32 was a freshman at a Baptist college which is now part of Colgate Rochester Divinity School. A course in casework changed my direction and in '59 got my Master's in social work at CWRU. That year I was hired at the Family Service Association of America and was there until I joined the staff of The Legal Aid Society in '69. In '67 Judge Burt Griffin, then head of LAS asked Family Service to find a volunteer to start a pilot social service project. When I volunteered I never dreamed I would be there this long. One never knows what detours life will take.

In these 51 years you have shared so many life experiences with me. Beginning in '83 you traveled with me to Europe, Scandinavia, Canadian Rockies, National Parks out West, England, Hawaii and Alaska. You agonized with me on various home improvement projects; except for hiring the NRA to get rid of pigeons on my new roof, my home is in order. You learned of the joy I found in service at church while teaching, serving as Superintendent of the Church School 12 years, Deacon, Chairman of the Board of Christian Education, and being "God's Neatnik." This year I retired my voice after many years in choir. You shared my college days and work experiences. I've been glad to tell you how many great attorneys are out there helping people. I've enjoyed working with them and was tremendously surprised when I was given awards by the Cleveland Academy of Trial Attorneys in '90 and the Liberty Bell Award last year by the Cleveland Bar Association. For seven years you got reports on the progress my brother made building a Volmer Amphibian in our back yard. One Christmas I sent you a picture of it in the air. I took the picture while flying in a two-place coop with the canopy down. The pilot warned me not to lean over too far. It was no secret how much I loved all "my kids." My friends raised them and I enjoyed them.

They have all been successful but it was Drew Carey who made it big. For a long time his mother would say "Would you believe this?" What a thrill it was for me to be an extra on the show which is still being seen in re-runs. I'll always be grateful to him for a wonderful week in L.A. You shared sad times with me in the illnesses and deaths of all my immediate family and many friends. This year I lost my friend Dorothy whom I met in '46 and my cousin, Margaret. I heard it said that "a person never dies as long as there is someone who remembers them." What a comforting thought.

One of the best parts of Christmas is your sharing what has happened to you and yours with notes and pictures. My friends, whether neighbors, on the bus, at work, or at church — anywhere — are precious to me and have added so much to my life. Truly, friendship is a gift that we too often take for granted!

Now for this year! It started out quietly with no plans for the house or travel but it certainly picked up steam along the way. I am learning one is never too old for surprises. In July, my "English son," Barry, came with his two boys, 11 and seven. The week they stayed with me the house was full of laughter and the antics of Michael and Matthew. There were visits to Tower City, the Zoo, The Natural History and Crawford Museums, the Science Center and Omnimax Theater. I enjoyed it as much as they did. They visited another family for a week and were taken to Niagara Falls, so it was a great two weeks for the boys.

One Sunday my pastor asked me if I would be willing to have a minister from the Philippines stay with me for several weeks until she could find a place to live near the Cleveland Clinic. Daisy Basiliano arrived on September 18th and was with me three weeks. She is a hospital Chaplain but with the training she is getting she will be certified to teach others. She was a delightful house guest and I have a bed ready for her anytime she needs a change of scenery. She was in Dallas in the winter on a previous stay but has never experienced a Cleveland winter. She is petite so I was able to lend her an extra raincoat with an inner lining and will make sure she is prepared for her first experience with snow. So far we have had mild weather and I keep hoping, for her sake, it will continue that way.

Out of the blue I got a call in June from a friend at RTA saying she had given my name to a committee which was looking for someone who had a positive experience riding buses to be in an advertisement in *The Plain Dealer*. She knew about the bus group; this year there were 17 at my home for an evening of chatting and eating. Most were friends from the bus, along with their spouses. She didn't know that my grandfather was one of the first motormen when streetcars began and I had an aunt, uncle, and cousin who worked for the old Cleveland Railway. It became Cleveland Transit, and now for 25 years Regional Transit Authority. I thought an interview was all they wanted but discovered they also wanted a picture for their 25th anniversary ad. I told them they would be lucky if they got one good picture out of the two rolls of film they took; the photographer worked a miracle. I had no idea what they would do with all this and had a good laugh when I saw the ad, which covered ¾ of a page, with the heading stating I had run all over town with a 25-year-old. I assured people I don't live that interesting a life. I did it just as a favor not expecting anything but they gave me a free bus pass from July to December and all of 2001. I'll have to work until I'm 80 to use the pass as I hit 79 this year. Later I wrote to the new General Manager of RTA requesting a bus stop on the North side of Madison. Lo and behold, two weeks later my request was granted much to the delight of many other passengers and a few shocked bus drivers.

No Christmas letter would be complete without environmental messages. We don't realize that when we push other species to extinction, humanity is also threatened with extinction. We disrespect God when we disrespect His creation!

As I think about all that we have shared, I realize I have been given gifts that money cannot buy. I've had health, service to God, and you have added something special to my life! I pray that Christmas and Hanukkah will bring you joy and renew your many blessings. And now, I would like to leave you with this simple, but profound message:

"Somehow not only for Christmas but all the long year through, the joy that you give others is the joy that comes back to you." — Whittier

With all my love to all of you, Alida

# 52$^{nd}$ Christmas Letter, November 1, 2001 (At Home)

"We are all travelers in the wilderness of this world, and the best we can find in our travels is an honest friend. He is a fortunate traveler who can find many...They are the end and reward of life." — Robert Louis Stevenson

My dear family and friends,

For most of this year my life was uneventful. I thank God everyday for health which allows me to work at The Legal Aid Society everyday; allows me to continue to be active in church on the Board of Deacons, as "God's Neatnik" and President of Twidelphia; and allows me to enjoy so many wonderful friends. My 87-year-old house needed very little done but I did get gutter helmets so the leaves can now fall where they may. In May there was an article about the bus group in *The Plain Dealer* Sunday Magazine and I hit the gossip column in October because of flowers sent to me by Drew Carey and his family. It's a good thing this publicity doesn't go to my head!

Thanks to Tom Ollie who helped me, I got online and now have an email address. Send me your email address if you have one, though I don't have time to look at the computer every night. I've surprised myself and mastered the necessary programs at work, but there are things about computers I will never know.

My Philippine friend, Daisy, has returned to her homeland but while she was here would spend some weekends with me. Prior to her leaving she was with me three weeks in June and three-and-a-half weeks in August. I was glad to share my home with her and it took me a while to get used to being alone again.

The big event was the weeklong celebration of my 80$^{th}$ birthday. I still don't know how I got to be 80. Everyone has been so kind to me, I decided I wanted to treat them. If I could have rented the Public Auditorium I would have invited everyone I know at church, my attorneys, all the bus group, every neighbor, everyone at work, etc. But because I could get only 100 people into the party room at Sweetwater Landing in the Rocky River Marina, I did the next best thing. I had cake and punch on September 30$^{th}$ for everyone at church. On my birthday, October 4$^{th}$, I wanted to treat them at work because they treated me for my 70$^{th}$, but they wouldn't let me. The office was closed at 3:00 p.m. and there was cake, punch, balloons, purple mums, and lists of things that happened in 1921 taken from the Internet, plus songs from 1942. At my 70$^{th}$ I thought I was kidding when I said, "I think I'll work until I'm 80." At this party I said, "I think I'll work until I'm 90." Only God knows if that will happen!

Months before, I decided I was going to do it up right for my 80$^{th}$ and rented the party room at the Marina. I was a bit nervous hoping the party would go well and, from the response I got, it did. Hope you don't mind my sharing a bit of the party with you. When people die there is often a poster of pictures of the person from infancy to later life. Why wait until you die to do that? I went through family albums and found pictures of my parents, my brother, and the aunt who lived with us, and even a bare bottom baby picture of me taken by a professional photographer. My how times have changed! I told them it was the only porno picture they would ever see of me. There were pictures at various times of my life, pictures of friends, my brother's Volmer amphibian he built (I won't drive but flew in it when it had only flown three hours), and the 22-foot Colorado spruce tree I took to my favorite farm in Hanoverton, Ohio as a twig.

Background music was furnished by a couple who played the accordion and violin; they provided semi-classical and big-band era music. Two lovely bouquets were sent to the party room: white roses from Drew Carey and red roses from his mother and brother, Roger. His other brother, Neal, sent me a lovely basket at home and I got several other arrangements as well. The catered meal was delicious and there were hors d'oeuvres when people arrived. Lori and her mother, Cindy, decided I should be queen for the day and bought a beautiful pink feather boa and a lovely crown which added to the fun. Tom Ollie took a video of the entire evening and I will enjoy looking at it from time to time and remembering the happy event. I was delighted that Tom and "my kid," Susan, brought their three-month-old son, Philip. He was as good as gold all evening.

After the meal I explained the pictures on the poster and then told my guests I considered this my family reunion. Being alone except for two cousins, both out of town, I consider all my friends, whether at work, on the bus, in the diner, at church, my neighbors, and even my attorneys, my family. The Mosers in Hanoverton are kind of step-family and the Eilert family seemed like cousins. Other than that, just as a store in Lakewood is called Create a Cake, I created a family. At each table they got to know one another but I wanted everyone to know who was there and introduced everyone. After that my piano teacher read a poem and Dave McKissock from my church roasted me a bit. The party was over but I will always treasure the warm, wonderful feeling I had that night surrounded by "my family." This event reminded me of the following words of Marcel Proust: "Let us be grateful to people who make us happy — they are the charming gardeners who make our souls blossom." Thanks to all of you, for you have made my soul blossom! My wish for all of you is that one day you will have as happy an 80th week-long birthday as I had!

Adding to my birthday was a 12-day visit from "my kid," Tom Whitmer, from Arizona. He calls every few months to be sure I'm OK and when he learned I was having this party said he would like to be there and I was delighted to have him. It was like having a son with me and I missed him when he flew home.

At least once a year I visit "my kids" on the farm in Hanoverton (near Salem) and check on the majestic tree. They have purchased a new, more up-to-date farm, and assured me if they sell the old one they will have a clause put in that the tree cannot be torn down. I have seen to it that they can purchase a "twig" for the new farm. It is always so refreshing to be in the country enveloped by nature.

As I come to the end of this letter I thank God for all of you and your part in my life. None of us can predict what will happen in 2002, and after 9/11 we may not feel as secure as before. I intend to live life to the fullest knowing that God, who has brought me this far, will continue to be with you and me no matter what happens. As we celebrate Christmas and Hanukkah let's "Live well, laugh often, love much."

With all my love to all of you, Alida

# 53<sup>rd</sup> Christmas Letter, November, 2002 (At Home)

My dear family and friends,

When I was in the 8<sup>th</sup> grade we read the classic story, *The Maelstrom* (a famous whirlpool). A later assignment was to write a poem. With that story in mind I started the poem with the words, "Life is a whirlpool of trouble and joy which meet as the tides come in." I don't know how the rest of it went but remember the teacher feeling it was terribly deep for an 8<sup>th</sup> grader. Those words describe the past year which was full of sorrow and Joy. Let me share both with you in this 53<sup>rd</sup> Christmas letter.

In January I learned of the death of a favorite client I saw in 1968, my Tessie, I called her. We kept in touch all these years and I miss her. I'm so glad I had my 80<sup>th</sup> birthday party last October, especially for those who enjoyed what turned out to be their last happy party. By December Norman Roglin and Ann "Cookie" Jasko, friends for many years, were in nursing homes.

The month of March, 2002 I would like to have erased from the calendar. My dear friend, Beulah (Drew Carey's mother and my friend since 1941) died on the 15<sup>th</sup> after suffering from cancer. For the sake of privacy, there was no announcement in the paper until after Drew left Cleveland. My neighbors of 34 years, Dan and Dara Rosette, jolted me in January when they informed me they would be moving. I shed plenty of tears and am glad I wasn't home to see the moving van on "Maundy Thursday," the 28<sup>th</sup>. That night when I came home from church I learned my neighbor of 30 years, Elaine Firestone, had died the day before. For a week or two I was understandably depressed and decided getting old is for the birds because there are too many goodbyes. In May another friend of 68 years, Frank Zaffarano, died after months of dialysis. All of them were at my party, and I'm glad they were!

Later in the year I was saddened when a tree I planted at church in '83, and was so beautiful, was killed by someone who stripped all the bark off the trunk. Only a tree! For me a tree is like a person whose beauty and character are enhanced by age. It hurt to see the tree putting out branches at the bottom in an effort to stay alive. I will plant another in the spring and pray for whoever destroyed this one.

So it seemed as if the year would be a real bummer, but wait! The joy came late, but it came! I never prayed so hard as I did that I would get new neighbors who would be quiet (no loud music) and friendly. My prayers were answered. A young, single man of 25 purchased the house. Not only is he a nice person, but he has a wonderful family who have shared with me all the goodies from their garden in Portage County.

Early in August it was a real joy for me and the committee I chaired to plan a celebration honoring the 25<sup>th</sup> anniversary of our pastor's ministry with us. All our plans unfolded beautifully on October 13<sup>th</sup>. The worship service was followed immediately by the celebration in the sanctuary and then we had lunch. We furnished chicken, dessert, and beverage and everyone brought salads or vegetable of some kind. The turnout was great and the pastor was surprised when he got letters of congratulations from Congressmen Voinovich, De Wine, and Kucinich, State Representative Bryan Flannery and State Senator

Eric Fingerhut. The City of Lakewood proclaimed Oct 23<sup>rd</sup>, the day he was installed, "Dr. William G. Noyes Day." There were other greetings from the Cleveland Baptist Association and our headquarters in Valley Forge. A basket of cards and gifts were presented to him at the end, but during the celebration we gave him a book about lighthouses and a family certificate to a restaurant.

Another joy was sharing my home with our new associate pastor. Erin is to be the pastor for our contemporary service and also work with our youth. She should do well because she is vivacious and full of fun. She came on September 21$^{st}$ and stayed with me until her apartment was ready on October 7$^{th}$. The house seemed empty after she left.

Ten days after Erin left, my friend Rita, who worked at the Federal Reserve Bank with Beulah and me in the early 40's, came to Cleveland for her 64$^{th}$ class reunion, and stayed with me four days. We had a great visit and I hope she comes back next year. She always calls me Lee. That is one of only three nicknames I ever had. My Polish friends call me "Lidka" and in Canada someone couldn't remember my name and said, "Why don't you have an easy name like Fred?" And Fred it was with my Canadian friends!

The only traveling I did was on one of the last beautiful days in October when I went to see "my kids" on the farm in Salem, Ohio. A good friend, Peter, took me and, having grown up on a farm, he thoroughly enjoyed the memories it brought back. We went to the old farm in Hanoverton to see the Colorado spruce tree I planted 25 or 30 years ago. It gets more beautiful all the time. Peter said it must be 16 to 18 inches in diameter at the base and 30 feet tall. More trees of all kinds should be planted to help the environment.

I'm still working at The Legal Aid Society where there will be many changes. We bought the building which is near all the courts. There is going to be a lot of renovation, which will make working a bit difficult. Last year I said I would work until I'm 90, so I have only nine more years to go. I love being with people and would hate staying home, but I'll see what happens.

At the risk of sounding a bit preachy, I come to the end of this letter with a few insights I gained from my experiences this year. Don't put off doing things you feel the urge to do because if you wait it could be too late to make someone happy. Maintain friendships through phone calls, letters (if only a Christmas letter) because the older you get the more precious your friends become. When they are gone a bit of your history goes with them. Never give up hope because despite times of despair and sorrow there can be joy around the corner. Above all, treasure your faith, whatever your religion may be, because it is the one thing we have to cling to no matter what happens in our lives or in this crazy, love-starved world!

In the book, *A Love Worth Giving,* author Max Lucado tells that we can't give what we don't have. I worry about children who are growing up without love and how they will influence the world in the future. "We love, because He first loved us." (1 John 4:19) I know the love you have been given you will share with others at Christmas, Hanukkah, and always!

With all my love to you and yours, Alida

# 54<sup>th</sup> Christmas Letter, November 3, 2003 (At Home)

"Let us be grateful to people who make us happy — they are the charming gardeners who make our souls blossom." — Marcel Proust

My dear family and friends,

The beginning of the year was rather uneventful so I wondered if I should write a letter this year; however, it wouldn't seem like Christmas if I didn't keep in touch with you, and many asked me to never stop the letter, so get ready for my 54<sup>th</sup>. Every year brings changes and how I hate change. The Ostromeks, a family that lived across the street from me for 30 years, moved to a ranch-style home because stairs had become a problem. I still miss the Rosettes who moved last year and hope the few old neighbors left will remain.

Yes, I'm still working everyday and changes have taken place at The Legal Aid Society. LAS bought the building we have been in since 1977 and we are now going through all the throes of renovation with staff being moved here and there until the work is completed. Internal changes to make things more efficient are also being done and we hope that turns out well. I was pleased when the work I do was evaluated by a team of attorneys from other cities. The attorneys to whom I refer volunteer cases gave my program an excellent rating. One reason I'm still working is because I would miss the dedicated staff at Legal Aid and my private attorneys. I've had such a good working relationship with so many kind and generous private attorneys that I find it difficult to contemplate retirement!

The change I hated most was that the diner in our building, where I ate breakfast and lunch since 1977, closed. George turned it into a bar, decorated it nicely and hopes to reap some financial rewards. I will miss the many people I met there; some were much younger than I but we enjoyed one another and it's like old times when I bump into them now and then. Some friendships formed there have become lasting ones. The bar won't get my business but George and I will remain friends. Some things haven't changed. The bus group meets at my home once a year even though we don't see each other on the bus as often because of work changes. Each year one or two more people get added to the group. Being greeted by friends makes the bus ride so much more enjoyable.

The lives of "my kids" are changing happily. Elizabeth Kingsbury graduated from Lakewood High and headed to college; Matt Nelan got married; I had a bridal shower for Becky Hinshaw who married on October 31<sup>st</sup>; and there was a baby shower for Neil Nelan's wife, Kara. Do you remember Casey? I met Casey and his dad on the Madison bus and for six months I kept Casey, a three-year-old, with me until the nursery school opened each morning. It was located across from Legal Aid. The bond that formed continues and I received an announcement to keep a date open next year for his wedding. How could all my little kids have gotten old enough for all this? I'm sure parents ask that question often. Thank God for all of them who have enriched my life tremendously!

After about seven years of doing other things, I finally took a short trip to Maine in October to see Ginny, with whom I used to travel. Kathy Todd, a friend at church, arranged a nonstop flight to

145

Manchester, New Hampshire in a Continental Express plane and Ginny picked us up there, driving 1½ hours to get us. The weather was nice the few days we were in Ocean Park and we enjoyed walking on the beach and watching the waves roll in. The fall leaves were beautiful and Ginny drove us to Camden and Freeport where L.L. Bean is located. The only time it rained we were in Portland watching a documentary titled *Winged Migration*, which won an Academy Award.

I was surprised when "my kid," Tom, who lives in Arizona, said he had to use vacation time and wanted to come and help me celebrate my 82nd birthday. He came September 29th and while I was in Maine he drove to Chicago to see the Science Museum. For two weeks he spoiled me by driving me to work every morning and picking me up at night. He took my friend, Ruth, and me to dinner at Ferris' Steak House on my birthday. The weather wasn't too good on my birthday but the many flowers, cards, and phone calls warmed my heart and made it a very special day. My brother never liked birthdays because he would say it means you have one less year to live. I always felt they were special because we were given the privilege to live on this wonderful planet and a chance to do something worthwhile with our lives.

Our summer was wonderfully cool with just enough rain so I didn't have to water the yard once. Nine counties in Ohio weren't so lucky and were declared disaster areas because of flooding. I worried about "my kids" on the farm in Salem, Ohio. When I visited them they said they had too much rain but the crops were OK. Of course they took me to the old farm to see the tree I gave them many years ago. It was a twig then but is huge now. In a few more years it will be mammoth.

One of my big concerns as you know is the environment and the fact that it is being destroyed bit by bit. Giving money to environmental groups is one way I help but I also call congressmen when I'm concerned. It only takes a minute to look up their number in the phone book and leave a message with the receptionist. Politicians know that polls show most Americans don't want drilling in the Arctic Wildlife Refuge, but the administration has sneaked a rider onto the Energy Bill which would allow drilling. You can bet I called and told them what I thought of that! Thank God we live in a country where we can express our opinions!

In addition to environmental concerns, I feel so sorry for all those out of work, for the homeless, many of whom are mentally ill, and for future generations who will be paying for the huge debt that has been accumulated. Some time ago friends were visiting and had their three-year-old with them. We were discussing how we no longer talk about millions but trillions being spent. I remarked that they must think money grows on trees. The child immediately said, "I would like that tree." We still laugh about that and wish we had that tree.

When I was in the 4th grade, at the end of the year the children and teacher wrote in an autograph book which I still have. The teacher wrote, "God's in His Heaven, all's right with the world." I'm not sure who the author was, but wonder if he would write the second part of that quote now. No matter what, we must continue to hope that somehow, some way, peace will come to all parts of this world. Hanukkah celebrates the miracle of eight days of light and at Christmas we celebrate the birth of Jesus whom Christians believe brought light to the world. As we face a new year, let's all pray for the miracle of peace which would bring light to people everywhere.

My prayer for you is that you will have peace, love, and joy in your life in 2004.

With all my love to you and yours, Alida

# 55<sup>th</sup> Christmas Letter, November, 2004 (At Home)

My dear family and friends,

What a year! It was full of change, surprises, and joy. It started out slowly but certainly picked up steam and my date book was full every month. I began to wonder if I would get this letter written before Easter. The renovation of three floors at Legal Aid was completed and by June we were all back in one building. Packing and unpacking convinced me I was smart to remain in my home for 70 years. How do people stand moving all the time?

One of the biggest surprises of my life came when I received at letter from the Lakewood High Alumni Foundation telling me I was chosen to be in the Distinguished Alumni Hall of Fame for years of service to people as a social worker. I was inducted on May 26<sup>th</sup> and honored to have many close friends as guests at a special luncheon. They included my friend of 70 years, Ruth Hinshaw. Also present were Tim and Jan Hinshaw, Judge Burt Griffin, Lyonel Jones who is the Executive Director of Legal Aid, my pastor, Dr. Noyes, and Pam Carson from SASS at CWRU. I appreciated the many cards and flowers from friends, my church, and Legal Aid. I don't feel distinguished. I'm just the same old me!

The day I was inducted a classmate said he hoped someone would plan a 65<sup>th</sup> class reunion. I got two others to help and on September 11<sup>th</sup> 35 of us met in the Alumni Room at Lakewood High School. We had big-band music, letters from those who couldn't attend, phone calls typed and posted, and some memorabilia. The meal was catered and after lunch there was a tour of the enlarged high school. One could feel the warmth of friendship and everyone who came was glad we got together. We're looking forward to number 70 in 2009 — God willing!

Changes can be joyous and they can be sad. Dr. Noyes, pastor at the Lakewood Baptist Church (American Baptist) announced in May that he would retire September 26<sup>th</sup>. He was with us 27 years so it is like losing a part of one's family. I was asked to chair a committee to plan a farewell the end of September. I was so busy with both events I didn't have time to host a bus group party this year. A super committee of five with great ideas planned a catered picnic on September 24<sup>th</sup> so we could have a happy time with Bill and Martha and their daughter Jenni. After church on September 26<sup>th</sup> a reception was held and people in the community who knew Bill and Martha were invited. During the worship service we presented Bill and Martha with a lovely bowl and a love gift. We wish them many happy years of retirement, though they will no doubt find ways of being of service.

We had one more joyous occasion with Bill and Martha when Jenni got married in Frankfort, Kentucky on October 9<sup>th</sup>. She met Kurt at the Seminary they attended in Louisville. Jenni was only seven when her dad became our pastor and it was a thrill to have her preach the sermon his last Sunday with us. Kurt wore his kilt at the wedding and at the end of the ceremony put a matching scarf over Jenni's shoulder. She is now part of his clan! What a joy it was to have so many of "my kids" join the rank of the married. Six weddings and four showers kept me busy this year. Remember my Casey, the three-year-old I met on the bus? I did his dad a favor for six months by keeping him with me at Legal Aid until the nursery school across the street opened. The bond we formed will always be there. He is now 24 and married Carmen Rinella in New Philadelphia. Gail Shammo Bischof's wedding I'll always remember because of all the roses. Whether carried on top of three separate layers of cake or on the altar, they stood out because every color of rose was used. Henry Ward Beecher said, "Flowers are the sweetest thing God ever made and forgot to put a soul into." Those roses touched my soul!

"My Arizona kid," Tom, decided he would like to come again this year to spend a week with me in October to help celebrate my 83$^{rd}$ birthday. After moving into a new home he needed a week's vacation. While I worked he enjoyed exploring Cleveland where he spent a good portion of his life. I was so glad he drove me to see "my kids" on their new dairy farm in Salem, Ohio. They may sell the cows because while we pay a big price for milk, they make very little profit. I love the trip to Salem! Just getting away from the city and being in the country and communing with nature is refreshing. Of course we went to see my Colorado spruce on their old farm in Hanoverton, Ohio. It is magnificent and now so big even the White House couldn't transport it for Christmas. I should get a professional photographer to take a picture of it. We also visited my Romanian friend, Valentina, who enjoyed having Tom there. He treated my friend, Ruth, and me to dinner for my birthday. He calls every other week to be sure his "mom" is OK. Cards and flowers added to a great birthday!

People keep asking me who are these persons I call "my kids," so I decided I would explain. I never married but through the years my friends have shared their children with me. I've met others in the neighborhood. Casey on the Madison bus and Tom used to come from school when he was about seven to see his mother who was a typist at Family Service where I worked as a caseworker in the 60's. I've also enjoyed the three children of my brother's stepson. Two are now in college. God keeps bringing new kids into my life, such as Danny who joined my church and calls me his "church mom." I'm looking forward to his December wedding. I counted one day and came up with about 25 I call "my kids." I love every one of them and my life would have been very dull without them. Love is the best thing in the world to share!

I close this 55$^{th}$ Christmas letter thankful for each of you who have been a meaningful part of my life. Both Hanukkah and Christmas celebrate joy and hope and I pray you will have some of both in the New Year. Let's hope that somehow our country and the world will be restored to a state of normalcy. Let's look forward to being healthy and happy and enjoying the company of our friends.

With all my love to you and yours, Alida

# 56<sup>th</sup> Christmas Letter, November, 2005 (At Home)

My Dear Family and Friends,

I started this letter on Columbus Day October 12$^{th}$, from the emergency room at Lakewood Hospital. A storm window somehow got loose and came down slashing my middle finger. I was bored and decided I might as well start my 56$^{th}$ Christmas letter. What else could I do while waiting five hours to get seven stitches?

Little did I know that I would be back in the emergency room on November 4$^{th}$, and finish this letter from a hospital bed. I was walking to the bus at 6:15 a.m., tripped, fell very hard on cement. I could not get up. Suddenly two people appeared (I call them angels). They were sitting on their porch, at that early hour, and saw me fall. They got me up and walked me back to the house. At this moment I have no idea how long I'll be out of work, though I do hope to do some work from home. The doctor will operate on a cracked knee cap November 9$^{th}$. I'm hoping for good results. I was treated like a museum piece when word got around to all the nurses that they have an 84-year-old who had never been in the hospital before and is still working every day. I'm disgusted because I'm not used to being dependent and my first experience with a bed pan is one I could have done without. I'm wondering what God wants me to learn from all of this. Thanks to everyone who has made my room look like a florist and card shop, and offered help.

Other than the above, this was a year of anniversaries, searches, endless meetings, and successful endings. The Legal Aid Society and Lakewood Baptist Church were twins. We both had 100$^{th}$ anniversaries and we both conducted searches for key personnel. Legal Aid searched for an Executive Director to replace C. Lyonel Jones who was at LAS 39 years, and my church searched to find a minister to follow Dr. William Noyes who shepherded us for 27 years. Legal Aid's anniversary was a gala event with Hillary Clinton the guest speaker. Whether you like her or not she had a wonderful speech praising Legal Aid for all it has done. I loved seeing so many of my wonderful attorneys there. The LBC anniversary which I chaired was a big success. Everything the committee planned turned out well, including banners, bookmarks, catered dinner, and reception. Legal Aid found a new Director in Colleen Cotter and at LBC we are at this moment nearing a choice for our new pastor. We had a retirement party for Lyonel October 28$^{th}$. He was a kind, caring boss.

"My Kids" continue to be a source of joy to me. Casey drove from New Philadelphia with his three-month-old son, Carter — an adorable baby. Hard for me to believe Casey is a father! "My Arizona kid," Tom, continues to call me every other week to be sure I'm OK and to have a chat. In August I visited Roger Carey and his family. Much to my surprise Drew showed up with his manager. They came to see a pre-season Brown's game. Drew's hobby is taking pictures of sports figures. It was so good to see Drew, Roger, and his family. I thank God for all "my kids" who make this world a better place.

Maine came to me when Ginny Noyes came to our 100$^{th}$ anniversary at LBC. She treated me to the show, *March of the Penguin*, and to dinner. I miss traveling with her but having her friendship for a day to celebrate my 84$^{th}$ birthday was a real gift.

Thanks to "my bus daughter" Christa and her husband Rich I got to see my "stepfamily" and beautiful tree in Hanoverton, Ohio. If the tree gets any bigger the man who now owns the farm will be able to sell tickets to see it. Christa and Rich also took me to see Ruth Seavers, a "step-relative" in Cherry Tree, PA, near Titusville. I hadn't seen her for 50 years or more. It was a delight to see her again. Through her niece Clara Bell, we arranged a surprise visit which caused Ruth, now in her 90's, to shed tears of joy.

This year I was glad to be an Ohioan. We escaped so many natural disasters, many of which we have brought on ourselves by destroying marshes and wetlands, cutting down trees causing mudslides, and not heeding the warning of scientists that global warming needs to be addressed. Our environment needs more protection. I didn't do a lot this year that was exciting but I enjoyed everything in which I was involved. In the midst of the business there were interludes that brought me joy and happiness. As we celebrate Christmas and Hanukkah, I pray that in the coming year you will, despite the mess the world is in, find ways to make your corner of the world better. May God be with us!

With all my love to you and yours, Alida

# 57<sup>th</sup> Christmas Letter, November, 2006 (At Home)

My dear family and friends,

It is a year since I tripped, had my knee cap removed and spent 12 days in the hospital. I always dreaded the thought of being in a hospital overnight but the nurses and aides were all so nice I almost hated leaving. I was released November 16<sup>th</sup> and stayed with "my kid," Gayle, until December 15<sup>th</sup>. She made me so comfortable, and by the time I went home I walked on my own. Our standing joke is that she had just bought a new couch and she had to make me go home so she could sit on it. I went back to work January 3<sup>rd</sup>, much to the surprise of the staff at Legal Aid. Beginning in February I had about 16 therapy sessions at Lakewood Hospital with Jeff Sord who was so patient and caring or I might not have done so well. Will always have trouble with steps but I can walk, am healthy, am blessed. Thanks again to all of you who were so supportive and helpful in many ways.

God always provides. I couldn't take the bus and wondered how I would get to work. A friend Ernie Vagi called, said he takes his wife to work downtown every day and they would pick me up, and he and Kathy have done just that. My neighbor, Jim, uses my '72 Buick Skylark, which I only drove to church and back, and he picks me up at work.

In October, 2004 a Search Committee at Lakewood Baptist Church began looking for a new pastor. We met every week and finally in December, 2005 the Committee invited Jonathan Glass Riley to preach at a nearby church after which we interviewed him and met his wife, Saskia, (Dutch name) and their little son, Jaxon. We voted unanimously to call him and he began serving our church in February. He is dedicated, creative, fearless in trying new things, has excellent sermons, and loves candles which he uses often. He has found ways of getting members involved and wants the church to be even more involved in the community. I believe he has a bright future!

This may sound strange to put in a Christmas letter but I've had long distance calls from friends who I might have missed when I sent my letter. Though I'm very healthy, things do happen. If you don't hear from me and want to check, you can always call my church at 216-221-4005. You can see I never forgot the Scout motto of "Always Be Prepared." That motto has served me well all my life.

This was an uneventful year but I won't forget getting an email from "my kid," Drew Carey, inviting me to the ballpark the night they had Drew Carey Bobblehead Night. His brother Neal flew with Drew from California and his brother, Roger, was there with his wife and three children. It was good to have "my three Carey kids" together. Drew's two business managers, his agent, his assistant, and his girlfriend were also there, as was Senator Voinovich, his wife, daughter, and her family. I didn't see much of the ball game; we were all so busy talking. It was a fun night. I saw no cameras but got calls from friends saying they saw me on TV wearing my baseball cap standing with Drew. He is now into sports photography and already had one of his photographs in Sports Illustrated. He didn't use his real name because he didn't want that to influence choices a magazine would make. Anything Drew does he does well!

Several things brought me joy this year. "My Arizona kid," Tom, stayed with me a week to celebrate my 85th birthday. I worked because Tom had a few places to go, but one day we went to the old farm in Salem, Ohio to see those I love there and to see my mammoth Colorado spruce tree. He couldn't wait to get a pizza at Peppers and ice cream at Malley's. He wishes both would open a place in Arizona. Tom's son, Jeff Whitmer, was chosen to be on the *Wheel of Fortune*. The show will air December 26th and you can then find out how well he did. Tom and family went to see the show taped.

"My kid" Gayle's happiness made me cry with joy. While I stayed with her, her dad passed away and I was glad I was there so she wasn't alone. Her parents were friends of mine since '46. Norm was a great ballroom dancer and I treasure the times I danced with him. Despite her grief, Gayle always looked happy when the phone rang and it was her high school sweetheart, Tom. I told her I had a feeling something was going to come of this and she should go for it. Life is too short not to be happy. They both had married, had a boy and a girl, and now because of death or divorce they were free. They had never forgotten their first love. They are going to be married in California, which is near both their daughters so it looks as if I will be flying in March for a St. Patrick's Day wedding in Pasadena. When I met Tom I said I wasn't going to call him Tom but "At Last." I found music to that World War II song which I copied for them. He is a Professor at Northwestern University and Gayle has a Master's in teaching. They are so happy and I'm happy for them, but a bit sad because Gayle will be living in Evanston, Illinois and I'll miss her.

I'm looking forward to the joy of two of "my kids" becoming parents. Tim's daughter, Becky, will make me "Great-Great-Aunt Alida" in December. I can remember when Tim was born, and it's hard to believe he will be a grandfather. Can't be when I still feel like 30! My "newest kids," Danny and Katie, will be proud parents in April and are looking forward to all the new experiences that will bring. How empty my life would be if I didn't have all "my kids" and the joy of sharing so much with them.

I'm still working every day, enjoy what I do and love talking with my attorneys in private practice who are so kind in taking volunteer cases. I'd miss them and the Legal Aid staff if I retired. I truly believe that working keeps me healthy. I need to be with people and would go crazy just sitting at home. Activities at church keep me busy. Currently I'm a deacon and Hospitality Chairperson. Joining my church changed my life and everything I've done for the church these 56 years has been a thank you for all God's blessings. I'm thinking of going back to choir but am not sure I will.

Another year is almost history and a troublesome year it was with unrest all over the world. Thank God that is tempered by the beauty around us: flowers, trees, the songs of birds, pets, which give so much love, and even the little squirrel banging on my door asking for peanuts. Nature is a healer so let's do what we can to protect it. Best of all, we have the joy of our faith in God which gives us the ability to see good amidst the storms of the present and gives us hope for the future.

We can offer Christmas no more than that which we have already received: Love for others to match God's love for us; Patience with others' failures to match His patience with ours; Striving for peace in every relation to fulfill His promise of peace on Earth. I pray my Jewish friends will have a happy Hanukkah and my Christian friends a joyous Christmas and all of you a safe and blessed journey in 2007.

With all my love to you and yours, Alida

# 58<sup>th</sup> Christmas Letter, November 1, 2007 (At Home)

My dear family and friends,

Every year on January 1<sup>st</sup>, I tell someone that the next thing we know it will be Christmas. It seems time goes by that fast. It's hard to believe I am writing my 58<sup>th</sup> Christmas letter. This has been a year of celebrations I'm happy to share with you.

In March I had the joy of planning a baby shower for "my kids" Katie and Danny Ezell. Forty women from the church came and it turned out as beautiful and joyous as I hoped it would. On April 26<sup>th</sup> we celebrated the birth of baby Grace, and for the first time I visited a maternity ward and felt honored to hold Grace when she was only six hours old. She is adorable and I can't wait to see her walk.

On March 15<sup>th</sup>, three of us flew to California to celebrate the March 16<sup>th</sup> wedding of "my kid," Gayle to her high school sweetheart Tom, whom I nicknamed, "At Last." Only 16 of us were there, seated outside at the lovely campus of Cal Tech where Tom's daughter is a student. We all enjoyed the wedding which was informal but meaningful, with Gayle and Tom exchanging tiny loons (loons mate for life). A delicious catered meal followed at the campus. The next morning we flew home. I got a cab at the airport, and went to a wedding anniversary celebration for Barbara and Dave McKissock. What a wonderful few days!

The epidemic of happiness continued because Gayle's son Rod married Teri in Vegas on July 7<sup>th</sup>, 2007, and Tom's daughter married in August. Gayle was busy making bridal gowns. She and Tom now live in Wilmette, Illinois, and are divinely happy. He still teaches at Northwestern University and she wants to continue sewing and maybe teach sewing to others.

Celebrations continued with the news that Gayle's daughter, Erin, is expecting a baby in April. I was thrilled to learn that Drew was selected to host *The Price Is Right*. This is most certainly a reason to celebrate. Ratings have been good — naturally!

Busy is my second name these days. I'm still working every day and enjoy conversations with all the wonderful attorneys who take volunteer cases. If I mention the word "retire," they tell me they want me to keep working. At church I'm on Homebound Communion and Visitation Committees, and Coordinator for the Hospitality Commission, and Twidelphia, a social group. Jonathan, our pastor, works so hard and surprises us with new programs and worship experiences. He was in art and theater before the ministry and his creativity is evidenced in bulletins which are never the same. His love of candles and beauty enhance the worship service. We love his wife, Saskia, and their two-year-old son, Jaxon.

I decided to renew my social work license for two more years and so far have taken four of the five required courses and enjoyed them immensely. At home, after much thought, I decided I couldn't stand my faded carpeting any longer. Now I am enjoying a plush, deep red raspberry which brightens the house and my spirits. The installers were happy with the color as they are tired of working with white and beige which are currently popular.

In October I celebrated my 86th birthday. I can't thank everyone enough for the cards and flowers. For a week I had one surprise after another and was so grateful for all my friends. The biggest gift was a visit from "my kids" in Hanoverton and Salem. I did get to see my Colorado Spruce tree, which must be 30 feet high, when I visited them in the spring, but for years wanted them to come to my home. Bob, who was born on my 19th birthday and is now on dialysis and oxygen, wanted to keep his promise to visit. So, on October 14th he, his wife, Cindy, and his siblings, Linda and Johnny, made the trip to my place and we had a great time together. Wish Don could have come. I have such fond memories of visiting their mother and grandmother when I was little and am so glad this third generation continues to value our friendship.

Cleveland celebrated many victories of the Cavaliers and Indians. We had high hopes that they would go the distance and come home with the big prizes, but we rejoiced that they got as far as they did. There is always next year! I was around to see the Indians win the World Series in 1948 and feel sorry for those who are still waiting for the same thrill.

They say most people have four or five really close friends as they get older. People you grew up with and know your history are invaluable friends. This year we lost Lillian Roglin Thomas, so my friend of 73 years Ruth Hinshaw and I are the last of that group. A man named Arthur Gordon said, "Death is simply putting out a candle because morning has come." That is a nice saying but as one gets older there are too many candles being put out.

I'm so glad Al Gore got the Nobel Prize. If people think he is wrong about global warming they should live in Georgia with a water shortage due to drought or be a polar bear or penguin that may become extinct because of melting ice in the Arctic. Someone said the next war will be over water. We should pray that all countries will try to do something to help Mother Nature. God created us to protect and not destroy all His wonderful creations.

Some of you know I have a '72 Buick Skylark which my neighbor, Jim McGrath, keeps in perfect condition. It is a classic which so many want to buy or just admire. Jim picks me up at work every night. On the way home on October 26th a young girl, 18, suddenly swerved and my car was hit. The police and firemen felt as bad as I did to see such a beautiful car damaged. They used a crowbar to lift the left fender off the tire so we could drive home. Thank God nobody was hurt! I hope it can he restored to its original beauty. I keep saying I can only compare it to someone punching a hole in a lovely Van Gogh painting. I have forgiven the girl and try to remember a quote given to me years ago: "Forgiveness is the perfume the trampled flower casts upon the foot that crushed it." Now to deal with insurance carriers; but, "this too shall pass."

A minister reminded me that in life we look back and regret "The Word Spoken, Time Wasted, and Opportunity Lost." If that is true for us in 2007, let's pray that we do better in 2008. We're living in scary times. I pray that God will keep you safe, well, and provide you with whatever it is you really need. At this special time of the year may my fellow Christians rejoice in the blessings and promises of Christmas, and may my Jewish friends celebrate a peaceful and joyful Hanukkah!

With all my love to you and yours, Alida

# 59<sup>th</sup> Christmas Letter, November, 2008 (At Home)

My dear family and friends,

It has occurred to me for several years that I have more friends than family. All my immediate family, including aunts and uncles, are deceased. So are all my very old friends, except for Dorothy in California, whom I met in the 1$^{st}$ grade 82 years ago. I also have two cousins in distant cities. I'm grateful for the Mosers, Ezells, Hinshaws, and Scholls, who treat me as if I am one of them. I'm also grateful for my church family, my Legal Aid family, my private attorneys, friends, neighbors — all who have been a special part of my life. I thank God everyday for sending me all "my kids." I'm now called mother, great-great-aunt, and even grandmother by my 20 kids! Or is it 27? I've lost count. The biggest Christmas gift is having all of you in my life.

Having mentioned "my kids," you can imagine my year was full of joy as I attended baby and wedding showers and two weddings. There was the birth of Cash Pruitt in Hawaii and Isaac Walker in Iowa. I had the honor of holding baby Luke Ezell six hours after his birth and held Sydney Lowe shortly after her birth. Then there was the first birthday party for Luke's sister, Grace, and Luke's christening. So much new life, new hope, and joy! Can you imagine how many sleepless nights there were in all those families? Love conquers all!

"My kid," Gayle, who married her high school sweetheart, Tom, last year, wanted me to see her new home in Wilmette, Illinois. For 10 years I traveled to Europe, Norway, Alaska, Hawaii, and other places in America, but I'm not too keen about flying now. Gayle came to Lakewood for the baby shower for Sydney and arranged for me to fly home with her and Tom. What a lovely visit! We toured Chicago where I went to college in '53 through '57. I couldn't believe the transformation in that city! I've never seen so many tall buildings in one place and they're building more even higher. We visited the exquisite Bahai Temple in Wilmette which I would urge everyone to see if in the area. It is one of the most beautiful ornate buildings I've ever seen! No wonder it took 30 years to build. The environmentalist in me enjoyed sitting on the deck at Gayle's home and watching all the birds which emptied five feeders in the few days I was there. I came home so happy because they are so delighted to be together at last!

One great thing about this year was that "my kid," Drew Carey, was honored by replacing Bob Barker on *The Price Is Right*. I'm so proud of him and his deceased mother would be saying, "Can you believe this?" I relish all the times people have told me how much they like him. One person told me she feels happier after the show because he is so nice to people. Drew joined the Cleveland Orchestra at Blossom Music Center and did humorous readings from Shakespeare. I didn't get there but heard nothing but good things about his performance. Anything Drew does he does well. His brothers, Neal and Roger, are bright wonderful men, but being in the limelight is not for them.

Last year I told you about my 1972 Buick Skylark being hit by an 18-year-old on October 26<sup>th</sup>. It finally came home looking like new October 9<sup>th</sup>, 2008. It took a while to find parts but "my kid," Tom, found the fender, fender pan, and core support in Arizona. The bumper came from California and the grill from Illinois. Classic Connections on Scranton Road did the work and I would highly recommend them if you ever need excellent repairs. John was so nice to work with and even took the car for inspection. I suspect he enjoyed driving it so he even brought it to my home.

Once or twice a year Christa and Rich Scholl take me to Salem, Ohio to see "my kids" there. It brings back memories of when I was a little girl and we would visit their grandmother in Lisbon about once a month and later their mother and dad in Hanoverton, Ohio. I love the country and enjoy getting away from the city for a day. Of course I make sure to go to their old farm in Hanoverton to see my Colorado spruce tree which the Mosers, Beulah Carey, and I planted as a twig 25 or 30 years ago. Minerva loved watching the birds fly in and out of the tree. I finally met the new owner and was delighted when he said he loves the tree and, though it was a job, he managed to get Christmas lights on it. It is so tall he could have used a helicopter. He will cut down a tree next to it so nothing will deter its continued growth.

I've been a member of my church 58 years and glad I still have the energy to be a deacon, in charge of hospitality, etc, etc. Our pastor, Jonathan, has been with us almost three years and is full of creative ideas. His sermons are interesting, challenging, full of surprises, and no one falls asleep!

This year I was at Legal Aid 41 years. I still love what I do in finding attorneys to take volunteer cases. Don't ever say anything negative about attorneys to me because we have some of the best at Legal Aid and the private attorneys who take volunteer cases deserve nothing but accolades. The Legal Aid attorneys working with a tremendous number of foreclosure cases and training other attorneys who are willing to take them on a volunteer basis also deserve praise for all the work they have done in this recession. I've enjoyed getting acquainted with all the new attorneys on the foreclosure panel.

"My Arizona kid," Tom, came to help me celebrate my 87th birthday. He loves Peppers pizza and Malley's sundaes. One day while in his car I used my cell phone. It must have slipped out of my pocket and we couldn't find it. Tom went out one night and came back with it. The battery was low, it beeped often, and the noise led Tom to it. I never heard of a cell phone giving clues to its whereabouts. We had a good laugh.

Soon we'll celebrate Christmas and Hanukkah. How did they sneak up on us? Do you remember when you were little and you thought all the holidays would never arrive for us to enjoy? Then we got older and now wonder how they got here so soon and we're not ready. The anticipation we had as children is gone. My mother always said the older you get the faster the years go and she was right. When I was little you didn't hear carols or see decorations until after Thanksgiving. I wish we would get back to that. I remember making something for my mother in school, wrapping it in tissue paper, and she loved it as much or more than the diamonds advertised today. Ah, memories!

As I come to the end of my 59th letter I would ask, if you are a praying person, to please pray for our country, our new president, and for all those suffering because of loss of jobs. Where are they going to find work?  It seems as if they will have to move to China or some other country. It would be easy to get depressed but we must have faith that somehow things WILL get better, after all, GOD IS IN CHARGE!

Walt Disney said, "All our dreams come true if we have the courage to pursue them." May your dreams come true in 2009 and may you know the love of family and friends — the greatest gifts of all!

With all my love to all of you and yours, Alida

# 60<sup>th</sup> Christmas Letter, November, 2009 (At Home)

**A YEAR TO REMEMBER!**

My dear family and friends,

This 60<sup>th</sup> letter could be three pages long. This year has been BUSY, HAPPY, AND FULL OF SURPRISES!

At the end of 2008 I was asked to do two things: I) Write the Alumni Annual Day of Prayer Service for BMTS. It was due early in 2009 in order to be mailed to 300 in April. 2) Someone who attended the Lakewood High class of 39's 65<sup>th</sup> class reunion asked me if I would plan a 70<sup>th</sup>. Two BIG assignments!

I agonized over what to write for the Prayer Service but finally decided to share how I feel every decision I made was really God shoving me to where He wanted me to be — helping people! I did things I never dreamed I would do. After 14 years in industry I went to college at the age of 32 (unheard of in 1953) to be a Director of Christian Education. A course in Casework changed that. At age 38 I got a Master's in Social Work from CWRU-SASS. In 1967, after years counseling at Family Service, I volunteered to start a pilot social service project at Legal Aid where I did nothing but counseling for 10 years. I was asked to take over the referral work in '77, so for 32 years have located volunteer attorneys I call "my attorneys," who have been so kind and caring. No wonder I love them as I do my Legal Aid attorneys and staff. UNBELIEVABLE! I HAD TO BE SHOVED!

The response to a letter about a 70<sup>th</sup> class of '39 reunion was more than I expected. January 1<sup>st</sup> through June 13<sup>th</sup> was full of planning, phone calls, post cards, and buying everything from tablecloths to pots of purple and gold flowers. Some flowers were planted in the yard, and a couple balloons were displayed on the porch. What a joy it was to have at our age (then 87) 22 classmates and nine guests/spouses or grown children. They enjoyed being in my home for three hours. I've been here 75 years, so it reminded them of the homes they lived in when they were young. A friend of mine was happy to help and made sure everyone had beverage and snacks. Channel 8 took pictures of the reunion and interviewed me. We were on the 6 o'clock and the 10 o'clock news. I said thanks to the TV when the anchor said, "She doesn't look 87," but everyone there looked great. At 5:00 p.m. we went to Pier W for a luscious dinner and even sang our alma mater song there. I prayed that they would all like what I had planned and they did; in fact, some suggested I plan a 75<sup>th</sup>. Who knows? We'll only be 92 then. As I left Pier W I had tears in my eyes and said "It's over." I must thank all of you who sent "Thank You" notes and pictures. I got home that night to find my friend had the house in order. What a gift!

Of course there were the other happy times celebrating Gracie Ezell's second birthday, brother Luke's first, Sydney Lowe's first, and the birth of Alexus Hinshaw. Graduation parties were held for Cindy Ellsworth and Nick Vagi on July 25<sup>th</sup>. On August 1<sup>st</sup> the wedding of Megan Carstenbrock took place in Chicago. On August 30<sup>th</sup> I attended Hannah Gray's wedding at my church, and two hours later attended Todd Hoskin's wedding near Ravenna.

I celebrated 59 years as a member of Lakewood Baptist Church (American Baptist) where I have been busy since I joined. Years of choir before I lost my voice were a joy! Teaching church school, being on Boards (deacon now), in charge of hospitality with some wonderful women helping, I can never repay what the church has done for me!

In October I celebrated my 88th birthday. I can't be that old because I still feel like 30. It couldn't have been better and I never felt so loved. Three beautiful vases of flowers and a planter, cards, and long distance calls were so appreciated. "My Arizona kid" came for 10 days. While I worked he traveled to Columbus and nearby places. After church on October 4th, at which I had cupcakes for refreshments after the service, Christa, Rich, Tom, and I went to Salem, Ohio. I always love that trip in the country and being on a farm. Most of the family was there including a new baby, Caroline. As usual I took some German potato salad and KFC and they had a cake for me. We missed Bob who was born on my 19th birthday. He died this year after much illness. Of course we went to Hanoverton to see the Colorado spruce tree I planted 25 or 30 years ago as a twig and is about 30 feet tall now. A great 88th finale was Monday when Katie, Tom, Danny, his mother and grandmother, and I had dinner at Danny's home. It was so nice to be with the children. The chocolate ice cream cake with real cake added was a real treat.

One big surprise made me realize ESP is for real. FORTY years ago one of my clients happened to be a minister. After months of counseling he got a teaching certificate and followed his wish to be a drama teacher. He took a job in a junior college in Kentucky. I knew his wife and three children went with him but that was the end of my contact. A few months ago he came to mind and out of curiosity I went to Google and found the name, but the description didn't fit. I figured that was the end of that. TWO WEEKS LATER my phone rang at work and a voice asked if I was sitting down. I said "No, but I will." Good thing I did. It was my client who found me at Legal Aid by going to Google. He said he had wanted to find me and let me know how much I had helped him. How rewarding for a social worker! When a church needs him, he still preaches but is now running and producing plays for a Drama Theater in Ohio. He e-mails me and hopes to get to Cleveland to have lunch. I'm glad I lived long enough to be amazed by ESP!

The next surprise — I surprised myself. I always said I would work until I was 90 or die, whichever came first. I can't believe I'm doing this, and have very mixed emotions, but have decided to officially retire as of December 31st of this year. As much as I truly love what I am doing and will miss "my attorneys" and my Legal Aid friends, I have come to believe God is shoving me once again. I am giving two months notice to give the agency time to find a replacement. I am also willing to continue working as a volunteer until they find one, or to help a new person until that person is comfortable with all that has to be done and known. It will take time to get used to not working, but I will not be a couch potato. In the 61st letter next year I'll let you know where I've been shoved this time.

My BIG surprise came October 29th when, at a reception for attorneys, I was given an award for "dedication to volunteer attorneys and Legal Aid clients." It was engraved on a beautiful vase. I was shocked, nearly speechless, and could only say "Thanks," which wasn't enough. As I said in an email to the staff, I've had other awards but this was special because it came from Legal Aid. The kind words from the staff the next day did make me cry. What a wonderful way to end 42 years of doing what I loved to do at Legal Aid!

I have been so blessed and I pray, as the holidays approach, that the year ahead for you will be rich with blessings as you "Live well, Laugh often, Love much!"

All my love to all of you and yours, Alida

Chapter Nine

**Five Christmas Letters
From 2010 to 2014**

# 61<sup>st</sup> Christmas Letter, October, 2010 (At Home)

**THE YEAR OF TRANSITION**

My dear family and friends,

It takes a while to get used to being retired after working from 18 to 88, with six years of college in between. I must begin this 61<sup>st</sup> Christmas letter with thanks to all who made my retirement such a special event. Channel 3 televised an interview with me by Dick Russ. The Metropolitan Bar Journal had a long article about my life and the work I did with volunteer attorneys whom I loved. I also received a framed Resolution of Congratulations and members of the Board gave a donation in my name to Legal Aid. I was overwhelmed with the wonderful party at Legal Aid. Some of my attorneys and a few friends were included. They had cheerleaders, a cake with my picture in frosting, a constant running film, flowers, gifts, and a microphone so guests could say what they wished to me. It was such a warm, fun night, filled with love and hugs, but I didn't cry.

December 31<sup>st</sup>, 2009 was "my first retirement." No replacement had been found so I volunteered for four months, three days a week, until April 30<sup>th</sup>, 2010 — which was "my second retirement." That day, when I said goodbye to the staff I needed a box of Kleenex. I thought I would get busy right away but took time to be a bit lazy. Did clean files and tossed a lot but have postponed writing and volunteering until 2011. I have enjoyed being able to have lunch with friends, actually read a few books, and am getting used to this new life. The HOT summer slowed me down a bit. I still miss being with people daily and all "my attorneys."

In January, Will and I were asked to do an Ethical Will for a patient at Deaconess Assisted Living. Talking with Dorothy about her life experiences was a real joy. The interview was eventually typed and given to her family who will have these wonderful stories and bits of wisdom from Dorothy to pass on to future generations. I will do another interview sometime in the future.

The month of July was sad. I knew Ginny, with whom I enjoyed so many wonderful tours, had cancer. I kept in touch with weekly letters and phone calls. She died July 24<sup>th</sup>. I hadn't gotten over that loss when I got a call on July 28<sup>th</sup> that my "first kid," Neal Carey, died of a heart attack that day. He was only 64! He had called me just two weeks before to make sure I was OK. I felt like a mother who lost a son. I'm SO GLAD Drew, now 52, has lost 84 pounds because I worried about him gaining weight. He looks great. Had lunch with Roger Carey (middle brother) and his wife and one of their daughters, and enjoyed that immensely.

In September we lost 93-year-old Viola Sewell, called "Nanny," who will be missed as will her lovely southern accent. She is with the God she loved.

At the end of September, the chair I was sitting on shook and I thought we had an earthquake. A neighbor informed me a huge branch on my maple tree had broken and was on my porch roof. I always said if I moved I wanted to take my bedroom and my tree because my tree kept me cool on the hottest nights. My house is 96-years-old so the tree is probably at least 90. It loved me as much as I loved it —

not a window nor a shingle was damaged. Another big branch is cracked so on November 2$^{nd}$ I will tearfully say goodbye to my tree. I already have made plans to get another, but I may not be here long enough to benefit from the shade it will eventually give.

"My Arizona kid," Tom, came for his annual October visit and stayed 10 days. He helped me celebrate my 89$^{th}$ birthday with dinner at Ferris Steak House. We enjoyed an evening with Danny and his family and I was treated to birthday cake and flowers. Being a railroad inspector Tom enjoyed a three-hour ride on the Cuyahoga Valley Scenic Railway, after which I introduced him to Sokolowski's University Inn in Tremont for lunch. He was amazed at the amount of delicious food they serve. Christa and Rich drove us to see "my kids" in Salem. It is always a joy to see them and I never leave without seeing my huge Colorado spruce on the farm they sold. Thanks to all of you who filled my buffet with cards, for all the phone calls, emails, and verbal greetings. I'm the luckiest woman in the world to have so many friends and "kids." I would be lost without all of you and my church family. "A friend is someone who reaches for your hand, but touches your heart." — Kathleen Grove

I'm so glad that I can still be busy at church. From the time I joined I have found joy in service, whether teaching, being Church School Superintendent for 12 years, or singing in the choir (wish I had my voice back), etc. I'm still at it with making sure potluck dinners are successful and I still go to classes. I just finished working at our bazaar, which helps many in the community find things they need for practically nothing. I pray I can continue to stay healthy so I can continue to serve. My schedule is getting full with church and social happenings.

In 2004 I was inducted into the Lakewood High Distinguished Alumni Hall of Fame. A nice honor but I felt my two neighbors across the street with whom I grew up deserved it more. These were truly two brilliant men. Frank helped create radar, which helped us win WWII, and he was given a Presidential Citation for his work. Secondly, Dan had a Ph.D. in Physics and was Dean of the Department at Iowa State University. There is a Scholarship Fund in Dan's name and a new building named for him. I bugged the Alumni Committee for six years to put them in the Hall of Fame posthumously. My greatest joy was seeing that done on October 14$^{th}$. Frank's son flew from California and accepted the award for Frank and I accepted the award for Dan, whose wife couldn't get here from Iowa. Their families are delighted that they have received their due recognition. It seems strange that three of us who lived on the same street are in the Lakewood High Hall of Fame: Dan from the class of '36, Frank from '38, and me from '39.

This has been a year of transition, grief, and joy, but as I come to the end of 2010 I thank God for all His blessings. No matter what happens I can't complain because I have had many years of good health, have been given strength through good and bad times, have loved my work helping people, loved the years at Legal Aid, loved "my attorneys," "my kids," and friends. Yes, I am content!

There is so much uncertainty in the world. Today we suffer political turmoil, wars, foreclosures, homelessness and joblessness. Saving 33 miners gave us a reprieve from all of this. One miner said that there were 34 in the mine — one was God! Both Christmas and Hanukkah remind us that God IS with us. Who knows what 2011 will bring. I pray when it ends we can say, "Thank you God — we made it!" Wishing you hope, love, and peace throughout the New Year!

With all my love to all of you and yours, Alida

# 62<sup>nd</sup> Christmas Letter, November 9, 2011 (At Home)

## THE BIG 90

My dear family and friends,

I usually have the letter ready to mail by Thanksgiving but here I am on November 9<sup>th</sup> just starting it. Despite resolutions, I'm coming to the end of the year realizing how much more I could have and should have done. Still haven't done the writing some friends want me to do. I will try to do better next year.

I've always said I think I was a cleaning lady in another life because I believe it makes life easier if we keep things organized. When I was Church School Superintendent for 12 years, the first thing I did was check cupboards and drawers. It appears that some feel you can't toss anything if it is in a church. My thinking is that there is no such thing as sacred junk. Unusable things got tossed to make room. I did the same at the beginning of this year and marked items we were able to put in our bazaar, which helped people because items got sold for a pittance.

Some of you may wonder why I give my Christmas letter to everyone. In the 4<sup>th</sup> grade I learned a life lesson. The teacher had girls put a boy's name on a Valentine. I put one boy's name on and then erased it and put another name. The boy whose name I erased was the only one that didn't get a Valentine. I never forgot the sad, hurt look on his face and how bad I felt. I will NEVER leave anyone out so whether they want the letter or not, they get one. This letter has a life of its own. I was shocked to learn it gets read at a book club, is shared with others and if I accidentally miss sending it to someone I get phone calls wondering if I am OK. Maybe part of the reason this simple, ordinary letter is accepted is because email is used so much. People are glad to get an old-fashioned letter. I know I am glad to get one.

For some reason I never found volunteer work, but believe God had a special plan. There are several families which include me as a family member and I'm so grateful to be a part of them. One is the family of "my kid," Danny. On July 13<sup>th</sup> Danny had a seizure and was life-flighted to the Metro Trauma Unit. I was so glad I was free to stay with his mother several weeks while Danny was in an induced coma. If Katie needed a babysitter we would spend a day with Gracie, almost five, and Luke, three. What adorable, bright children. "Aunt Alida" was happy to spend some time with them and wished I had their energy. If I never believed in God and prayer before, having witnessed Danny's gradual recovery would have made a believer of me. With the help of God and therapy he learned to walk, talk, and swallow again. He came home September 1<sup>st</sup>. He is still on medication, gets therapy, and needs plenty of rest.

I could be the old woman who lived in a shoe with all my wonderful "kids," but without giving birth. I have so many "kids" I love. I could write one letter about all of them. They know who they are. Life would be dull without all of them.

You may recall when I turned 80 I invited 100 for dinner at what I called a Family Reunion, followed a week later with a lunch for my church family. Why not do the same for my 90<sup>th</sup>? On October 2<sup>nd</sup>, despite it being a chilly, rainy night, all but four who were ill, arrived. My former piano teacher played songs of my era during appetizers. I had table assignments and those from Legal Aid and my volunteer attorneys I had at various tables so others would get to know them. The owners of Peppers Restaurant who have been so kind were there. A big surprise came when my former neighbor announced she asked a student from her belly dancing class to entertain us. She did a lovely dance and I invited her to stay for dinner. After we ate I said something about everyone there and then Dave McKKissock had a program in which he said something about my life. He put words to the tune of *Hello Dolly* and then gave the microphone to others who may have had something to say. I came home feeling humble and wondering how I could live up to all the nice things said. There was such a warm feeling in the room and I was so glad Tom came from Arizona and Gayle and Tom from Wilmette. Danny's mother sent flowers to the restaurant and Drew Carey sent a lovely arrangement to my home. He was going to Haiti for Save the Children. Tom and his daughter sent me a Shutterfly book of pictures he and Tim Hinshaw took which I will treasure.

On October 9th I had lunch for 150 after church. I was happy to include 60 Karen (pronounced "Ka-rin") we are delighted to have attending our church. They are legal refugees who the State Department brought here. They suffered in Burma with a dictator who burned their villages and they escaped by going through the jungle for weeks to get to a refugee camp in Thailand. They were so happy to be invited when they were with us only two weeks that they sang their birthday song in Karen to me that Sunday. I was almost in tears!  They are an asset to the Lakewood Baptist Church.

On October 31st my last celebration was a pizza party at the downtown office of Legal Aid. I hadn't been back since I retired. I was overwhelmed with all the hugs I got and it was nice to know they missed me. Several told me that my referral attorneys have asked about me and I certainly still miss them. They were like family to me. It was SO GOOD to see everyone. WHAT A JOY MY 90th WAS! I loved sharing it with so many and hope I gave joy to them!

As you know I love nature and try to help environmental causes. If you mention them in your will, when a representative comes to town they invite you to lunch or dinner. They are always such nice people. Morgan Dodd was here for the National Parks Conservation Association. We talked about the fact that so many animal habitats are being destroyed because of over population. Millions of acres of rain forests are no more. Oceans are polluted and coral is dying, and recent catches of shrimp have been damaged by the B.P. oil spill. Several weeks later Morgan called and asked me to fill out some interview questions related to the National Parks. My answers, along with a picture, will be sent to a professional writer who will put what I wrote in letter form. It will be sent to me to OK and then mailed to 50,000 people. I can't give them a million dollars but feel this is a simple way for me to help NPCA, whose budget has been cut. I want all of nature saved for future generations. Every Christmas I think of a lovely African-American homecare aid who stayed with my mother and aunt a few weeks so I could go to work. She knew my last name, which I admit is difficult for people, but she didn't hear it exactly right. Christmas came and I got a card from her addressed to "Miss Alida Scrooge." She is deceased but I still have that card and envelope. It was, after all, in keeping with the holiday. Soon Christmas and Hanukkah will be here.

The main purpose of this letter is to let you know I'm remembering you with love and prayer. This past year had joyous moments sufficient to make up for any challenging ones. I don't know how we can live these days without faith.

With all my love to you and yours, Alida

# 63<sup>rd</sup> Christmas Letter, November, 2012 (At Home)

"We can do no great things — only small things with great love." — Mother Teresa

My dear family and friends,

Can it be November? It seems as if I just wrote a Christmas letter and I keep wondering now that I am 91 how many more I can write? I'll see what each year brings. This year started by my getting a call on January 4<sup>th</sup> that my last immediate relative with whom I have memories had died and with her went a lot of my history. Making up for that are all the wonderful relationships I have with all of you, "my kids" I've borrowed, my church family, my friends, and my attorneys whom I still miss. God keeps bringing new kids into my life. I now have the titles of "mom," "Aunt Alida," and "grandma," and I love it.

Having so many "kids" means I have the joy of going to weddings. This year Josh Hinshaw married Whitney, Andy Hinshaw married Donna, and Michael Wallace married Courtney. There were children's birthdays and for his 60<sup>th</sup>, Roger Carey had a party. It was a snowy night but Drew Carey managed to get there and I was delighted to see him. He looks so good minus 84 pounds. He was happy to see "Aunt Alida" and I was happy to tell him how much people like him on *The Price is Right*. I'm so proud of him but am proud of all "my kids."

When you have lived in a house 78 years you sadly lose old neighbors who moved. I'm glad Ron and Teri Firestone intend to stay put and Jim McGrath is not moving. Jim has been my neighbor since we were 18. He was 91 October 14<sup>th</sup>, ten days after my 91<sup>st</sup> on October 4<sup>th</sup>. We should be in the *Guinness World Records* book.

Speaking of birthdays, I must thank all of you for making my birthday so special. Thanks for the cards, phone calls, emails, meals, and grandma plaque. I even got a bag that had on it "Happy Birthday Spring Chicken" with a fluffy chicken inside that plays the chicken dance song while it dances. We're never too old to enjoy something so cute. A lovely plant and flowers added to the joyful day. Relationships make life worthwhile. I love the relationships I have with people of different nationalities. Gia Hoa (Jahwah) is an amazing Vietnamese friend. She bought an old rundown building and in three months turned it into a palace called the Sai Gon Plaza. Many events take place there and now Joe Meissner, who retired (he calls it transitioned) from Legal Aid, will have an office there. At the Thai Kitchen I met Suriya (Jim) and Numtip (Joom) who now spend six months in Thailand and six months here. I'm sure to see them when they leave and when they come back from Thailand. They sold the Kitchen to her cousin, Kwan, who is an excellent cook and makes sure I get a cup of tea if I have to wait for a take home order.

In my last letter I told you about 60 or more Karens (pronounced "Ka-rins") the State Department rescued from a Thai refugee camp. They had fled from their homes in Myanmar when their villages were burned by the dictator. Many were Baptists there and found Lakewood Baptist. God sent us these wonderful people who are now part of our church family — our new ministry. I am "mom" to Thomas Kate (po bleh do) and his family and "grandma" to Jonathan Hla's family. I'm honored! On October 21<sup>st</sup> our pastor married two Karen couples and Jonathan interpreted the ceremony. Some of the service was in the Karen tradition. All these friends have made my life so much richer and make *The King and I* song *"Getting to know you,"* more meaningful.

It was one of those years when I felt I did nothing, but my appointment book would be full, At times I felt I could use a secretary. The National Parks Conservation Association did use my quotes and picture in their Legacy paper. A few weeks later I was asked if they could use one quote and my picture in the first ad they would include in their magazine which goes to 300,000. It has been in two issues so far. There are oil companies who care less about the environment and want to drill in and around national parks and in lakes in Alaska. I leave messages in my senators' local offices asking them to protect the parks and the entire environment. Also had a visit from Gayle and son, Garrett, from Florida. We took a ride on Lolly the Trolley on one of our many 90 degree days. I was amazed at the progress being made on our Medical Mart and Convention Center. We hope Cleveland is on the way up again. Sports? Glad I saw the Indians win the World Series in 1948.

I usually don't recommend books but one you will never forget is *Messenger* by Jeni Stepanek. She writes about her son, Mattie, who died just before his 14th birthday. He was writing stories and poems when three-years-old and had two to three books called *Heartsongs* on the best seller list. He was known around the world for promoting peace. He was in a wheelchair with all kinds of medical equipment because he had a rare form of muscular dystrophy. Oprah gave him permission to call her day or night. Maya Angelou wrote the Foreword to *Messenger*, he was on the Jerry Lewis show, and he and President Jimmy Carter became friends. President Carter spoke at his funeral and called him an angel. Mattie's book, *Just Peace*, edited by Jimmy Carter, and published after Mattie's death, is so full of wisdom you would think it was written by an adult, not a child.

Strange things happen to all of us. I want to share two of my strangest. Years ago I promised my aunt who lived with us that I would never get rid of a jardinière (a stand with a big vase). I collected paper for a church which used the money to beautify Rapid Transit slopes. A woman collecting paper saw the jardinière in my basement, was thrilled, had been looking for one, and wanted to buy it. She was disappointed when I told her of my promise. All week I thought of how she would treasure it and if I died I had no idea what would happen to it. One very happy woman came to pick it up. I still had some guilty feelings, looked up at the heavens and said, "I hope Pinkie doesn't mind." The woman exclaimed, "Pinkie?" I told her that was the name my brother and I gave her and the only name she was known by. Chills went up my spine when she said, "But that is my name and the only name I'm known by." I had tears in my eyes when I said, "If Pinkie is your name, surely this belongs to you," and all guilt was gone. It was as if my Pinkie had reached down and said, "It's Ok, Sis." How often would that happen?

Then in '96 a trip to Hawaii ended with a BIG SURPRISE. The tour group was divided in three to help hotels, but one evening we were together for a buffet dinner. Ruth Hinshaw and I saw the only two seats left and asked the ladies if we could eat with them. We had a lovely conversation about the tour but DID NOT exchange names. The two women lived in the same apartment and at Christmas, as was my custom, I sent a letter with a paragraph about the tour to one of the women who shared it with her companion. The signature "Alida" was the WOW factor! In January a woman on the phone asked if I was Alida and then asked if my mother's name was Elizabeth, my father's Walter, and my aunt's Min? I was stunned! How did this person know all this? When she told me her name was Nadine S, I was shocked!

I knew her folks lived next to me when I was a child. My dad and uncle went fishing with her dad but didn't keep in touch after we moved to Parma. I almost cried when she said, "I was looking out my bedroom window and saw you when your parents brought you home for the first time as their adopted baby." This nameless woman in Hawaii was part of my past. I went to see her as she lived near and kept in touch until she died. How often would that happen?

Christmas and Hanukkah seem to be here so soon. I'm already being asked if I'm sending a letter. This is my 63$^{rd}$ and I'll continue as long as I can. I get good reports from doctors and between steps at home and running around church, get Dr. Oz's 10,000 steps. I'm sure we'll all enjoy the holidays more with the election over so we can look at Christmas movies on TV rather than campaign ads. Thank God for the mute button! I'm so grateful you are all in my life and always love your greetings, notes, and pictures at Christmas. I pray that God who loves us, always has and always will, will be close to you, bless you, and may friendship light a candle in your heart in 2013.

"Don't walk in front of me, I may not follow. Don't walk behind me, I may not lead. Just walk beside me, and be my friend." — Author unknown

With all my love to all of you, Alida

# 64<sup>th</sup> Christmas Letter, November 1, 2013 (At Home)

My dear family and friends,

The widow of Dan Zaffarano, a childhood friend, told me that when my Christmas letter arrived early in December, he would always say, "Now it's Christmas." I hope the letter is a harbinger of a peaceful and happy holiday for you.

Years are always full of some of the same things but even those have a different twist or flavor. Four weddings and two showers were full of joy. The first, early in the year, was very brief because the couple decided to have the Mayor of Lakewood marry them. Mayor Summers was surprised to see me. We were both inducted into the Lakewood High Alumni Hall of Fame the same day in 2004 but never dreamed he would be Mayor some day. It was brief, but they are happy. I also enjoyed the fabulous weddings of Emily Carstenbrock and Alison Carey. Emily's gave me the three-day getaway I needed. A Karen wedding at our church was a new experience.

You know how much I love the environment and do what I can to protect it. Last year I told you National Parks asked me to do an ad for their magazine. I thought it was for one issue but it has been in many. This year on a whim I scribbled answers to a survey National Wildlife Foundation sent in a mailing. Two weeks later I got a call from Tim Brady saying in his words, "We loved your survey." He asked if their writer could talk to me and use some of my thoughts in an article he was writing about seniors and the environment. If it will help — why not! The article by John Carey is in the October/November magazine as *Natures Long-Term Benefits*.

Recently I received a mailing from the African Wildlife Foundation and included was a booklet. On the front of a shiny brown cover were the words, WHAT DID AN ELEPHANT LOOK LIKE? What a potent message! It told of how the Africans lived in harmony with elephants, giraffes, rhinos, and leopards. Now because of poachers killing animals for tusks and rhino horns the numbers have dwindled. The fear is that if this continues, soon we will see animals only in zoos. I wanted to cry because soon we may be saying WHAT DID IT LOOK LIKE about birds, bees, wolves, butterflies, national parks, rain forests and all of nature. Please think about calling your senators and ask them to put more money in the budget for our parks and ask them to protect the forests and the entire environment. Mother Nature will love you!

Last year the gardener I had for 30 years or more disappeared, and this year Ernie died. Because I let him use my garage, the minute we had two inches of snow I would hear him plowing my drive. His wife, Kathy, had a lovely celebration and had a tree planted in his memory in Lakewood Park. I had no idea that evening would bring one of two strange meetings. We didn't know a soul so we just sat at an empty table and got some food. A young man joined us and then a couple came. I swear I had NEVER seen them before so imagine my shock when the man said, "Alida Struze, what are you doing here?" When I came to, I asked him how he knew me. He is an attorney and Kathy works in his firm. He also knows people at Legal Aid and has seen my picture in agency mailings. I still think it is a long shot for him to recognize me just from my pictures when we had never met. I'm either famous or infamous because the second shock is almost the same.

My church was involved at a Community Festival in Madison Park a block from my home. As I crossed Madison Avenue, two men were heading in the direction of the park and they said "Good morning" to me. I responded, then the older man said, "Aren't you Miss Struze?" When he saw the questioning look on my face, he told me his name and said he had been a counseling client of mine at Legal Aid. He said he has thought of me often because he was grateful for the help he got. Counselors never know whether they have helped clients or not, so it was nice to know he thought I did. My question was, "How long ago did I see you?" He said, "This is my son, he was a baby and he is now 34." Thirty four years and just by chance I meet this man on Madison Avenue on a Saturday morning. He and his son just moved into the area. We never know what a day will bring and surprises like that are sweeteners to our life.

There is always something to do at church and it gives me joy to serve God as I serve the church and its members. I've been a member 63 years and whether it was singing in choir, teaching, or being Superintendent of the Church School, anything I did enriched my life. "My Arizona kid," Tom came for seven days to help me celebrate my 92$^{nd}$ year of life. We both enjoyed a trip downtown and couldn't believe all the changes. Adding to all "my American kids," I now have Karen ones. No matter where I see the Karens, at the bank or store, I hear them calling me "Pepe" (grandma), and love it.

Now for my third and best surprise: Baw Htoo and his wife Htoo Wah Paw had their second child October 18$^{th}$. What a thrill it was when they told me they named the baby Alida Moo Thaw. I was named for an Alida my aunt worked with who knew my mother had to give me up for adoption. She gave me a little picture, now 92-years-old, and on the back it says, "To little Alida from Alida. I will give it to this little Alida. She is beautiful." It seems strange that the Jewish holiday Hanukkah is the same day as Thanksgiving this year. It has been close to Christmas for a while. It's rather fitting because we are both so thankful for freedom. I wish all stores would respect the holidays and stay closed.

Who knows if I will get a letter written next year! If I get one done, it would help if you would send me your email address and I would try to learn how to mail it to you. It wouldn't seem quite as personal but I send at least 300 and sometimes more. I order 600 to 700 copies and hand one to everybody in church. I don't miss anyone, remembering the little boy in elementary school that was the only one in class who didn't get a Valentine because I had erased and replaced his name. I have never forgotten his sad face. It was not done intentionally of course but it was a life lesson learned. Nobody gets missed!

If this should become my last Christmas letter, believe me when I say I never dreamed when I sent the first one that I would continue for 63 years. The Christmas letters have helped me keep in touch with very old friends (one from the 1$^{st}$ grade I lost a year ago) and with new friends. I've shared my travels, being on *The Drew Carey Show*, "my kids," my joys and my sorrows in losing all my immediate family and becoming the "Last of the Mohicans." I have been so blessed having all of you in my life and have enjoyed your cards, notes, family pictures, and best of all your friendship and love. My letters always seemed so simple to me. I never quite understood why people liked them and wanted me to continue. The first ones were mimeographed. Remember those? Suffice it to say, one reason I wrote the letters is because I loved you and wanted you in my life. That will never change, letter or no letter!

The world isn't at peace but we can be if we put our lives in God's hands! 2014, here we come whether you are ready for us or not!

With all my love to you and yours, Alida

# 65<sup>th</sup> Christmas Letter, November 9, 2014 (At Home)

My dear family and friends,

Only one other time in the 65 years of writing this letter have I been so late getting it written. I'm nervous wondering if I can get it in the mail by December 1<sup>st</sup>. I'm sure you will forgive me if I'm late. The year started out well but after a month or two I had no energy; everything was a chore, plus for the first time in my 93 years I had discomfort in my back. I went to a chiropractor who released me after seven treatments. The back discomfort was still there so I decided I had joined the "Arthritis Club" and used mineral ice, which helped. I still had no energy so went to my family doctor and a test showed I had been fighting an infection for months. I've been so healthy I can't complain no matter what happens.

I was feeling guilty because I kept being asked when I was going to write the book many wanted. For years I would start writing but always felt I needed some help. Because I had a full schedule I decided to wait until things settled down to think about the book.

In April there was a wedding shower for Sarah Hinshaw. I was so glad she was getting married but also glad that she is no longer in Turkey. She was a missionary for the Campus Crusade. Her love for Josiah brought her home to America. The way things are, we could use a missionary here. Two weeks after Sarah's shower we had a baby shower for her cousin, Amy. Her baby was due July 4<sup>th</sup> and Sarah's wedding July 5<sup>th</sup>. Baby Isabell waited until July 8<sup>th</sup> so mama could enjoy Sarah's wedding reception.

Our former Music Director, Michael, felt God's call to become a minister and three years ago went to a Seminary in Pittsburgh, Pennsylvania. What a difference it made in his life. Through a friend there he met Courtney who became his wife. Four of us from church had the joy of seeing him graduate and were doubly happy because he and Courtney were graduating into being parents in October. In the meantime Lakewood Baptist decided we would like Michael to come home to be associate pastor and he accepted. During worship on September 28<sup>th</sup> we got the news that Theophilus James Wallace had arrived.

For months, and when I had little energy, I was planning the Lakewood High's Class of 39's 75<sup>th</sup> Class Reunion. If you recall five years ago 19 classmates came from Florida, California, and four other states. We were all 87 and 88 and most in pretty good health. In five years things changed. Now that we are 92 and 93 I decided to simplify things and reserved the party room at Pier W and ordered a beautiful purple and gold center piece. How many were there June 21<sup>st</sup>? SEVEN classmates arrived, along with two wives and two children who brought their parent. Only one from Illinois! The number didn't matter because we were just happy to be together. I brought our year book and other memorabilia and they were laughing and having a great time remembering the good old days and friendships. I was happy because they were happy. Will we have an 80<sup>th</sup> class reunion? Only God knows.

With the reunion over I could think about the book. I'm asked what things were like when I was little and what happened as I grew up. Don't expect a novel but more of an autobiography and possibly articles. I'm not writing for the public but to answer your questions. Last Christmas I was invited to a Christmas gathering by Gia Hoa at the Sai Gon Plaza. She had authors there who spoke about their books. I talked to one author because I agreed with his ideas. I gave him my Christmas letter and he gave me his business card. When I looked at Michael Petro's card it said, "Writing, Editing, Publishing Services." I felt God was not only guiding me but providing the help I needed to get the book organized. We are working on it but have no idea when it will be done.

My 93$^{rd}$ birthday could not have been nicer. My dining room table was full of cards, and phone calls from Vermont and Florida were nice surprises. It was special to have Danny's family and his mother spend the afternoon with me. Gwen took us to lunch and brought a cake for us to eat when we got home. Grace and Luke gave me four balloons and made cards which had school pictures in them. Gwen sent me flowers as did "my kid" Gayle in Illinois. Actually I had two birthdays because my Karen Alida Moo Thaw was ONE on October 18$^{th}$ and the Karen's always have a worship service for birthdays of small children. They had a small cake for little Alida and a larger one for me, plus a bouquet of flowers. How sweet! They had pizza, pork, chicken, pineapple and grapes. I was enjoying something new to me when suddenly I realized I was eating HOT Karen food. I reached for a bottle of water quickly. I was sorry "my Arizona kid," Tom, couldn't be here but we both felt with health issues he should be near his doctors, which proved to be the right decision.

I couldn't stand the way my basement looked so finally got the walls and floor painted. I asked my friend Peter to look at some things and let me know if they were any good or should be recycled. Right now I have the cleanest, emptiest basement ever. I thought I would charge if anyone wants to see it to be inspired to do the same. Kidding of course! The fruit cellar is next. In June I lived in this house 80 years! If I ever thought of leaving I don't know what I would do with all my things. I'm starting to get rid of things. Colin, husband of "my kid," Becky, opened a bookstore on Madison Avenue, and I was happy to give him two big boxes of books. The books were old, but in good condition. I had them in my Barristers bookcase in the attic for years. He will get more.

Everything I read makes me more and more worried about the environment. An article in *The Plain Dealer* said that from 1970 to 2010 half of the world's wildlife was killed. There has been loss of habitat for animals because of too much building, and even climate change. One article said 1,000 elephants were killed in one year. Soon there won't be any. Richard, Christa, and I took our annual trip to Salem, Ohio to see "my kids" there. Of course I saw my Colorado spruce on their old farm in Hanoverton, Ohio. I was told it is now 50-feet tall. I enjoy the trip each year as if it is the first time and it brings back so many memories. As long as the tree is there I feel a little bit of me is also there.

LOVE AND KINDNESS are stressed at Christmas but we should be stressing them all year. A few stores are actually closing to give their employees Thanksgiving Day off so they can be with their families. About time some stores were kind enough to do that. "My Arizona kid," Tom, had an experience with kindness, and I want to end this letter sharing it with you. He has many health issues. A week ago he went to get his mail, was at the mailbox when with no warning he just crumbled. A woman, we call an angel, had never driven on that street before. She saw him fall, got out of her car and called her husband to help get him home. She worried about him after she got home so went back to his house and found he had fallen again in the house. He looked so bad she called 911. After the firemen left she realized the dog was frightened so she took Ginger home with her. She even went to the hospital to check on him. How many people would be that loving and kind? May God send you an angel in 2015 — if you need one! Merry Christmas and Happy Hanukkah!

All my love to you and yours, Alida

# Part Three:

# More Memories Of My Life

# Chapter Ten

# Walt's Amphibian

In my Christmas letters I often mentioned my brother building a Volmer Amphibian plane. In this chapter I want to expand on what I wrote in those letters. In the Christmas letters the reader is presented with small portions of the story, but in this chapter you will find the complete story in condensed form.

Walt was a very creative person. He painted beautifully, built two guitars that worked, and could have been a cartoonist. I was shocked when he asked me, who couldn't pound a nail or draw a straight line, what I thought of him building an airplane. Knowing how he loved creating things, I told him to go ahead, not knowing it would be an adventure for me as well. I'm glad I made a photo album showing the progress we made step by step. I still treasure those photos. This plane was not built from a pre-fabricated kit. Every piece of wood came from the highest mountains, as if nature had created them to fly. The project was started with bulkheads built in the house and then transferred to a 4 X 4 in the garage. The next time Walt was home, we decided to get sledge hammers and knock down the one-car "chicken coop" of a garage, which had to have the front extended. A neighbor and his crew of real craftsmen built a 2½ car garage complete with a furnace! Construction of Walt's airplane began around November 30th, 1965.

Being in the Merchant Marine, sometimes Walt was home for several months at a time. He would get up in the morning when I got up to go to work and he would work on the plane all day. I would babysit the plane when Walt was away for extended periods performing his Merchant Marine duties. We went to Pittsburgh where he bought the wings, and he gave me the job of cleaning them. I spent most of a vacation taking out hundreds of screws and cleaning the wings. It was not fun! When it came time to place cloth on the wings I helped with the rib-stitching. Walt would be on one side of the wing and me on the other, each with long needles. Sometimes I got men together to turn the plane over so Walt could waterproof the bottom and then turn it back when dry. There was always something to do until one day it was finished and ready to leave home. I really enjoyed what I could do.

For safety reasons, when it came time to test fly the plane, it had to be transported to Portage County Airport in a rural community. We were lucky Walt had a friend who flew hot B-26s in World War II. His friend not only made sure the engine was in good shape, but was also willing to be the test pilot. The yard seemed empty with the plane gone. I often wondered what pilots flying overhead thought when they saw the "Puddle Jumper," as Walt called it, in our yard. The first time we turned the ignition on our neighbors must have been startled by the roar of the engine!

A Federal Aviation Administration (FAA) official inspected Walt's plane at the airport, and said it was one of the best planes that he had examined and it was ready to fly. I would pack Walt lunches, and when I went with him I swept the hanger floor. I laugh when I recall men asking me questions that men typically ask about how the plane operates. I sounded as if I knew what I was talking about, but my answers were merely what I had heard Walt and his friends say many times.

After taking it for a short run on the ground, Bill decided he would do some lift-offs the next week. Because he felt the plane was ready to fly, we were surprised to see years of work in the air. It was November 13th, 1971. Walt built it with the intention of flying it to Canada and fishing from the plane on one of Canada's beautiful lakes. He wanted to leave the plane in Canada, but discovered that would not be permitted. His interest waned a bit when he discovered he would have to bring it home each year and not store it there.

Next Walt wanted to test the plane to see if it would take off from the water while he piloted it. Some who built amphibian aircraft made them so heavy they would not lift off from a body of water. They were doomed to failure! Being a perfectionist, Walt's plane took off from water with no problems. He flew the plane for a while, but I always thought he enjoyed building the plane more than he enjoyed flying it! He finally decided to sell the plane to a man from Baltimore, who also wanted to fish from it. I had tears in my eyes as I watched it take off from the airport at 1:15 p.m. on Saturday, October 15th, 1977, heading for its new home, but was happy it arrived safely at 5:45 p.m.

Naturally I wanted to fly in the plane, but because my mother was living decided to fly with our test pilot. I trusted Walt's craftsmanship and had the joy of flying despite the fact that the plane had only flown three hours. It should not have had a passenger until after 50 hours of flight time.

I have many lovely memories of Walt's plane. I wanted a picture of the plane to put in my Christmas letter. I thought Walt would fly with someone to get the picture while Bill flew his plane. But Walt insisted I take the picture. There I was in a two-place coop with the canopy down and the pilot I just met telling me not to lean over too far. I'm no photographer, so was happy the picture tuned out well.

I'm grateful for what I call the "plane years!" Working on a plane was a new experience and I was proud to be of help to my brother.

# Chapter Eleven

# **My Love Story**

I just happened to be there with my brother and other friends when a new boy on the street joined the group looking for new friends. I was in the 4th or 5th grade and he was about three years older than most of us. His brown eyes smiled before he did, and there was something very captivating about him. I was smitten! From that moment on Ned was part of my life and my life's pattern was set. Of course I wondered if he could possibly feel the same about me. My answer came one night when a lot of us were playing ping pong at a neighbor's home. My hand was beneath the table where no one could see it. I felt someone put something in it. When I got home and looked at it, it was a small dime store picture of Ned, which I put in my *Bible* where I knew it would not be found. It is still there today, exactly where I put it more than 80 years ago. As young as we were, there were always feelings between us that were more than just friendship. Was it "Puppy Love?" A professor I had in college once said, "Don't laugh at Puppy Love, it could be real." He was right! Ned collected baseball cards and the one he wanted and couldn't get was that of Joe Vosmik. How happy I was when I got the one baseball card Ned so eagerly wanted. I couldn't wait to give it to him. It was another bit of cement in our childhood relationship.

My brother Walt and I had what I would consider a happy childhood. We liked our school and enjoyed our friends — who were all very much like us. Our neighbors were like an extended family, and for us as children life was serene; but things were about to change.

I was in the 6th grade and had just turned 11 years old in October of 1932. Walt and I knew something ominous was in the air and it wasn't too long before the Great Depression, which began in 1929, really impacted our family. Like many other Americans, we were losing our home and would have to move to a less expensive residence. We were despondent thinking about losing contact with our friends, neighbors, and the community we loved. It was a low blow to know we couldn't take our dog, Chester, and the two cats, Jake and Lena, named after two radio characters we heard every morning. Our aunt who lived with us would have to abandon her beautiful flower garden, and dad would have to surrender the vegetable garden he faithfully planted every year. Most importantly for me, it meant not seeing Ned.

My parents located the upstairs of a double house on Easton Avenue off East 93rd and Kinsman. In the 1930's it was a German neighborhood, but it lacked fields filled with the wild flowers we loved so dearly. Walt went to an elementary school in the 6th grade and I went to Audubon Junior High for my seventh year of school. It was known to be a rough school, and for the first time I was with children of many cultures. That was a unique experience for young Alida, and helped to expand my perspective of humanity. However, unlike my previously safe neighborhood, I would run home through Woodland Hills Park because I heard girls had been assaulted in that area. That alone, was a life-altering experience!

It didn't help that in the one year we lived at that location mom had three operations for which she needed special nurses. Our aunt was like a second mother and kept the home running while mom was unable to perform her normal routine. Many nights I dreamed we were going back to the home we loved. I also missed the little church where I went forward to say I wanted to follow Christ. We moved shortly after that and I never found a replacement church, but I didn't forget God. It helped a bit that mom enrolled me in tap dancing classes — which I loved! In those classes I discovered that I truly had a natural talent for tap dancing! Just once I threatened to run away from our new home, but I knew better. To ease our conspicuous sadness, dad would drive us about once a week to visit an aunt and uncle who lived in our old neighborhood. While there I would peer out a window at every opportunity, hoping I might see Ned once again. To my disappointment, he was often nowhere to be found!

However, from time to time Ned and I would make contact when our family visited our old neighborhood. My Aunt Mil knew Ned and I liked each other and would pass notes between us. I'm not sure how long that lasted, but on one visit when mom and Pinkie found out about the note passing, they were furious. From that point on there were no more notes to be passed. I don't know what harm they felt those notes would do, but they probably felt they were being protective of me — and boys were out of the picture!

We never know what fate has in store for us. On one of our trips back to the old neighborhood I was going to visit my best friend — even though it was getting dark. As I was approaching the house someone came walking toward me. To my sheer delight, it was Ned! We were so glad to see each other. He took my hand and led me to a bench by a trellis in his backyard. We talked a while and then he gave me my first kiss — which neither of us ever forgot. We even had a secret name for it: "Flavors!" I wasn't gone very long, but when I got back they wondered why my brother couldn't find me when he yelled at my friend's home. I didn't want anyone reprimanding me and ruining the joy I felt in my heart just knowing that Ned stilled cared for me. I lied and said we were playing records so loud I couldn't hear him calling. Recently I found greeting cards Ned had sent to me a while later. Instead of signing his name, he signed with our secret code, "Flavors!"

We were so grateful when my aunt bought this home I've lived in now for some 80 years. It was so good to live in our own home again, and I was in a better school when starting the 8th grade. Ned and one of his friends came to see me a number of times when I was in my teens. He phoned several times asking me for a date. We were still in the Great Depression, and I didn't have nice clothes to wear. I didn't want to look poorly dressed, so I always made some excuse not to go out with him. To this day I wonder how different my life would have been had I accepted his invitations!

I didn't date in high school because I didn't want to be with anyone but Ned. I graduated in 1939, and it took a while to find a job. After much searching I landed a position at a bank with the "generous salary" of $60 a month. Shortly thereafter our world fell apart when the Japanese bombed Pearl Harbor and America entered World War II. I dreaded the thought of my brother, Walt, going to the Merchant Marine. At that time I heard Ned had gotten engaged to a friend of my best childhood friend. Ned entered the Army, and I was so glad he telephoned me before he left.

To help America's war effort, I wrote letters to all the men I knew — and that included Ned. He wrote back and sent pictures of himself. When his mother died, I wrote a supportive letter which reached him before he received a notification from the American Red Cross. He never forgot that letter. He said it meant a lot to him. A friend at work asked me to write to her brother, Chuck, who had gotten a "Dear John" letter from his girlfriend when he joined the Army. I knew some of their family members, but had never met Chuck. My Royal typewriter should have gotten a medal. At Christmas I sent them all a check and a "Petty Girl" calendar. I thank God they all came home safely.

It was not unusual for an engaged girl to have the wedding all planned when her fiancée came home from the service. Ned wasn't home too long when I got an invitation to their wedding. It was a Saturday event. The day before the wedding I was called down to the bank's first floor to see a visitor. I had no idea who would be there to greet me. I had to walk down an aisle that had the desks of six Vice Presidents on either side. Hollywood couldn't have done it better. Standing at the end of the aisle in uniform was Ned, waiting for me. I can't remember most of what we said but I do remember him saying, "I'm sorry it turned out this way." Later I asked his father, who knew I loved Ned, if he had made him come to see me. He assured me it was Ned's idea. I found someone to take me to the wedding. While waiting for the newlyweds to come out of the church, people from the old neighborhood threw rice on *me*. Looking back, that was a hurtful gesture and not the least bit funny. We didn't stay long at the reception and I don't remember if I had one dance with Ned. I do know I cried all the way home.

Years went by when I had little contact with Ned except to send him a birthday card like I did for all my old friends. Once in a while we would be at the same wedding and I would chat with him and his wife, Marilyn. She was a lovely person and raised four children. Ned was a good husband and father. I was glad for them. When we danced at those later occasions we would, at some point, smile at one another and both say, "Flavors!"

Years later one of my dearest friends suggested I have dinner with them and go to the alley where her husband, Jack, bowled with Ned. It just happened to be Valentine's Day. Betty and I arrived after bowling started and we sat in the last row at the top. I don't know if Jack told Ned I was there or if he just glanced up and saw me, but I never saw anyone run up stairs as fast as he did to see me. When bowling was over Betty and Jack, without a word, went to their car to wait for me. Ned and I went to his car and we kissed and hugged for a half-hour. Some would say what we did was wrong. I knew we were never going to repeat that romantic encounter. We were both expressing romantic feelings that we had repressed for many, many years. It was a Valentine's Day gift I would treasure for the rest of my life!

Did I ever have a chance to marry? The brother, Chuck, I had been asked to write to during the war sent me flowers as soon as he got home. I dated him for a while and eventually he wanted to marry me, but he also wanted me to live with his mother. I knew his mother and liked her, but didn't like the idea of living with her. I guess I really used that as an excuse to bow out of the proposal. Truthfully, I did not want to marry anyone but Ned, and was willing to be a single woman the rest of my life rather than live with a man I did not truly love!

In 1994 my brother was killed instantly in a traffic accident. I called Ned to let him know, just as he had once called to let me know that an old friend from our childhood had passed away. I was talking to my boss when Ned arrived at the funeral parlor. I got a bit rattled when I looked up and saw him there. To this day I have persistent feelings of regret because I never gave him a hug like everyone else got. "Let me introduce you to my first love," I said to my boss. He looked at Ned and said, "How did you let her get away?" Ned's simple but profound answer was, "Her mother and aunt." I was a bit surprised, but glad he realized it wasn't because I didn't care. I didn't know it at that time, but that funeral parlor encounter turned out to be the last opportunity I would have to enjoy Ned's company, and I would never again gaze upon his smiling brown eyes!

I had plans to go to Alaska in September or October of 1995. In AUGUST I felt compelled to look for Ned's name in the death notices. I thought it was strange, but I could not refrain from doing so. I asked my neighbor to save my papers so I could check the notices when I returned home. WHY WAS I DOING THIS? It began to drive me crazy! Was something wrong with Ned? Or, was something wrong with me? By October I couldn't stand it so I called the house and Marilyn answered. I told her I had been thinking of them and wondered how they were. She said she was fine but Ned didn't feel good early in the year but several doctors couldn't find the cause. He went to one of the big hospitals where in AUGUST cancer was diagnosed and it had already spread. Was it intuition, or was there a bond between us that made me know Ned was going to die?

Another shock came when Ned's wife told me the day I called was the date of their 50th Wedding Anniversary. I truly felt saddened for her predicament. I told her I was at their wedding. Of course she wouldn't remember, but I did. Initially I decided to send some flowers for the anniversary, but sent fresh fruit instead. When she sent a "thank you" note she said she was glad I sent fruit because it was the only thing Ned enjoyed at that point in time. Intuitively, I knew what he needed. Marilyn had Ned talk to me that day and he said he would like me to come to visit him, and Marilyn agreed. One day I made food and dessert for her. When I phoned to see if it was OK to visit, they were installing a hospital bed. Marilyn was exhausted, so I didn't visit and gave the food to someone else. I didn't want to impose upon her. I kept in touch with Marilyn. I wanted to give her some support and she appreciated the references to various supportive resources that I had supplied to her.

The last time I called their home there was no response. I suspected Ned was in the hospital, so I left a message. Marilyn replied and said Ned had deteriorated to the point that he had to be hospitalized. She didn't mind if I tried to visit him. When I called to see if he could have visitors the operator asked who I was, so I knew he was dying. She put me through to one of the daughters who said he was very ill, and she didn't think he would survive much longer. I told her my thoughts and prayers were with them. The next morning his son called to say Ned had died. I went to the wake, but I didn't feel it was appropriate for me to attend the funeral.

I only talked to Ned twice on the phone after the first time I called in October. The last time, for some reason, I felt I must tell him I never married because he was the only man I ever truly loved. He said he always knew that. There was a slight pause, and then he said, "You know I always loved you." I knew he loved me, but it was so endearing to hear him speak those words. Those were his last words to me and I will always treasure them.

Our childhood love never ended, and Ned and I went our separate ways as adults. However, I truly believe we both enjoyed rich, full lives, and we followed the paths that God had planned for each of us!

# Chapter Twelve

# World War II

It was Sunday, December 7<sup>th</sup>, 1941. Our parents and Pinkie had decided to visit friends, but Walt and I stayed home. We were watching TV when an announcement cut into the program: PEARL HARBOR HAD BEEN BOMBED BY THE JAPANESE! I don't remember either of us saying anything we were so shocked, but both of us knew this was the beginning of a big change in our lives. We weren't out of the Great Depression and now we were probably going to war. When I look back I believe the war got us out of the Great Depression. I ran upstairs, fell on my bed and cried because I knew Walt would probably have to go to war.

I started working at the Federal Reserve Bank January 1<sup>st</sup>, 1940 as a clerk. At the entrance there was a coffee stand run by a blind man and he had a radio. Everyone in the bank gathered around the stand to hear President Roosevelt ask Congress to declare war on Japan. It was December 8<sup>th</sup>, my brother's 19<sup>th</sup> birthday. As the men left the bank to join the armed forces and the Merchant Marine, we women took over some of their positions and worked long hours. It might be 7:00 p.m. or 8:00 p.m. when we went home and often walked alone at night from East 6<sup>th</sup> Street to the Public Square to wait for a streetcar. We were cautious but not afraid. We wouldn't do that now. We worked all day Saturday and a half a day Sunday so there was little time for fun. Women in the neighborhood, including my mother, who had only been homemakers, went to work in factories to help the war effort.

Walt's hobby had been Ham radio. He and his friend across the street somehow got a wire across the street so they could communicate, and I spent hours helping Walt learn the Morse Code. Because of his Ham radio experience, he decided to join the Merchant Marine and use his skills to be a radio officer on a ship. It was an important position because ships had to be totally dark at night. The operators were given zigzag signals and if they didn't get them correctly could cause ships to collide at night and sink. Walt went to Gallup's Island for training and soon was on a ship with the Captain being the only person to whom he had to report. Thank God he made it through all the war years safely but with a few scary incidents. Like many veterans, he didn't talk about the war. Only once he mentioned falling to the deck with tracer bullets flying over his head.

Of course we at home knew nothing of Navy talk. When he was getting training he wrote and said he had been made Captain of the head. I'm ashamed to say we thought he had some kind of promotion until we learned the head was the latrine. And to this day I feel bad because we didn't know they could get mail on board and didn't write thinking they would get it when they got back to the States. When I found out he was the only one who didn't get mail one trip, I wrote V MAIL letters EVERY morning before work started.

My typing got really good because I would write many letters every week to friends in the service — sometimes 10 a week. My Royal typewriter should have gotten a medal! It was my part of the war effort. When Ned's mother died, my letter telling him the sad news reached him before the letter from the American Red Cross. At Christmastime I would send them all a check and a *Petty Girl* calendar that had pictures of pretty girls on them. One time I sent them a picture of me, and one fellow put it in his airplane. The plane got back to the base — but my picture had a bullet hole in it! I'm grateful that everyone I wrote to came home in good shape.

We in this country were blessed because bombs never reached us as they did in England and other countries. Just in case, precautions were taken. Many nights at a signal we had to turn off all lights and not even light a match during a blackout session. At another signal we could turn the lights back on.

Many things were rationed such as gas, meat, and liquor. My Uncle Henry started raising chickens which became many Sunday meals. Sometimes he was naughty and drove to the country to get black market meat. Many people began growing "victory gardens," which were also called "war gardens."

One night a neighbor invited me to go with them to a place where people gathered to dance. It was good to get away from war news for an evening and dance the night away. The war brought me two lasting friends, Dorothy and Norman Roglin. They were friends of my neighbor and became lasting friends of mine. A few years later they asked me to go to church with them. Never dreamed I would join that church some day. Their first daughter visits me several times a year from Illinois. Sadly, her sister died at age 14 from Hodgkin's lymphoma many years ago. Today's medicine probably would have saved her life.

I don't remember hearing anything about the Holocaust until the war was over and the horror was discovered. So much time has gone by that there are people today who say it never happened. But that denial just adds to the horror!

I'm proud of the way everyone in this country worked together, sacrificed, and prayed together, determined to beat the enemies. It was no easy task to fight Hitler and Japan at the same time, but because we were united in our effort we won. God Bless America!

# Chapter Thirteen

# Discovery And Decisions

June 22$^{nd}$, 1951. It was an ordinary day in the lives of most people and it began like every other day in my life. The alarm clock announced it was time for me to get up and I obeyed. It was my custom to get to work an hour early to write letters and checks which my busy schedule didn't allow me to do at night.

One of the things I intended to do this particular morning was to sort through some papers my dad had given me the night before to put in our new safe deposit box. Mother was in a mental hospital having had a nervous breakdown and dad wasn't feeling well. I had never looked at the papers they kept in a buffet drawer. Inasmuch as dad and I were the only ones with keys to the box, I felt it would be wise for me to see what insurance policies were there. Little did I know how revealing this sorting would be!

In a routine way I leafed through the policies quickly, and in the same way picked up a folded piece of paper which I thought was some ordinary correspondence concerning a policy. As I unfolded the paper I realized it wasn't a letter, but because I saw my name I continued to read. I didn't know when I picked up that piece of paper that I was discovering the secret that had been kept from me for 29 years:

**I was an adopted child!**

As I put the paper on my desk I suddenly felt weak. Now I could understand the gulf that had always separated me from the rest of the family. My ideas were not their ideas and my dreams were not their dreams. It occurred to me I need no longer be afraid of inheriting my mother's mental illness as had once been implied. I was free at last from that worry and I wanted to shout with joy because I was so relieved!

Another reaction quickly replaced my relief. Sheer unmitigated anger welled up within me when I realized my parents had lied to me for years just as my aunt and uncle lied to my cousin who was also an adopted child. How could they let me believe I was something I wasn't? I always had different ideas but I had a right to be different.

Within a few moments my entire being was a storm of confused emotion and the tears which came didn't stop all day. I wondered how I could go home and face my "folks." How could I sit across the supper table from them knowing the truth? How could I call my brother whom I loved "brother" when he wasn't my real brother? Should I tell my adoptive parents I knew the truth? Would it be too much of a shock to my mother and cause more illness? Did everybody else know the truth?

As the day wore on, I knew I could not tell my folks that I had discovered the truth. I knew them well enough that if I told them they would be upset and tell me how much they had wanted me and loved me. At that moment I didn't want to hear the worn out, pat phrases so often used to explain adoption. I called mother's psychiatrist, who felt this was not a good time to tell her the truth. The secret had nothing to do with her illness and all the family knew but me.

The following weeks were filled with a feverish search to find out all I could about my natural parents. I consulted the City Directories of the past 30 years at the library. I wanted to know where the persons whose names I found that morning among the papers had lived when I was born. My birth mother's name, which sounded German, did not appear in any Directory after I was born, but a previous Directory had both parents names and they apparently worked in the same place. My natural father had a name that could have been Welsh, and the kind that could be easily traced. It was a shock to learn he was living only a mile and a half from me. More questions came to my mind. Should I find some excuse for visiting him and hope he came to the door so I could just see him? What if I looked like my mother? Would he have a heart attack? He was married but I didn't think it was to my birth mother. I didn't want to take a chance of disrupting a family, so once again I decided to keep my secret.

My search was not complete until I consulted an attorney where I worked at that time. Original birth certificates were not available at that time to just anyone, but an attorney would have access to them. At first he told me he couldn't find anything. He confirmed my adoption ONLY after I nonchalantly said that I knew I was illegitimate. He breathed a huge sigh of relief saying, "You know that?" I said I knew from the names I found, and it didn't bother me nor did I judge girls who had babies out of wedlock. He had worried all day wondering what to tell me because so many people had very bad reactions when they learned such a controversial truth. His staff told him to tell me he couldn't find anything. Now he was free to tell me the truth. He did find an original birth certificate with the names I already had in my possession. How kind of them to want to protect me!

As time passed, my original feelings of shock and anger were replaced with a feeling of gratitude toward my adoptive parents. They had taken me as a baby and raised me to the best of their ability. True, I had never been completely happy because of a lack of understanding between us, but who is ever completely happy? The love they showered on me was a binding kind of love, but at least I knew I was loved and I loved all my family no matter what. They had not had easy childhoods and they had done their best for me and my brother and I knew it. By their example they taught us to value education, to be kind, honest, and generous, to have a good work ethic, and not to be afraid to show or voice our love. For those valuable life lessons, I am eternally grateful!

My search for my natural parents had come to an end and once and for all I decided that even though I may have an eternal question about who I am, I'm satisfied with building on who I am now. My heritage will always be a mystery but it is sufficient to know that someone gave birth to me; someone with love and kindness raised me; I am glad to be alive.

### SEQUEL

My father died before I could find a way to say "Thank You" to him for all he had done for me. I was determined that somehow I would find the right way and the right moment to let my mother know I knew her secret. It was sixteen years from the time I discovered the truth that I found a Christmas card that said "Thank You To Mother" on the deep green cover. Each page expressed thanks for things mothers do in preparation for Christmas. I found parchment paper that matched the paper used and inserted another page on which I wrote, "Thank you for adopting me and giving me such a good home." Before I went to church that Christmas Sunday I handed her the card with the plea that I wanted no dramatics when I got home.

When I got home nothing was said by mom nor my aunt. Her eyes were bad so I wondered if she had not seen the sheet I inserted. I even looked around the parlor floor thinking it may have fallen out. It was the next evening before she was able to ask me very calmly how I found out. I told her and asked why they had kept my adoption such a secret. I'm sure it was partly the thing to do in those days. Her answer was, "Because we were afraid you would leave." I assured her they were my family and casually said, "Where would I go?" She could give me no information about my identity, and others who might have known had passed away. I was glad she could hear the word adoption now and know that I knew the truth. Nothing more has been said. It was finished!

(I originally authored this story at a Writer's Conference at the Baptist Assembly at Green Lake, Wisconsin. The assignment was to write about one day in our life. The teacher felt it should be published.)

# Chapter Fourteen

# Euclid Beach Park

Euclid Beach Park, located in Cleveland, Ohio, was a family park the likes of which we'll never see again. It was a family attraction from 1895 to 1969 and today it is remembered every year with a picnic and memorabilia. A newsletter titled *Euclid Beach Now: The Arch,* is sent to those who wish to be members, and I am one. Before and during the Great Depression looking forward to going to the Park was as exciting as holidays. The Al Sirat Grotto and Cleveland Railway (now RTA) picnics were the two we attended. If rain kept us from going we were devastated. When it closed in 1969 everything was removed except the entrance — which stands like a monument. I'm glad I have a picture of a streetcar at the Park entrance with a roller coaster in the background.

We had to take a dinky to get to Brookpark Road. The dinky was a little car which ran from Brookpark Road to Snow Road and was operated at either end. It had a coal stove used in the winter, along with wicker seats. At Brookpark Road we took a streetcar to downtown Cleveland where we waited for another streetcar to take us to Euclid Beach Park. We would get there around noon and my dad would come from work to eat with us, enjoy a few rides, and take us home.

After receiving a stamp on our hand, Walt and I could go on every ride all day. Mom could let us go just as long as we would be back at the table in time for supper. She didn't have to worry about us being kidnapped. Sadly, if the Park was open today, children could not be as free!

Rides like the Thriller seemed so fierce then, but were nothing compared to the huge coasters at parks today. The first time I went on the Thriller, my dad took me so I felt safe but oh, how I screamed going down the first downhill. The racing coasters were fun but my favorite was The Bug. If you needed a little cooling on a hot day there was the Over The Falls and Laff In The Dark. The Flying Turns was supposed to be the worst ride, causing some people to be sick to their stomach when they got off. I never went on it until the last night the Park was open when my neighbor and I went on every ride. To my surprise it wasn't as bad as its reputation. Who would not like the Carousel? We all loved the music as we went round and round on it. The Carousel itself went round and round from one city to another until it finally found its home again in Cleveland. I couldn't resist buying a large paver in memory of Euclid Beach Park and the joy we found there!

Laughing Sal with her infectious laugh is still laughing at events. Stores sometimes have the real taffy kisses as made in the Park. I warn people not to chew them if they want to keep their teeth and fillings. Just put them in one's mouth and enjoy the flavor as the kiss melts. The popcorn balls are still available and one never left the Park without having the delicious Frozen Whip, which someone said is being brought back to the Euclid Mall.

One of the loveliest attractions was the Dance Pavilion. I regret I never was on that dance floor but loved watching people dance a waltz or fox-trot to the beautiful music of Glenn Miller or other big bands. Ballroom dancing was so beautiful compared to the calisthenics they call dancing today, and the music was not loud but romantic. It was a sad day when the Pavilion closed. When I got older I was a good dancer and would say, "I would rather dance than eat."

This is a strange memory, but some years bugs called Canadian soldiers came off the lake and occupied the Park a short time. They had long wings which we children would put together and gently pull the bug off the bench or tree, hold them for a second, and put them back without harming them.

I have a miniature facsimile of the entrance to the Park on my buffet so I can see it every day and rekindle those many cherished childhood feelings that are lodged in my heart.

Other parks may be bigger and rides higher and faster, but Euclid Beach Park had a unique family feeling that made it unforgettable!

# Chapter Fifteen

# Pinkie

Our aunt who lived with us, and was like a second mother, was nicknamed "Pinkie" by us. Why little children would find it easier to say Pinkie than Aunt Min is a mystery, but for my brother Walt and I, that's just the way it was? The nickname stuck and relatives and friends used that term exclusively when referring to our Aunt Min.

Pinkie had few material possessions which she valued, but among them was a jardinière. From where she got it and how long she had it I do not know, but it decorated our home for many years. The jardinière was a deep pink, rather heavy ceramic stand. Four lion heads encircled the stand, and a large pink vase sat on top. At one time it was on our porch with a huge fern inside the vase. From the porch it was moved to the living room and eventually got relegated to the basement where it occupied a corner unnoticed. An antique dealer passed it by because one of the lion heads was damaged.

Pinkie's affection for the jardinière never dimmed. One day, as we were cleaning the basement, she requested that I keep the jardinière in my possession if anything ever happened to her. I promised to honor her request!

A few years after Pinkie's death, I read of a church group that wished to beautify the Rapid slopes. The Rapid Transit, a train-like means of local transportation, is operated by the Greater Cleveland Regional Transit Authority. In order to raise money for this beautification project they were going to collect and sell old newspapers. It pleased me to think some group was going to take action because morning after morning I rode the Rapid to work, and my love of beauty and nature was assaulted by the trash along the slopes. In the recent past I had written a Letter to the Editor of *The Plain Dealer*, suggesting clean-up projects to remove this eyesore! I also contacted the youth group that was collecting newspapers for this project, and arranged to have my newspapers picked up once each month.

A couple picked up my newspapers for the first few months, but they were replaced by Mr. and Mrs. "J." On the first Saturday they collected newspapers, it was on her second trip down the basement that I heard Mr. J say, "Look over in that corner!" Mrs. J let out a cry when she saw the jardinière. She told me excitedly that she had been searching for a jardinière for years but never found one! I was not surprised when she asked if I would sell it to her. She was disappointed, but understood, when I told her of my promise to my late aunt. The basement also housed an old treadle sewing machine my aunt had used for 70 years. I also rejected her offer to buy that cherished family possession as well! For a week I was haunted by Mrs. J's joy at the sight of the jardinière. Though my promise to Pinkie was uppermost on my mind, I wondered what would happen to the jardinière if anything happened to me! Would someone get it who truly appreciated it? Pinkie was a practical person, so I wondered if she would really mind if I sold it or gave it away to someone who would cherish it as much as she did!

Still ambivalent, but feeling it was something I was compelled to do, I telephoned Mrs. J. She was elated when she heard my voice. She said she had thought about the jardinière all week, but had not contacted me because she respected my promise to my aunt. She was so sincere during our conversation that I decided I would like the jardinière to find a home with this woman. I knew she would treasure it and pass it on to her children. We agreed that the next time she and her husband arrived to pick up my old newspapers she could have both the jardinière and the sewing machine!

As the two long-cherished family treasures were placed in their van, I remarked almost under my breath and still feeling a bit guilty, "I hope Pinkie doesn't mind." Hearing those softly spoken words Mrs. J asked, "Did you say Pinkie?" I replied, "Yes, that was the only name my aunt was known by." I felt a chill run through me when Mrs. J said, "But that is my name. My father always called me Pinkie, and it is the only name I have been known by."

With tears in my eyes I said, "If Pinkie is your name, then the jardinière and sewing machine truly belong to you." At that moment I felt my Pinkie was saying, "It's OK Sis!" I have felt peace and have not had a moment of guilt since that day!

# Chapter Sixteen

# The Other Side Of Hell

My first experience with nursing homes was when I had to find a suitable one for my Aunt Pinkie, who had always lived with us. The nine homes I visited before making a decision ranged from very good to absolutely horrible. No matter how good or bad they were, after the visits I was depressed. Before and after I placed Pinkie, who was like a second mother, I cried and cried. The tears were because I hated separating her from our family the last days of her life; the tears were for those elderly I saw who had to spend their sunset years in places where they were warehoused and not loved; the tears were for a society which permitted substandard nursing homes to exist; the tears were for myself because I hated to do this to someone I loved; the tears were expressions of my fear that one day I might end up in such a place.

The home I selected was one that assured maximum safety to an ambulatory person, and one surrounded with the beauty of nature which Pinkie loved. It was one I could walk into without hating myself because I knew it was the best I could find. One night they didn't see her at the dinner table. In the nick of time they discovered her walking half way up the driveway to Detroit Road. I never got to know the other patients very well because the nursing home was some distance from where I lived. I could visit only once a week and friends would take me. Mercifully, my aunt's stay was a short one of four months.

The second time was no easier. In 1978 I was forced to find a nursing home for my mother. I felt as if I were placing a child because she was totally dependent on me for the last seven years she was home. Day after day I cried. The tears were for mom, who had always said she never wanted to go to a nursing home; the tears were because I felt helpless and defeated when I had to break my promise to never put her in one; the tears were expressions of anger because it wasn't fair to have to go through the trauma of placing someone I loved a second time; the tears were the early stages of mourning for I knew my mother would never come home again.

This time I found a place in my neighborhood so that I could visit after work every night. It took a relatively short time for the other patients to realize I was coming every day, and I could tell they began to expect me. As I walked to my mother's room, I would wave to them. Later as I wheeled her down the corridors, we would stop and chat with some. Sometimes we would join those in wheelchairs who were watching the pet Chinese pheasant, which was the sole inhabitant of the lovely open court which was filled with trees and flowers. The pheasant convinced me nursing homes need pets.

As days went by, I found my dread of walking into the home and my sadness each time I left were eased by the expressions of appreciation when I was able to do something for a patient and by the concern they showered on me. The relationship we developed helped me to see the patients as persons, each with his or her own way of coping. While I can't say that my relationship with these people totally erased my personal trauma, it did help to ease it.

I thank God for mom's first roommate. She was a refined, kind woman with a sense of humor. She realized, before the nurses did, that mom could not feed herself so she would lovingly feed her. How good it was to know that there was someone in the room who cared and would be alert to mom's needs. When Valentine's Day rolled around, I made sure Mrs. A shared in the remembrances. We missed her when she went home to try once again to live alone. Later I learned she had to go to another facility where she would remain permanently.

There was a sweet Slovak lady who could not speak nor understand English. When I used the few Slovak words I knew, her face would light up. Before I left her, she would reach for my hand and kiss it.

I gave the name "Operator" to one woman because when she called for a nurse, very often loudly, that is what she called them. She was usually sitting in a wheelchair in the hall finishing her dinner when I arrived. She was always interested in what I was wearing, and it was worth dressing up for her because she would tell me how nice I looked. A purple dress was her favorite so I would wear it once in a while just for her. I suspect she had an excellent wardrobe at one time. It amused me to find out that twice a day Operator was treated to a highball. There were times when she was very angry. If one listened carefully, the tirades were often followed with veiled remarks about no one in her family visiting her. She was like many others who never saw their family after they were placed in the home. Money was sent for the bill, but the family never appeared.

Mr. N always had a twinkle in his eyes and constantly wore a large apron and a hat. He looked as if he was ready to go outside and start a barbeque grill. The aura of business that he created belied the fact that actually he had nothing to do.

Because I was there so often, some of the patients might have thought I was one of the staff. In contrast to Mr. N, Mr. C was a slow moving, quiet man with a sad look in his eyes. I don't know if he could talk or not, but I never heard him say anything. One day as I was leaving another patient's room, he was waiting for me. At first I couldn't tell what he was trying to tell me. He just stood there with his arms outstretched and his palms up as if he was pleading for me to do something. Then I noticed his trousers were wet. He had had an accident and wanted me to help him find dry clothing. I led him to one of the nurses.

The woman who had the room next to my mother's was a feisty lady who had been there a long time, and probably would be for many more years. She was forever "helping" patients by wheeling them down the corridors. Her "helpfulness" became dangerous when she would untie their restraints which were there for protection. Her room was her castle and she made it clear no one was to enter it. I felt honored when she invited me in one day.

Mrs. B dressed so beautifully I imagined she must have been listed in the social register at one time. Her favorite game was finding ways of sneaking out of the nursing home. One day she and two others were missing. The "Three Musketeers" were found taking a leisurely stroll many blocks away.

One of my favorites was one whom I referred to in thought as the striptease artist. She had a wizened, pixy look that for some reason always brought a smile to my face. One never knew what stage of undress she would be in. She would take off her house coat and parade down the hall with her fanny exposed. One night as I was leaving with my neighbor who came to take me home, she walked out of one of the dining rooms stark naked. The nurses were kept busy trying to keep her presentable, but you couldn't get angry with her. After she learned my name, she made sure she didn't forget it. Every night when she first saw me, she would point her finger at me and say, "You are Alida?" and then walk on down the hall. I had a sense of loss when I learned she had died.

Nursing home residents Mrs. M and Mrs. J shared a room which it seemed neither of them ever left. I saw them in wheelchairs next to their beds. Both were very alert. They were impressed because I visited my mother every day but worried because they knew how tired I must be after working all day. One of them shared that she had looked after her mother for years and never regretted it, and she knew I wouldn't either. Once in a while I would buy a sandwich, my supper, and eat it while talking to them. Their concern and understanding were unexpected blessings.

The stereotype of nursing home patients is that of old people who are always on the receiving end and having nothing to give. In the period from February 2$^{nd}$, 1978 until June 28$^{th}$, 1978 when my mother died, the patients in that home gave me something I will always treasure. I never dreamed when I placed my mother there that I would find, in what I would have considered the most unlikely of all places, warmth, humor, understanding, and affection. New strength was given to me by those who seemingly had nothing at all to give. But they did have something after all: themselves!

(The material in this chapter was printed in the *Baptist Leader* in August 1983, under the title, "Discovering That Real Person In A Nursing Home." As the author, I am the copyright holder.)

# Chapter Seventeen

# The Legal Aid Society Of Cleveland

I thought I was going to be a Director of Christian Education when I went to The Baptist Missionary Training School (BMTS) at age 32 to earn a Bachelor's degree. But a course in Casework made me feel that was really where God wanted me to give my life. I was accepted at the School of Applied Social Sciences (SASS) at Case Western Reserve University and received a scholarship for two years. I went right from graduation at BMTS in 1957 to SASS, from which I graduated with a Master's degree in social work in 1959. I was happy to start a new career at the Family Service of America at age 38. It was a wonderful agency and the training I got there was the best.

At one of our training sessions we were told that The Legal Aid Society of Cleveland was hoping one of us would start a pilot social service project there. They had so many people with problems they would suggest they get to an agency, but didn't know if they ever went. Having a social worker on board would take care of that. One worker said she would take the job and would teach the attorneys. Having worked with men in industry for 14 years before going to college, I didn't think that would work. It was NOT LIKE ME to start a new project but I heard myself saying I would do it when the first woman backed down. My bosses, knowing my work background, said I was the one they hoped would do it. For the year The Legal Aid Society got a grant for the project, I was still an employee of Family Service, but when the grant ended I was asked to stay at The Legal Aid Society, and I did. I didn't know much about The Legal Aid Society but soon learned to be proud that I was a part of that agency. Without the Society and its attorneys, thousands of people would have no representation. The staff attorneys are dedicated, and the private attorneys who work outside the agency who take volunteer cases can't be thanked enough for their help.

The first 10 years I did nothing but counseling. If the attorneys had a client they felt needed some social service they would bring the person to me. I was grateful for the training I had at Family Service. It is one thing to be surrounded with other workers and another thing to be alone. One or two clients followed me from Family Service to The Legal Aid Society, but I had hundreds of new ones.

When the person who did the referral work died, they asked me if I would do that too until they found someone else. They never did! If The Legal Aid Society couldn't handle a case or if the person was over the financial guideline, I would refer them to a private attorney. I would still talk to the clients, but now I was also getting to know many attorneys. I never stopped doing referrals but still did some social work.

There were hundreds of volunteer attorneys on my Referral Panel. They volunteered when I asked because they wanted to give something back to the community. The newspaper often wrote about attorneys who did something wrong, but there was very little about those who were so kind and generous. I sent several Letters to the Editor so they would get the praise they deserved. Sometimes clients were frightened to go to a private attorney. To ease their fear I would call the attorney and, while the client listened, tell the attorney about the problem so the client felt the attorney understood what was needed. It helped the client to feel more comfortable when meeting the attorney for the first time. Sometimes clients would send me a thank you note for referring them to their attorney. One attorney took a will and worked on it for four years because of complications. From that experience I learned never to say a case was simple! The relationship I developed with "my attorneys" made it difficult for me to retire because I thought of them as family!

In January of 1991 an article in the *Cleveland Bar Journal* had the title, "Meet the Lady Who Loves Lawyers." Some of them told me I am the only one who does love them. How could I not love attorneys whom I knew did so much for their clients! Awards I got from the Cleveland Bar Association (as it was once called), the Cleveland Academy of Trial Attorneys, and The Legal Aid Society, I deeply appreciated. But the years of helping clients as a social worker at The Legal Aid Society and working with dedicated attorneys who helped so many people made my 42 years extremely rewarding!

Readers of my Christmas letters said they would like to know something about my clients. Of course I will not mention names nor the problem. That would not be ethical, but I will try to share some general things that made me remember them. Of the hundreds of former clients I served, I am now writing about a few who have given me permission to share this information.

One lady, now deceased, came for counseling because of a marital problem. When I started to set a date for the next interview, she said, "Are you going to let me go?" I asked her why she thought I wouldn't. She said her husband told her if she went for help they would send her to a mental hospital. How cruel! They finally got divorced and she would find reasons to keep coming back. I didn't keep clients when they felt it was time to stop. I called it the "Bo Peep" counseling. Leave them alone and they will come home, and she did over and over again. One time I was in another office when she came for counseling because mine was being painted. Now we, in those days, didn't laugh with clients. She started to cry, I reached in a drawer for Kleenex and when I brought it out we both went into hysterics. It was the most beat up box of Kleenex we had ever seen. She always said she couldn't have raised her three boys without my help. She stayed in my life until she passed away.

One man had worked at a manufacturing plant until he was let go. He went from dressing well to looking shabby. He would take trips and lose his luggage, and his family had a rough time looking after him. He blamed someone else repeatedly for his job loss and whenever he came to see me he sounded like a broken record. He would call me "Miss Tuze." One of my attorneys was about his size and gave me clothes for him, and a tailor on West 6th Street altered them at no charge! There was little I could do for him but be kind. He must have felt welcomed because he came frequently. It got so when he came to the agency I would simply greet him, he would use the restroom and then he would leave. I kept in touch with his family and they got him into a nursing home where he was safe.

An attorney brought me a woman who he was sure needed a social worker. She told him she was rather afraid to come to the agency because she thought the Mafia would follow her across the square. She became one of my dearest clients. I called her "My Tessie." She had four children. If she found work she would take money to welfare hoping someone would buy clothes for them. She had been in a hospital from which she left and wasn't getting welfare. She was walking from wherever she lived near downtown in winter boots in the summer. I made sure she got some bus tickets. The first interview she said, "I must be the dirtiest, filthiest person you ever saw." How sad! When she finally got on welfare she had me keep food stamps because she feared they would be stolen, and she was right! I got her some clothes and eventually whatever money she got we opened a bank account so she could buy her own things. One time when I visited her, she was in the gym where they had a piano. I was shocked when I saw her fingering the keys to play a church hymn. She loved to read, and I would bring her copies of *Reader's Digest*. This woman had more substance to her than anyone knew. When I supervised students I would take them to her spotless home, which someone at welfare found for her in a project. She was eventually placed in a nursing home and I was happy when I got rides to see her several times before she died.

I also had a 22-year-old woman who managed to come to Cleveland and survive. I don't know how she did it! She tried to work but would have anxiety attacks if around too many people. She tried many places but just couldn't last. An attorney and I went to a disability hearing. The judge wanted her to get a job. We were able to tell him she has tried many which made her anxiety attacks worse. He put her on Disability. She is now 72 and in a nursing home, which has taken good care of her. I'm glad the nursing home allows her to have the birds she loves and has devotions with them. Because I have cared about her for 50 years she calls me "Mommy." Since a lot of stress has been lifted she has shown more strength, faith, and ability than some might have recognized. When you speak with her you wonder if she ever had an anxiety problem. She loved to watch baseball games, was on top of all the news, and was aware of what was going on in her family. She is a caring, loving person, and gave me permission to write about her.

One lady, in her 80's, wanted to make a will and was referred to an attorney who saw her once, had trouble figuring out what she wanted to put in the will. He eventually closed the case because she didn't return. It wasn't long before she was back at Legal Aid, and still wanting help making a will. I decided there was no point in referring her again until I talked to her long enough to see if I could figure out what she wanted. She was so grateful to have someone take the time to talk with her, and one day she said, "God said He would send us a Comforter and He sent me you!" When I thought I knew what her problem was in making her will, I called an attorney I knew would go into distressed neighborhoods to help elderly people. Her house was one of the few that had not been torn down on her street. The attorney helped get a will made that satisfied her. When it came time to have her sign, he asked me to go with him as a witness. Of course she didn't recognize me because we had never seen each other. When he asked her to listen to my voice she was happy to meet me in person. Her face lit up and I got a hug. She wasn't too well and her daughter thought she should move out of the house. I tried phoning her before I retired but her phone was no longer working. I always think of her as a sweet lady who wanted to do the best for her children.

When I was at Family Service I had a client who wanted to change his vocation, and did. During the period in which I counseled him, he had written a book. I spoke to him only once after he left the city with his family, and he was doing well. Years later I wondered if he had given me a copy of his book. I searched my library and could not find a copy. I wondered what happened to him and decided to do a Google search of his name. I located his name, but the description did not match. I decided to give up the search. Two weeks later my office phone rang and someone said, "Are you sitting down?" I said "No, but I will." I was shocked! It was the former client I had just tried to locate. He was thinking about something I had said to him during a counseling session, and decided he wanted to speak with me once again. He, too, went to Google and found that I was working at The Legal Aid Society. We figured it was 48 years since he was my client. We decided ESP works. His wife is very ill and he is now in assisted living. He still keeps in touch.

It's hard to believe one of my first clients when I started the pilot social service project at The Legal Aid Society in 1967 had kept in touch with me. She was sent to me by an attorney who worked at Legal Aid for a short time while working on her law degree. The client was in the midst of a divorce and very anxious about a number of things. She needed someone to whom she could express her emotions and still feel accepted. A second marriage to a good husband has lasted almost 50 years. Despite some of her concerns, they raised four children who have excelled. Two he adopted from her first marriage. I can sometimes quell her fears by pointing out what a good job of parenting they did. The children are all married and have made them grandparents. One of the things that may have wanted her to keep in touch with me was that her mother's name was Alida. Her mother had MS from the time the client was born and for a while cared for the child while in a wheelchair. When her mother became bedridden the client was older and looked after her mother with the help of her aunts. Having such an ill mother, she must have had very little mothering. She admits she practically raised herself. She and her husband moved to a nearby city, but she still calls when she is anxious or just wants to have a chat. She was glad to give me permission to include her in my book.

It is always nice when former clients still remember you many years later. The Legal Aid Society got a call from a woman in Florida recently trying to locate me. She was a former client and wanted to know if they had my permission to give her my home phone number and address. Forty years later we have had several phone conversations.

In one of my Christmas letters I wrote about crossing the street to go to Madison Park. Two men, heading in the direction I was going, said "Good Morning," to which I replied the same. The older man asked if I was Miss Struze. A bit shocked, I said I was! Then he told me he had been a client of mine. I asked how long ago that was. He said, "When my son, who is with me, was a baby — and he is now 34!" I have not seen him nor his son again although they said they had moved into my neighborhood.

A number of years ago on my way home, a man sitting across from me on the bus, heard my voice and said he had been my client. He spoke loudly about how I had helped him years ago. It was nice, but embarrassing, because everyone on the bus could hear him speak!

A social worker seldom knows if what he or she said or did may have helped? I'm just grateful to know that the assistance I provided to some of my clients did some good. I do believe that, the fact that a person truly cares gets through to the clients — more so than any words!

# Chapter Eighteen

# Hawaii Brought More Than Beauty

One place I always wanted to see was Hawaii, but I didn't want to go alone. I wanted someone with me with whom I could share all that beauty. I thought of my friend Ruth. We met in the 8th grade and had known each other 62 years. Ruth had never been on a tour and, despite having some health problems, was happy to accept my invitation. Plans were made and we boarded the plane in Cleveland in October, 1996.

When we got to Hawaii, those on the tour were divided into three groups at the request of hotels, which could not accommodate so many at once. It was a wonderful tour. We visited four islands as did the other three groups and enjoyed every minute. One night, near the end of the tour, every group met in a very large building where we had a buffet-style meal. It was nice to have everyone together though, of course, we didn't know other tourists as well as those in our group. Ruth and I filled our trays and tried to find a place to sit. I saw two ladies, one of them was from another group, who were sitting at a table with two vacant chairs. "Would you mind if we joined you?" I asked. They welcomed our company. We chatted about all the places we had been and how delighted we were that we had taken the tour. For some reason we didn't exchange names.

As was my custom, I sent my Christmas letter to those I got to know on the tour. I would summarize the tour and figured they might like the memories I had documented. I sent the Christmas letter to the lady who was in our group, and she shared it with the other lady. Little did I know what a shock that letter would bring!

In January my phone rang and a female voice said, "You are Alida?" When I acknowledged that I was, the voice said she was a friend of the woman to whom I sent the letter. They lived in the same building and her friend shared my letter with her. Then came the shock. She asked, "Was your mother's name Elizabeth, your father's name Walter, and your aunt who lived with them named Min?" How could this woman I had dinner with in Hawaii know all this? She went on to say, "I'm Nadine Stahl. We lived next door to your parents. I was looking out my bedroom window and saw them bringing you home that first day when they adopted you." Unbelievable!

Memories flooded back. My father and uncle went fishing with Nadine's father and I have a picture of the three of them waiting for fish to bite. Her dad worked nights and slept days and I heard stories of my brother and me joining him for a nap. I would hear about Nadine and may have a picture of her with me when I was a baby. How wonderful it was to meet someone who saw me welcomed into a loving home 75 years earlier.

Nadine had married and had one son. We planned to get together and friends drove me to see her. What a lovely evening that was. Over and over we talked about what a miracle it was that a tour to Hawaii brought us together. I kept in touch with Nadine by phone. The last time I spoke with her she was in her 90's, knew her days of traveling were over, but seemed to be alright. A few months after that, in 2010, I phoned and the line was disconnected. What happened to Nadine?

There weren't too many in the phone book with her last name so I phoned to see if any of them were related. Several replied but never had a Nadine in their family. I wrote to the Building Manager but got no reply. I was determined to try again so wrote to the Rental Agent. It felt like another miracle when the Rental Agent, Mary Alice, called me. She told me that three months earlier Nadine, on her way to a hairdresser, fell in the parking lot, broke a hip, had surgery, went to rehab, seemed to be doing well but suddenly died. Mary Alice had been friendly with Nadine and has a few of her belongings her son didn't want. I was so grateful to know what had happened to Nadine, glad that I had kept in touch with her, but sad that I wasn't able to say goodbye to my "Hawaiian miracle." I asked Mary Alice to let her son know I would like to talk with him and give him a picture of his grandfather. I'm saddened by the fact that I never heard from Nadine's son.

# Chapter Nineteen

# Me And The Bookies

My father had two sisters and two brothers, but we were not close to any of them. When we were little dad would take my brother and me to see Uncle Steve once in a while and he was always glad to see us. He had a shop where he fixed cars and I learned he would lock up at noon and go to the race track. He loved horses and in the winter he would follow them to southern states. My dad's other brother, Jeff, married, but our families didn't mingle. One of my father's sisters lived in another state and I never saw her, but his other sister, my Aunt Hazel, I got to know in later life.

I have no recollection of Uncle Steve visiting our home even though he was welcome. I saw him only three times in my adult life. He was at a relative's wedding when I was about 18. Somehow we got together to go to Aunt Hazel's husband's funeral. We were the last ones at the grave and he said to me, "When I die, just bury me and have a bookie say a few nice words." Little did he know how close he was to predicting the future! The third time I saw him was when my dad died in 1956. He came to the funeral and we gave him a lot of dad's clothes, including a coat that became part of his story later. We had no contact with him after that.

I had gotten to know Aunt Hazel when she and Uncle Pat moved to this area. Not long before she died she changed her will and made me executrix of her estate because her husband had died and she knew Uncle Steve would be hard to find. I found an attorney in Florida where she lived to take care of everything and had her remains placed in a grave close to my family's graves. There was very little money of hers left, but I saved it as I suspected I might have to bury Uncle Steve some day. The big problem was how to find Uncle Steve to let him know his sister had died, as I had no address for him. Where does he spend his time when in Cleveland? I called Thistledown Race Track, told them who I was and asked if they would page him. I gave them my phone number in case they found him. It wasn't too long before the phone rang. Yes, it was Uncle Steve! I told him of his sister's death, that I had found an attorney and made arrangements for visitation, cremation, interment, and a marker. He was sad that his sister died though they hadn't been in touch. He was grateful that I had taken care of all the arrangements. We didn't see each other and once more Uncle Steve returned to his very private life, and I still had no address.

**January 30<sup>th</sup>, 1995**

There I was sitting at my desk at The Legal Aid Society of Cleveland interviewing a client. I had started a pilot Social Service Project there. Little did I know what was ahead of me when the phone rang! It was the Coroner's Office notifying me that Uncle Steve had been found dead in his car a few days earlier, apparently on his way to breakfast. My first question was, "How did you find me?" It seems my cousin's husband would go to the race track with Uncle Steve and they found a card in the car with his name and Florida address. My Aunt June was the only one on dad's side of the family I had contact with. She was with her daughter in Florida and knew I had buried Aunt Hazel. She told the Coroner he could find me at Legal Aid. He certainly did.

I was told I would have to identify the body, which made me a little anxious, but it was only the beginning of experiences I never dreamed I would have. My neighbor worked for funeral homes so went to the Coroner's with me the next morning. He checked the body to see if it was in good shape for me to see. Although I hadn't seen him in years, I identified my uncle. The Coroner gave me a tiny billfold big enough for the dime in it. I knew other money had been lifted but said nothing. I was given a key to the apartment Uncle Steve was living in so I thought the apartment was his, and I was told a couple across the street would help us if needed. Before going to the apartment, we went to the lot where the car had been taken. None of his tools were in the car but there was no point worrying about that. I was grateful when I found out that while he was driving the car, it was not in his name. It was up to someone else to get the car back and I had no idea who that was. One less worry!

The third place we went that morning was to the apartment which I thought was my uncle's. The main reason I went to the apartment was to find a Social Security number which the funeral director needed. My plan was to have Uncle Steve cremated and buried with his sister Hazel. I was about to put the key in the door but told Mark I would feel better if we asked the Polish woman the Coroner mentioned to come with us. She was willing, and told me what a nice person Uncle Steve was, and suggested I look in pockets and hems. Why? Little did I know I was walking into a bookie place! Why did Uncle Steve have them there?

Someone had told the bookies a relative had surfaced. Mattresses were over-turned, drawers were opened, and it was obvious someone didn't have time to pick up things on the floor. But, they had cleaned up other stuff as fast as they could before this previously unknown relative got there. I was tired, frustrated, and had to get back to work. I hurriedly picked up some clothes I would clean and donate to the City Mission. I also picked up a license plate and some coins. Hanging from a door was a coat I recognized as one of my dad's that I had given to Uncle Steve at my dad's funeral. It really needed to be cleaned and I took it only for sentimental reasons. The Polish lady's husband suddenly appeared just as the phone rang. He told me not to answer it. I decided we should leave because I had not found a Social Security number. My hands were dirty and I asked the lady if I could come to her home to wash them. She said there was a kitchen which I missed. The house had been a photographer's studio and was a maze of rooms. I was told the downstairs was used by a barber to cut a priest's hair. I washed my hands, opened a cupboard door and there was a Social Security card and some money which I took still believing they were Uncle Steve's.

Mark dropped me off at work by noon and I asked him to take the clothes to the dry cleaner. It wasn't long before he called me at work to tell me when he picked up the coat, some slips fell out. He assumed they were bookie slips. Now what do I do? As soon as I got home, Mark took me to the police station. I turned in the license plate, told them about the money I took and was informed if anyone called to say I took only $27.

The next day, a Saturday, I got a call at home. The person said the place was so cold they needed the key so they could turn the heat on. How did they get my phone number? Maybe from the Coroner! I told them my attorney said I shouldn't give the key to anyone but the landlord. The Post Office was open until noon and I had time to mail the key. Reluctant as they were, they gave me the address and the key got sent. I was also asked how Uncle Steve was to be buried and I told them he would be cremated. That led to my being asked which crematory and I didn't know. They probably would have looked through his clothing for the slips. A number of them must have been given my address and phone number. Just once one of them got testy with me. By then I was getting a little scared and a bit angry. I told the person I never saw my uncle and new nothing about his life except I knew he liked horses. I said, "I don't know the front end of a horse from the back end." I heard no more but did have my porch light on and the police watching my house for several weeks.

When all this was going on, I had a mother who was not well and I was working. I was going through so much at home and with an extended family that needed help. I didn't need this! I would have given the money and slips to them but didn't want to meet them. They were kind to Uncle Steve giving him a place to stay when he wasn't well. I found a slip with appointment times at Mt. Sinai Hospital. The death certificate said cause of death was probable arteriosclerotic heart disease. Because the Polish lady told me he often carried a lot of money, probably bookie money, I checked with banks and found he had only one account with one having $523 in it. The bank put a hold on the money which I would have given to a relative who needed help. I had to get an attorney to get the money because mine was on vacation. The attorney's fee was half the amount in the account. I told the attorney no matter what he might find I didn't want to make waves. My showing up probably got them in enough trouble. They were his friends and gave Uncle Steve a place to stay. One last shock came when I could not get burial help from Social Security because the card I found was not Uncle Steve's. I don't know if he ever had one! By now I realized the apartment was not Uncle Steve's but belonged to his friends.

I had his name in the death notice one day. I learned a woman called the parlor and said Uncle Steve was kind to her husband when he was dying of cancer and her children loved him. She had a mass said for him. People really liked Uncle Steve, who was a quiet, gentle man. As a family we never saw him and he never asked for anything. He was no problem during his life. I'm glad I was able to bury him with dignity. How well I remembered him saying, "When I die just bury me and have a bookie say a few nice words." Little did I know the bookies were going to help pay for his funeral with the little money I took — thinking it was his. I'm sure they had nice words for him but not sure they had nice ones for me!

# Chapter Twenty

# Angels In The Morning

God sends angels in different forms and sometimes they appear as people. I know because on November 4th, 2004 I left my home at 6:20 a.m. as usual to catch a bus on Madison Avenue. I dressed in a nice suit because that night I was to be a receptionist after work at the Sai Gon Plaza.

The temperature was above normal for November so I had on a lined spring coat rather than a heavy one. There wasn't a soul around that morning and not a car drove up or down the street, which was unusual. I walked at a good pace up the east side of the street heading south and at some point crossed to the west side to continue heading south to cross Madison to the bus stop. That did it! I must have tripped over my two feet as I turned south. The next thing I knew, I was falling and heard something crack on the cement walk. I was carrying a bag and purse but unfortunately they weren't in front of me to save my knee.

There I was, totally alone, making an effort to get up when suddenly there were two people around me. I was shocked and said, "Where did you come from?" They said they were sitting on their porch having a cup of coffee and saw me fall. How many people would sit on their porch in November, and I certainly had not seen them as I rushed up the street? To this day I believe God sent them as angels to help me. At first I thought I would get the next bus, but decided I had better go home. They escorted me to my home eight houses away. My leg was beginning to hurt and I forgot to ask them which house they lived in. It turned out I never took another bus to work.

When I got in the house, I realized going home was the wise thing to do. My beige coat had blood on it, the frames of my glasses were bent, and there was blood on my nose and face from a nasty scratch an inch long. I managed to walk upstairs to change my clothes because I knew I would be going to the hospital for x-rays. A friend from church picked me up and by the time we got to the hospital someone had to help me out of the car into a wheelchair because the pain had started. The doctor wondered how on Earth I had managed to go up stairs three times before leaving home. I told him I had used my slacks to lift my right leg.

X-rays showed I had a fractured kneecap which would have to be removed. I, who said I would NEVER be in a hospital overnight, was licked and had my first experience as an inpatient. I had enough vicarious hospital experience through the years with family members and wanted none of it.

Because I was 84 at the time, the doctors insisted I had blacked out. I told them they were wrong — I knew I was falling and heard my knee crack. The operation went well and everyone was so nice to me. It got so I would laugh with every shift of nurses. Word must have gotten around because the nurses would come to me and say, "YOU'RE the 84-year-old that is still working and has not been in a hospital before!" I'm glad I showed them that not all seniors are frail.

I had so many flowers, one doctor asked if this was a hospital or floral shop. My friends lifted my spirits. I didn't know how I would get to work on the bus, but a friend called while I was still in the hospital. He said he takes his wife to work downtown every morning and would take me and did for several years until I retired. I spent a month with one of my kids and was home by Christmas. It was worth losing a knee cap to be with her when her father died so she wasn't alone. I was back to work on January 2$^{nd}$, 2005. My only regret is that I never found my angels to thank them. I have thanked God for sending them to me in my time of need.

# Chapter Twenty-One

# Why Me?

Did you ever wonder why you were born? Was there a purpose for your being here? Perhaps it will only be as you look back that you will see how you fulfilled the purpose God planned for your life. At a meeting as we discussed such things tears came to my eyes. Now, as the last one alive in my immediate and extended family, the question "Why Me?" came to mind. Strange that the last two family members to survive were the two who were adopted! When my cousin died I was the "Last of the Mohicans." It's sad to have no relative to whom to give pictures and family treasures, and no one with whom to share precious memories. You want to share something that happened with a relative or friend — but there is no phone in heaven!

Why me? Was I placed in this family because I was healthy and needed to help those in later years who took such good care of me as a child? Was I needed as the last matriarch in three or four families? One of "my kids" surprised me when she said she was glad I was still with them at family gatherings. She was with another part of her family one holiday and they all felt sad because all the parents were deceased and they missed having older people with them at the table. I was glad if just my presence gave her a more family feeling or eased the loss she felt. I never thought that just being alive could make a difference to someone!

Why Me? Why was I the only one in the entire family to find God, or did He find me? Many of them went to church when young but, though they believed in God, they just didn't go to church when older. Some people might think God may not welcome them but they were good people and I believe He did. When I taught 3rd year Primary children my father would drive me to church on Sunday with the car full of things for the lesson. I told him once that all he did for the children on Sunday he would get to heaven someday. I never preached to my family, but they supported my church activities. A hospice worker told me my cousin, who never talked about God, did mention God before she died, and was grateful for his prayers. Who knows if sometimes we are silent witnesses?

Why Me? My brother, being in the Merchant Marine, was gone a lot so it was up to me to make decisions about nursing homes for my aunt and seven years later for my mother. I kept both home as long as it was safe to do so. When a home-health aide told me it took two nurses to get my mother from the bed to a wheelchair, so it would be dangerous to take her home. I knew I was licked! We had talked about death and I knew she didn't fear it, but I didn't know how she would react to a nursing home. The night before she was transferred, I told her she would be going to another place. She said she trusted my decision. I wheeled her into a room that had a piano and hymn book. She loved to hear me play and sing. Before I wheeled her back to her room I said a prayer with her. Her words after the prayer I'll never forget: "I didn't know you loved me so much." The next day was not easy for either of us. Could part of the plan for my life be finding strength and patience through faith to face two traumatic nursing home experiences?

Why Me? Because I worked outside the home, my mother and aunt did the cooking and baking and I did most of the cleaning. Years went by and there came a time when they both had pneumonia at the same time, which meant keeping track of medications and temperatures. Now what to do about cooking? I learned in a hurry. I remember where I stood when I had the nerve to challenge God. I said, "God, you promised you would never leave us nor forsake us and I NEED YOU NOW! Little did I know this was just the beginning of years of one thing after another, and God never let me down! I like to think the healthy baby my parents adopted was part of the plan for my life.

Have you thought about the purpose and plan for your life?

# About The Author

Alida grew up in a loving home with parents who had good values and were kind, generous people. Her mother's sister, Pinkie, who was like a second mother, always lived with Alida's parents. Alida and her younger brother always remember her as a member of the household. Life was normal for the children until the Great Depression brought havoc to the family, causing them to lose their home. One year later Aunt Pinkie bought a home in Lakewood, Ohio.

After graduation from Lakewood High School she wanted to study voice, but lack of finances made college impossible. Beginning January 1st, 1940, she felt lucky to have a job at the Federal Reserve Bank, which she had during World War II. In 1946 she went to the Illuminating Company to work, which was next to the Old Stone Church. She attended noonday services there for seven years, which led to her joining Lakewood Baptist Church in 1950.

She got so busy she began writing Christmas letters which became very popular. She was inspired to go to the Baptist Missionary Training School at the age of 32, where she obtained a Bachelor's degree in Christian Education. In her junior year a course in Casework inspired her to earn a Master's degree in social work at age 38 from Case Western Reserve University in Cleveland, Ohio. Her greatest gift is loving people and she did just that at Family Service of America for 10 years. She then started a pilot Social Service project at The Legal Aid Society in 1967 and stayed there for 42 years.

The first 10 years she only did counseling, and then was asked to also refer clients Legal Aid couldn't help to private attorneys. They would represent the clients without charge. She was known as the lady who loved attorneys, and they began to feel like family to her. It took a box of Kleenex to say goodbye to the staff after so many years even though she volunteered about six months until they found a replacement. She is grateful she was healthy and able to work until 88 years of age. She has enjoyed a fulfilling career and a wonderful life!

Her prayer is that, as Grandma Moses became known for her art at an advanced age, the people who wanted her to write this book will enjoy sharing *My Life, My Letters, and My Loves!* This book was created for all the people she has loved, including the Karens, who called her "Pepe," which means "Grandma" in Karen!

# Videos Of The Author

A short video describing some of the volunteer work Alida has performed to help resettle Karen refugees from Burma is available on Youtube.com. To view this video at Youtube.com you can search the title *Alida by Paul Sobota* at the Youtube.com website, or you can type the following onto your web browser:

https://www.youtube.com/watch?v=N9ENo--UAPw

This video is also available at Vimeo.com under a different title. To view this video at Vimeo.com you can search the title *Extended Family: Alida and her Karen,* or you can type the following onto your web browser:

https://vimeo.com/132131167

Made in the USA
Charleston, SC
29 June 2016